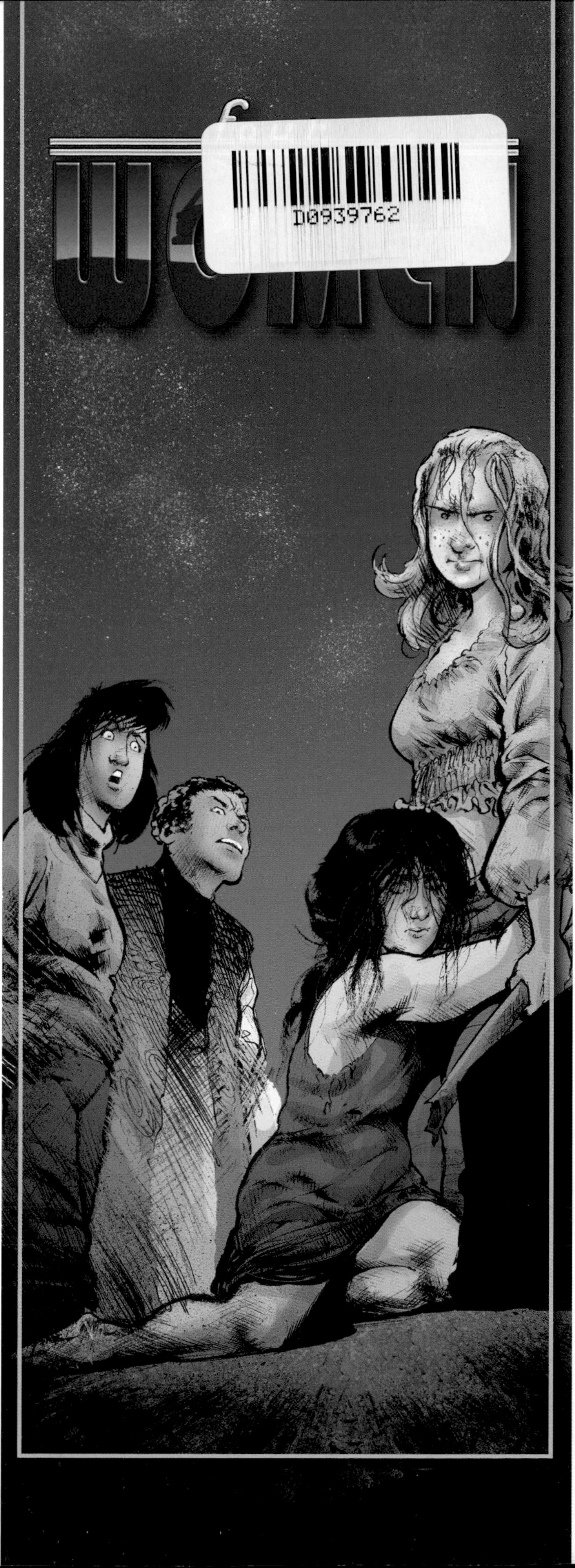
WOMEN

Four WOMEN

Become our fan on Facebook **facebook.com/idwpublishing**
Follow us on Twitter **@idwpublishing**
Subscribe to us on YouTube **youtube.com/idwpublishing**
See what's new on Tumblr **tumblr.idwpublishing.com**
Check us out on Instagram **instagram.com/idwpublishing**

IDW
www.IDWPUBLISHING.com

Ted Adams, CEO & Publisher
Greg Goldstein, President & COO
Robbie Robbins, EVP/Sr. Graphic Artist
Chris Ryall, Chief Creative Officer
David Hedgecock, Editor-in-Chief
Laurie Windrow, Sr. VP of Sales & Marketing
Matthew Ruzicka, CPA, Chief Financial Officer
Lorelei Bunjes, VP of Digital Services
Jerry Bennington, VP of New Product Development

ISBN: 978-1-68405-042-0 21 20 19 18 1 2 3 4

WRITER & ARTIST
SAM KIETH

COLORIST
ALEX SINCLAIR

LETTERING
NAGHMEH ZAND & SERGIO GARCIA

SERIES EDITOR
SCOTT DUNBIER

COVER ARTIST
SAM KIETH

COLLECTION EDITORS
JUSTIN EISINGER AND **ALONZO SIMON**

COLLECTION DESIGNER
CLAUDIA CHONG

PUBLISHER
TED ADAMS

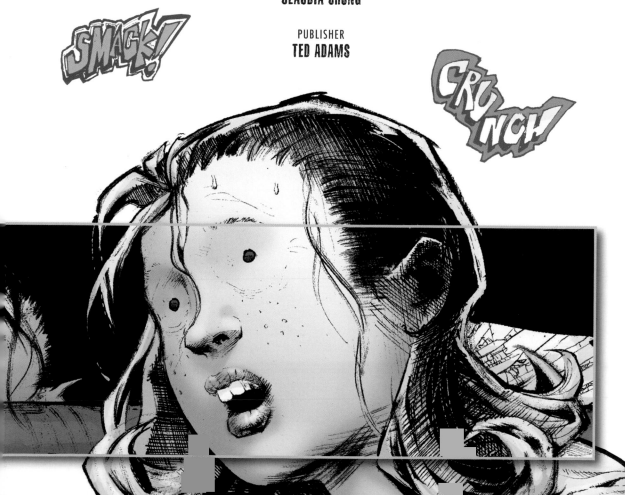

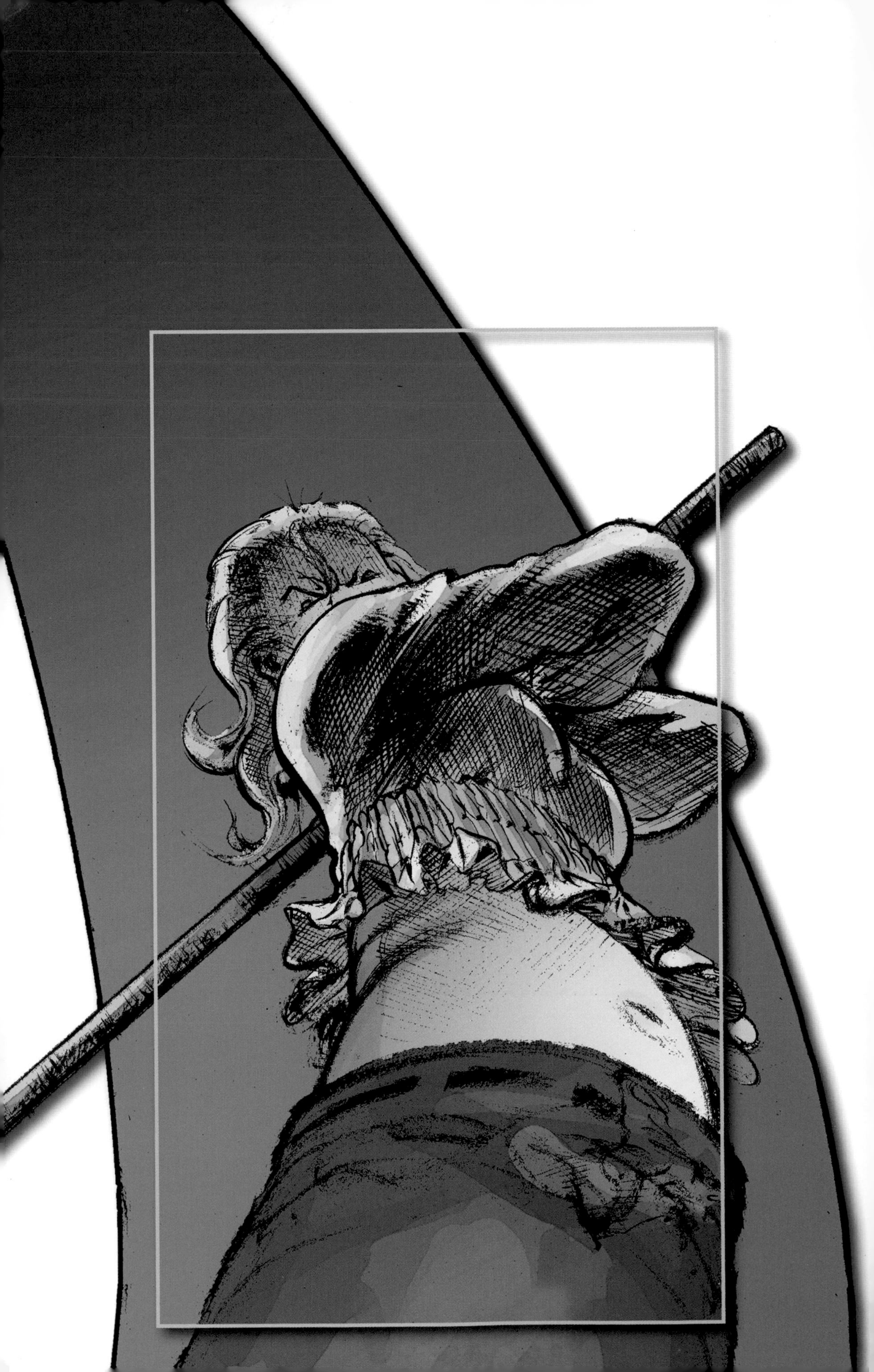

If you're familiar with my work, there's usually a surreal or magical quality to stories like *Maxx*, *Zero Girl*, or *My Inner Bimbo*. *Four Women* strays into grittier, darker territory than I usually write/draw. That's not to say it's all dark–hey, I wouldn't put the reader through all this emotional and physical ordeal without trying for some sense of closure towards the end.

Once again, as with *Zero Girl*, my dear old friend and ace editor Scott Dunbier is responsible for pushing me to stretch outside of my comfort level. First visually, trying to navigate between my usual cartoony style with the character Cindy balanced with a more realistic rendering of the other three women (as realistic as my style gets), seemed important with a story such as this.

I struggled with a satisfying ending in the last issue of the mini series, and even re-wrote, actually edited out, much of the dialogue between Donna and Marion in the last scene of the trade.

Less is more. Still working on that. So, though it's either finished, or maybe more like abandoned, it's much like everything else I strive to create, flounder to execute, struggle to draw and write, much like the author himself...

...it's a work in progress.

SAM KIETH
Nov. 2017

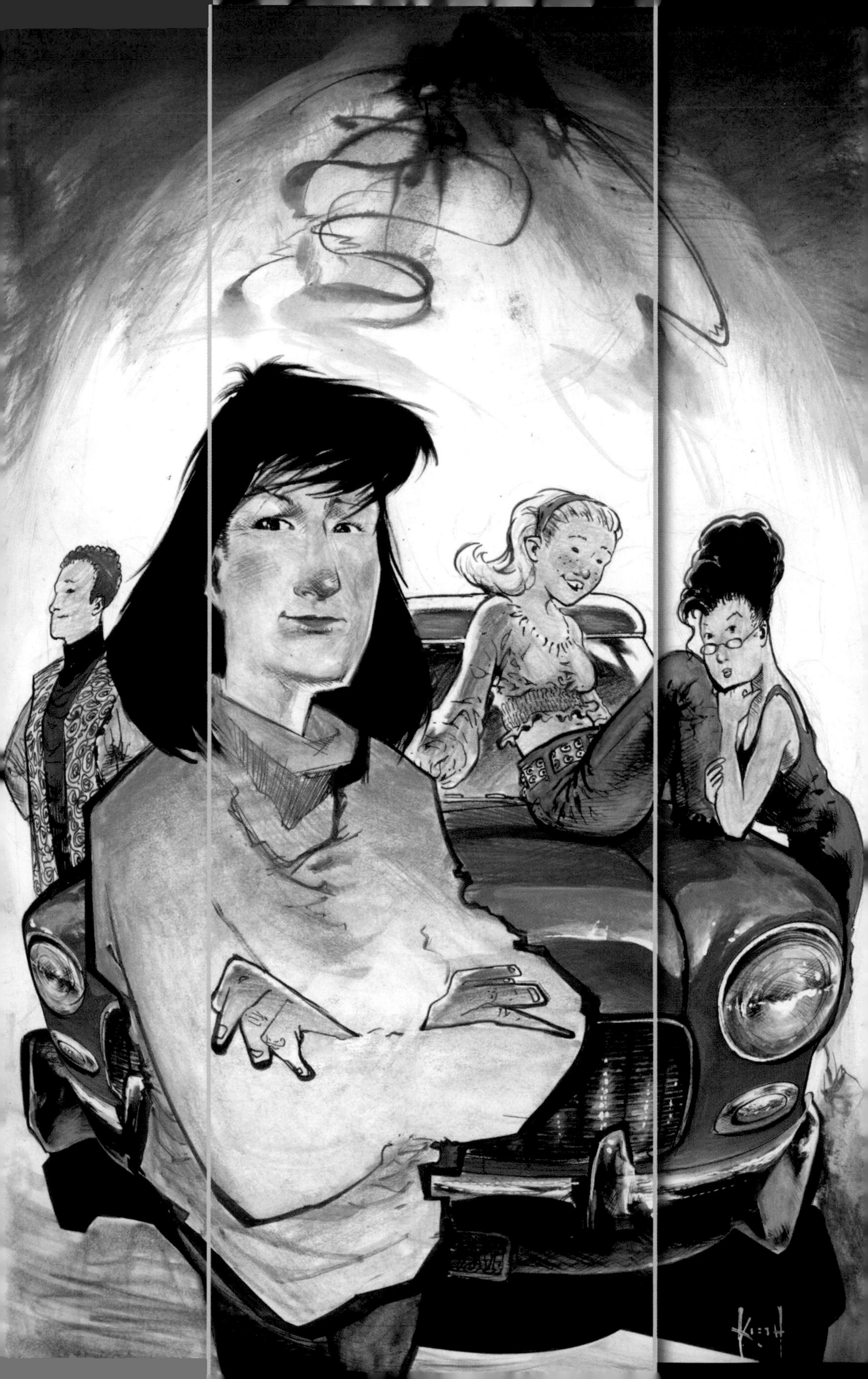

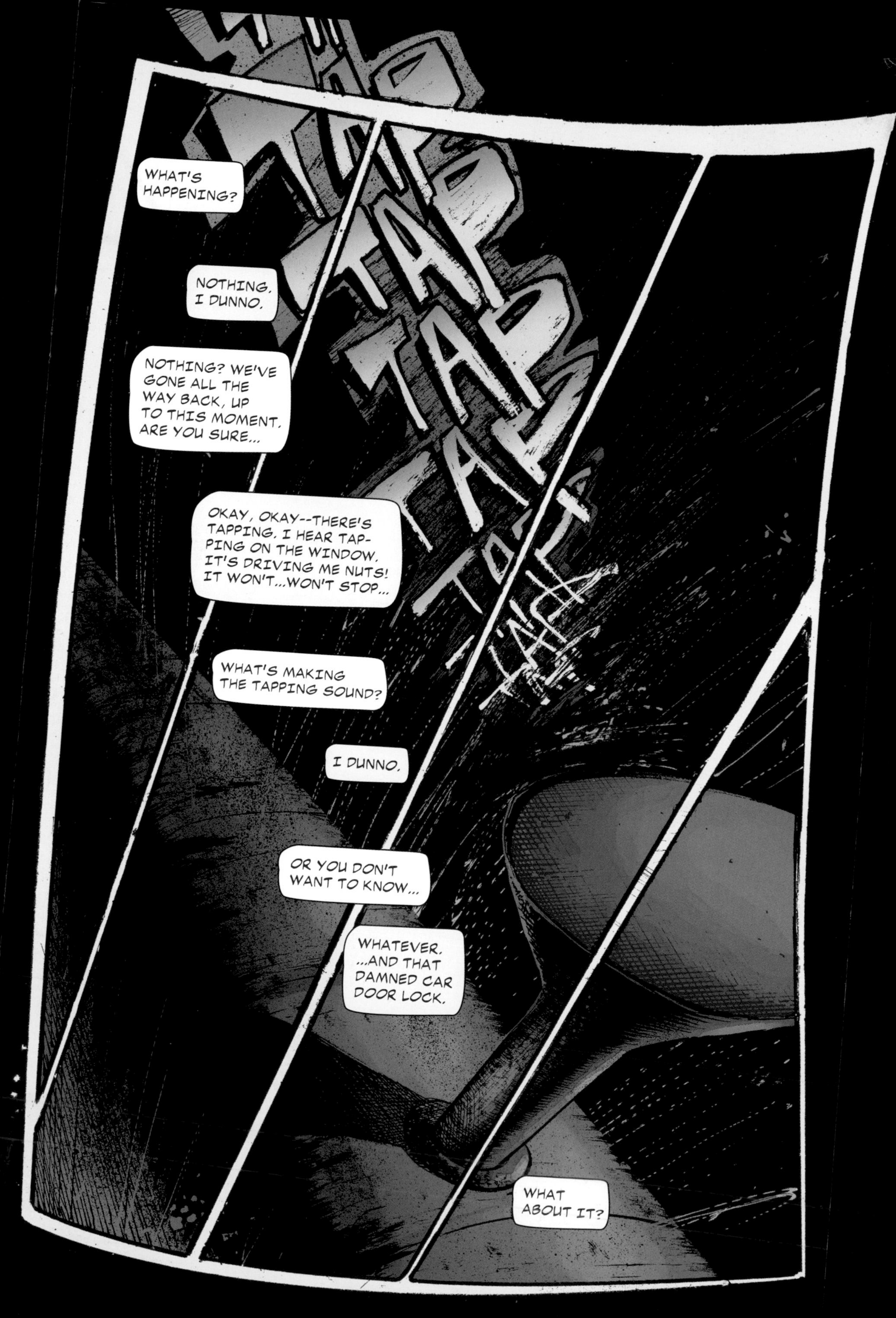
TAP TAP TAP TAP TAP
WHAT'S HAPPENING?
NOTHING. I DUNNO.
NOTHING? WE'VE GONE ALL THE WAY BACK, UP TO THIS MOMENT. ARE YOU SURE...
OKAY, OKAY--THERE'S TAPPING. I HEAR TAPPING ON THE WINDOW. IT'S DRIVING ME NUTS! IT WON'T...WON'T STOP...
WHAT'S MAKING THE TAPPING SOUND?
I DUNNO.
OR YOU DON'T WANT TO KNOW...
WHATEVER. ...AND THAT DAMNED CAR DOOR LOCK.
WHAT ABOUT IT?

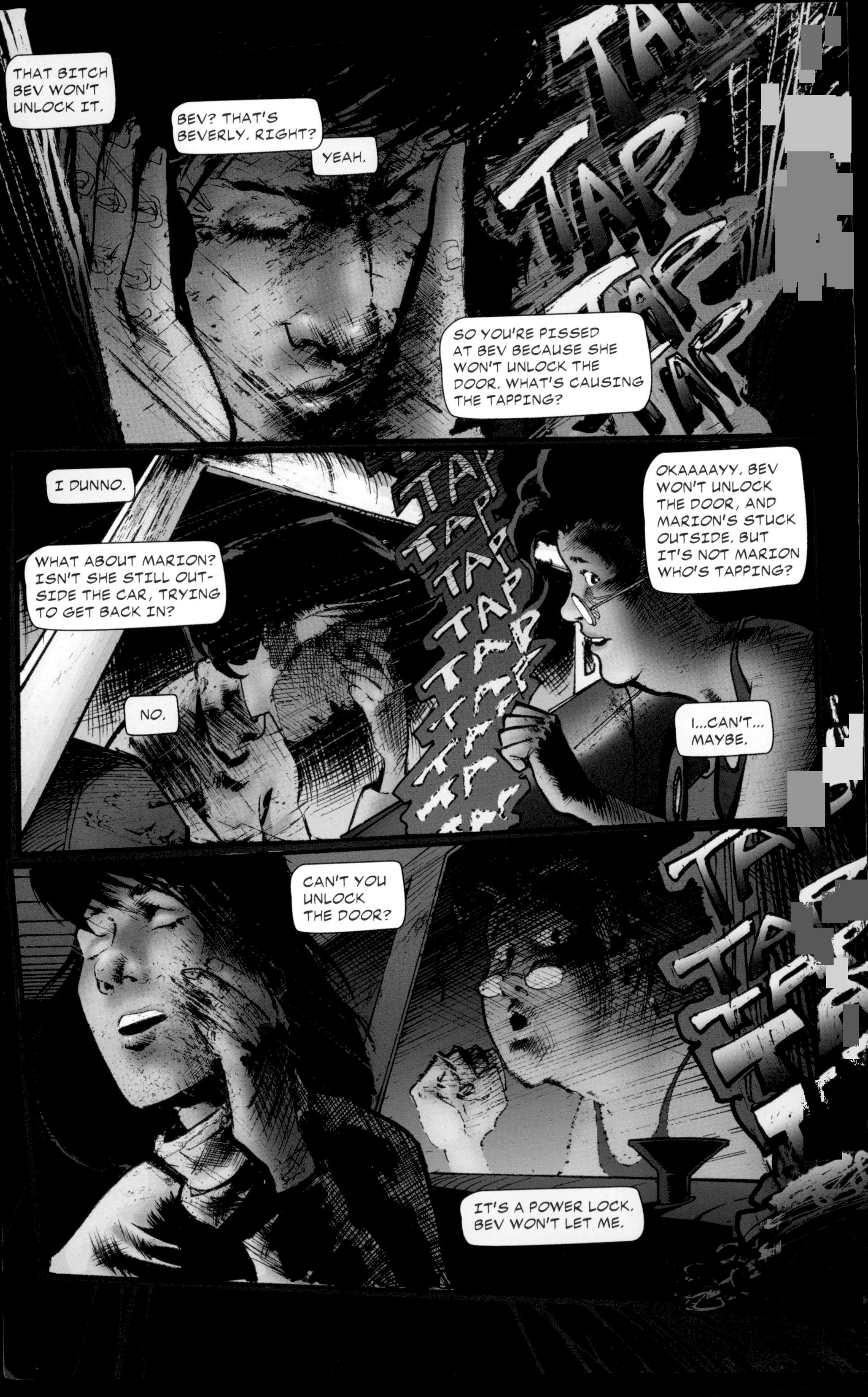
THAT BITCH BEV WON'T UNLOCK IT.
BEV? THAT'S BEVERLY, RIGHT?
YEAH.
TAP TAP TAP
SO YOU'RE PISSED AT BEV BECAUSE SHE WON'T UNLOCK THE DOOR. WHAT'S CAUSING THE TAPPING?
I DUNNO.
TAP TAP TAP TAP TAP
OKAAAAYY. BEV WON'T UNLOCK THE DOOR, AND MARION'S STUCK OUTSIDE. BUT IT'S NOT MARION WHO'S TAPPING?
WHAT ABOUT MARION? ISN'T SHE STILL OUT-SIDE THE CAR, TRYING TO GET BACK IN?
NO.
I...CAN'T... MAYBE.
CAN'T YOU UNLOCK THE DOOR?
IT'S A POWER LOCK. BEV WON'T LET ME.

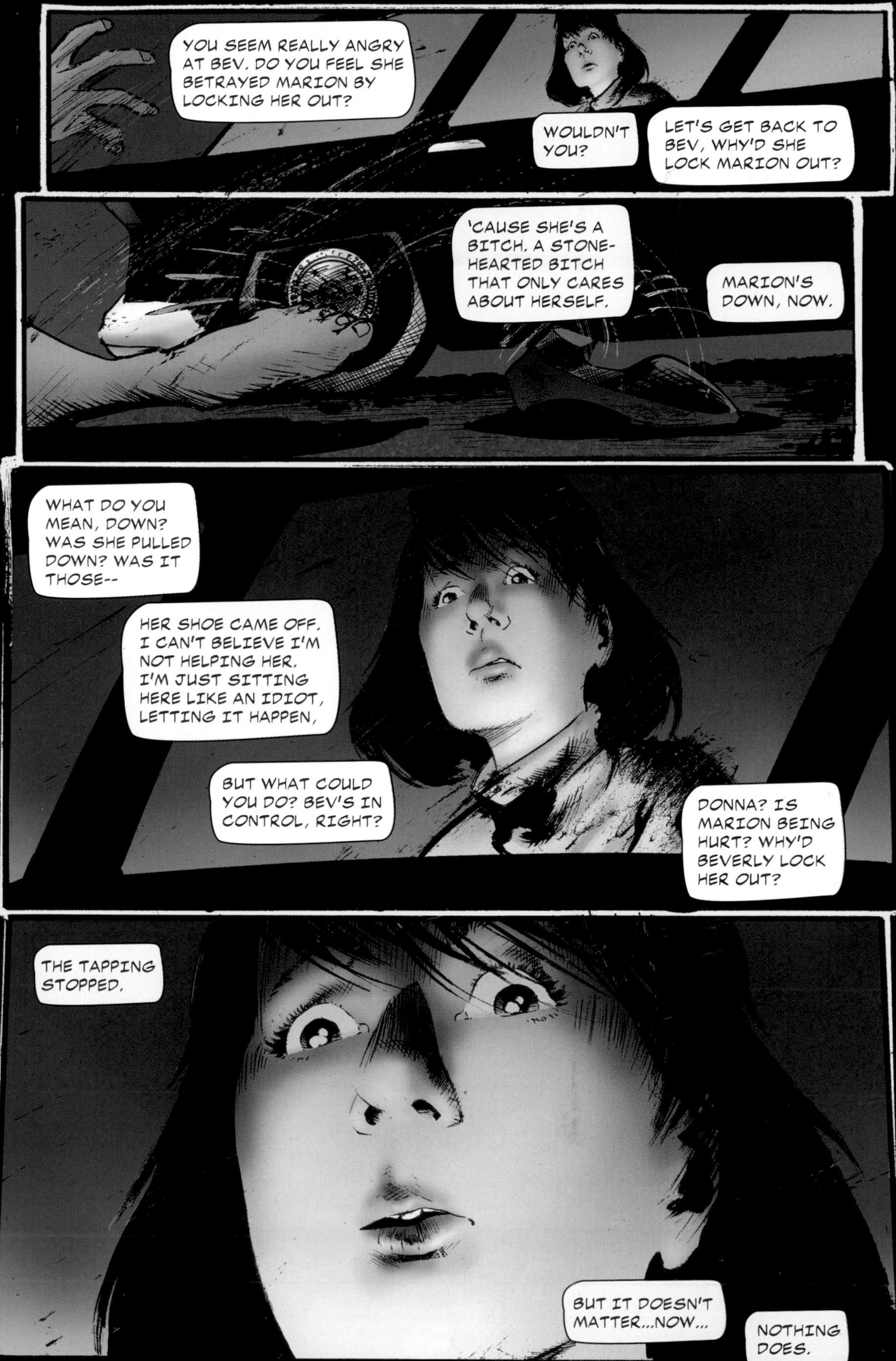

YOU SEEM REALLY ANGRY AT BEV. DO YOU FEEL SHE BETRAYED MARION BY LOCKING HER OUT?
WOULDN'T YOU?
LET'S GET BACK TO BEV, WHY'D SHE LOCK MARION OUT?
'CAUSE SHE'S A BITCH. A STONE-HEARTED BITCH THAT ONLY CARES ABOUT HERSELF.
MARION'S DOWN, NOW.
WHAT DO YOU MEAN, DOWN? WAS SHE PULLED DOWN? WAS IT THOSE--
HER SHOE CAME OFF. I CAN'T BELIEVE I'M NOT HELPING HER. I'M JUST SITTING HERE LIKE AN IDIOT, LETTING IT HAPPEN,
BUT WHAT COULD YOU DO? BEV'S IN CONTROL, RIGHT?
DONNA? IS MARION BEING HURT? WHY'D BEVERLY LOCK HER OUT?
THE TAPPING STOPPED.
BUT IT DOESN'T MATTER...NOW...
NOTHING DOES.

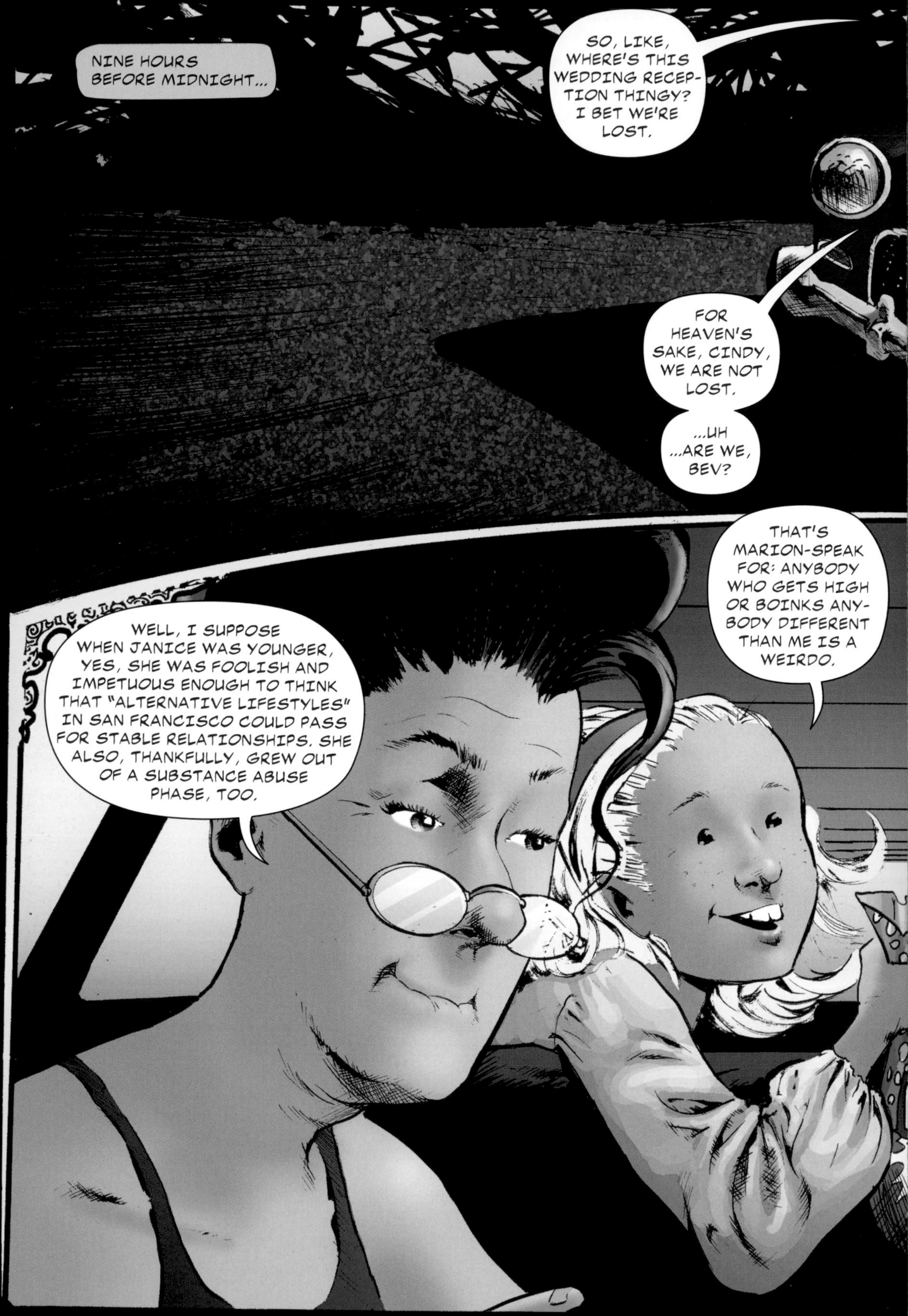
NINE HOURS BEFORE MIDNIGHT...
SO, LIKE, WHERE'S THIS WEDDING RECEPTION THINGY? I BET WE'RE LOST.
FOR HEAVEN'S SAKE, CINDY, WE ARE NOT LOST.
...UH ...ARE WE, BEV?
WELL, I SUPPOSE WHEN JANICE WAS YOUNGER, YES, SHE WAS FOOLISH AND IMPETUOUS ENOUGH TO THINK THAT "ALTERNATIVE LIFESTYLES" IN SAN FRANCISCO COULD PASS FOR STABLE RELATIONSHIPS. SHE ALSO, THANKFULLY, GREW OUT OF A SUBSTANCE ABUSE PHASE, TOO.
THAT'S MARION-SPEAK FOR: ANYBODY WHO GETS HIGH OR BOINKS ANYBODY DIFFERENT THAN ME IS A WEIRDO.

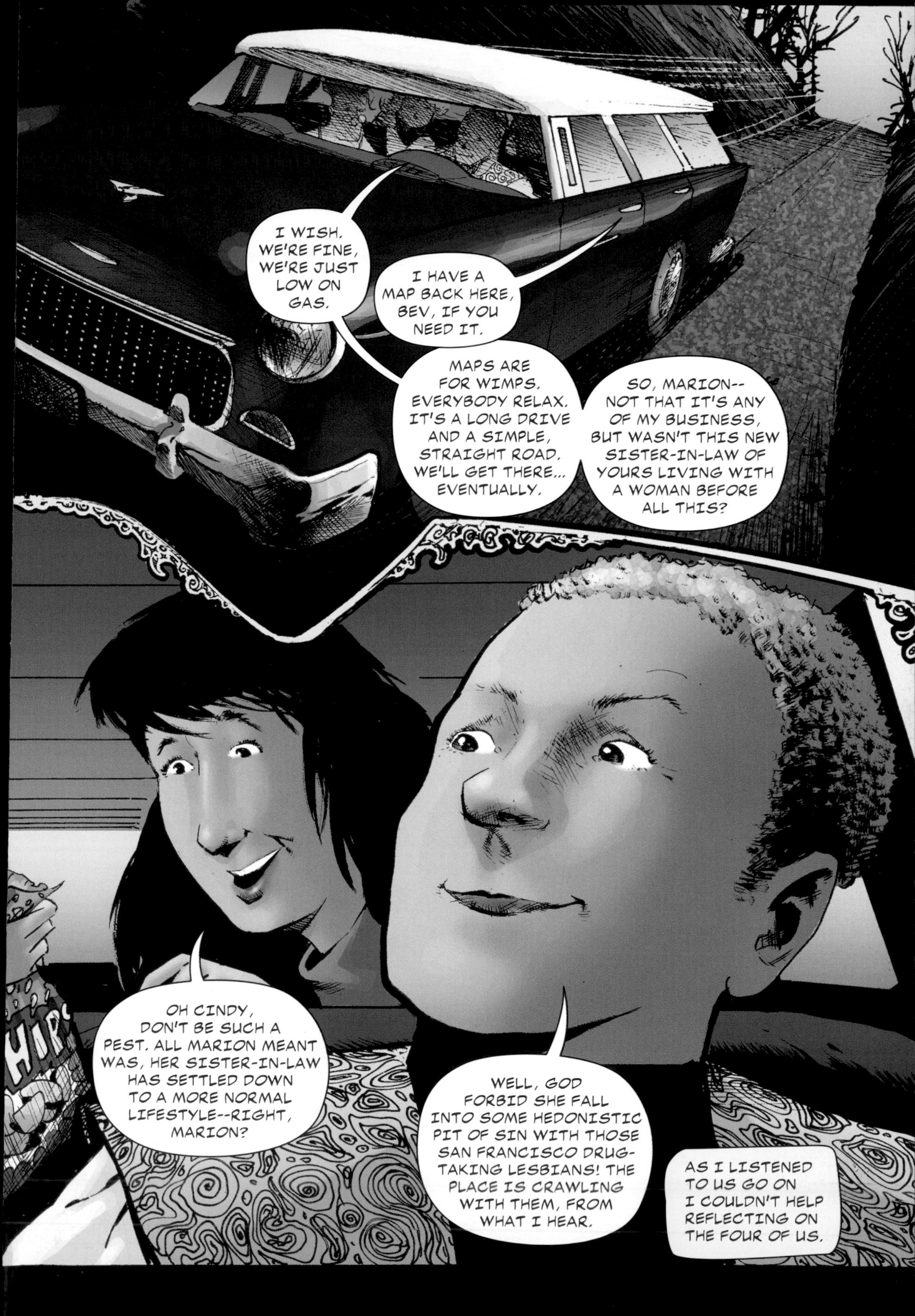
I WISH. WE'RE FINE, WE'RE JUST LOW ON GAS.
I HAVE A MAP BACK HERE, BEV, IF YOU NEED IT.
MAPS ARE FOR WIMPS. EVERYBODY RELAX. IT'S A LONG DRIVE AND A SIMPLE, STRAIGHT ROAD. WE'LL GET THERE... EVENTUALLY.
SO, MARION-- NOT THAT IT'S ANY OF MY BUSINESS, BUT WASN'T THIS NEW SISTER-IN-LAW OF YOURS LIVING WITH A WOMAN BEFORE ALL THIS?
OH CINDY, DON'T BE SUCH A PEST. ALL MARION MEANT WAS, HER SISTER-IN-LAW HAS SETTLED DOWN TO A MORE NORMAL LIFESTYLE--RIGHT, MARION?
WELL, GOD FORBID SHE FALL INTO SOME HEDONISTIC PIT OF SIN WITH THOSE SAN FRANCISCO DRUG-TAKING LESBIANS! THE PLACE IS CRAWLING WITH THEM, FROM WHAT I HEAR.
AS I LISTENED TO US GO ON I COULDN'T HELP REFLECTING ON THE FOUR OF US.

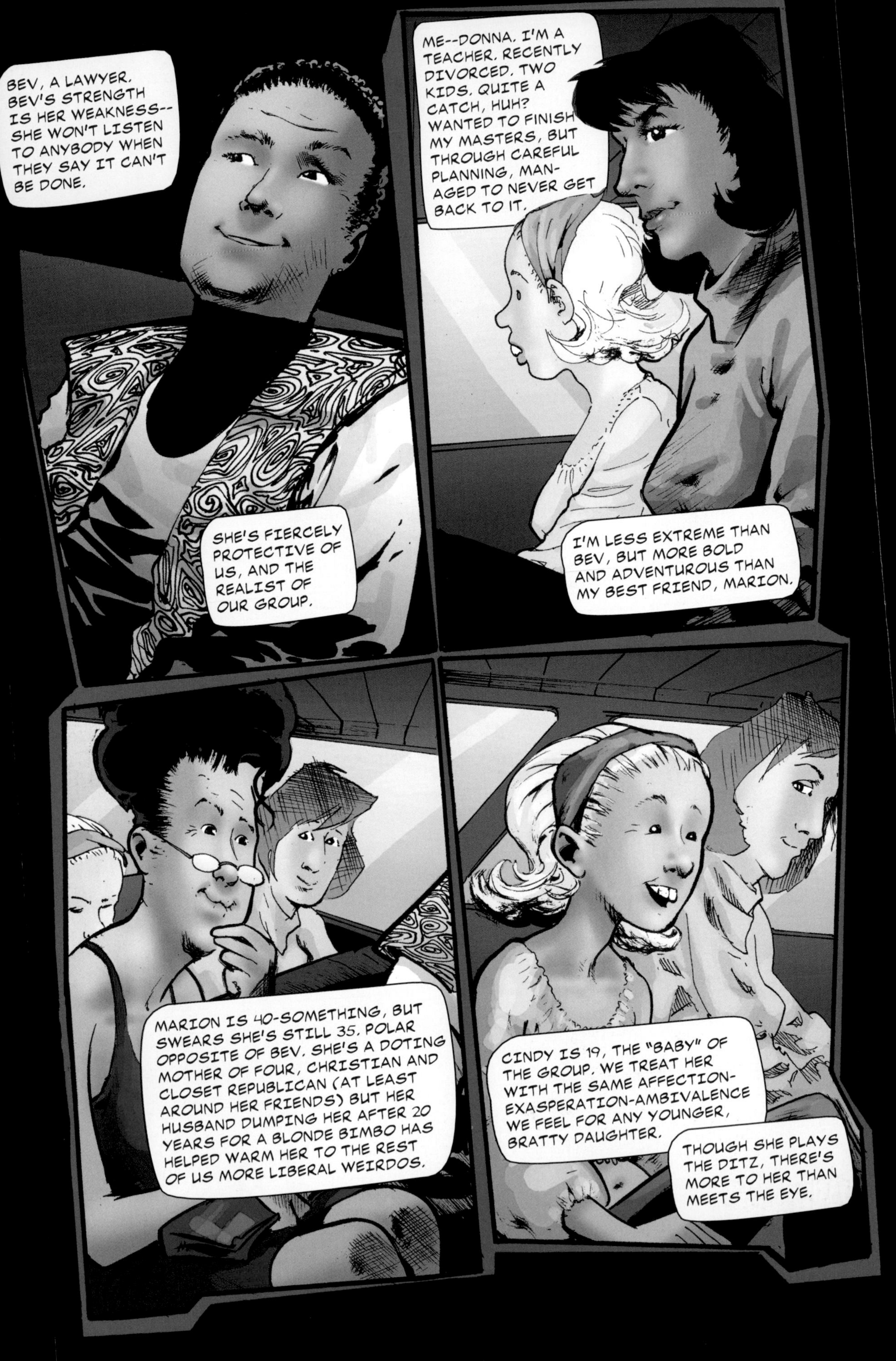
BEV, A LAWYER. BEV'S STRENGTH IS HER WEAKNESS--SHE WON'T LISTEN TO ANYBODY WHEN THEY SAY IT CAN'T BE DONE.
SHE'S FIERCELY PROTECTIVE OF US, AND THE REALIST OF OUR GROUP.
ME--DONNA. I'M A TEACHER. RECENTLY DIVORCED. TWO KIDS. QUITE A CATCH, HUH? WANTED TO FINISH MY MASTERS, BUT THROUGH CAREFUL PLANNING, MAN-AGED TO NEVER GET BACK TO IT.
I'M LESS EXTREME THAN BEV, BUT MORE BOLD AND ADVENTUROUS THAN MY BEST FRIEND, MARION.
MARION IS 40-SOMETHING, BUT SWEARS SHE'S STILL 35. POLAR OPPOSITE OF BEV. SHE'S A DOTING MOTHER OF FOUR, CHRISTIAN AND CLOSET REPUBLICAN (AT LEAST AROUND HER FRIENDS) BUT HER HUSBAND DUMPING HER AFTER 20 YEARS FOR A BLONDE BIMBO HAS HELPED WARM HER TO THE REST OF US MORE LIBERAL WEIRDOS.
CINDY IS 19, THE "BABY" OF THE GROUP. WE TREAT HER WITH THE SAME AFFECTION-EXASPERATION-AMBIVALENCE WE FEEL FOR ANY YOUNGER, BRATTY DAUGHTER.
THOUGH SHE PLAYS THE DITZ, THERE'S MORE TO HER THAN MEETS THE EYE.

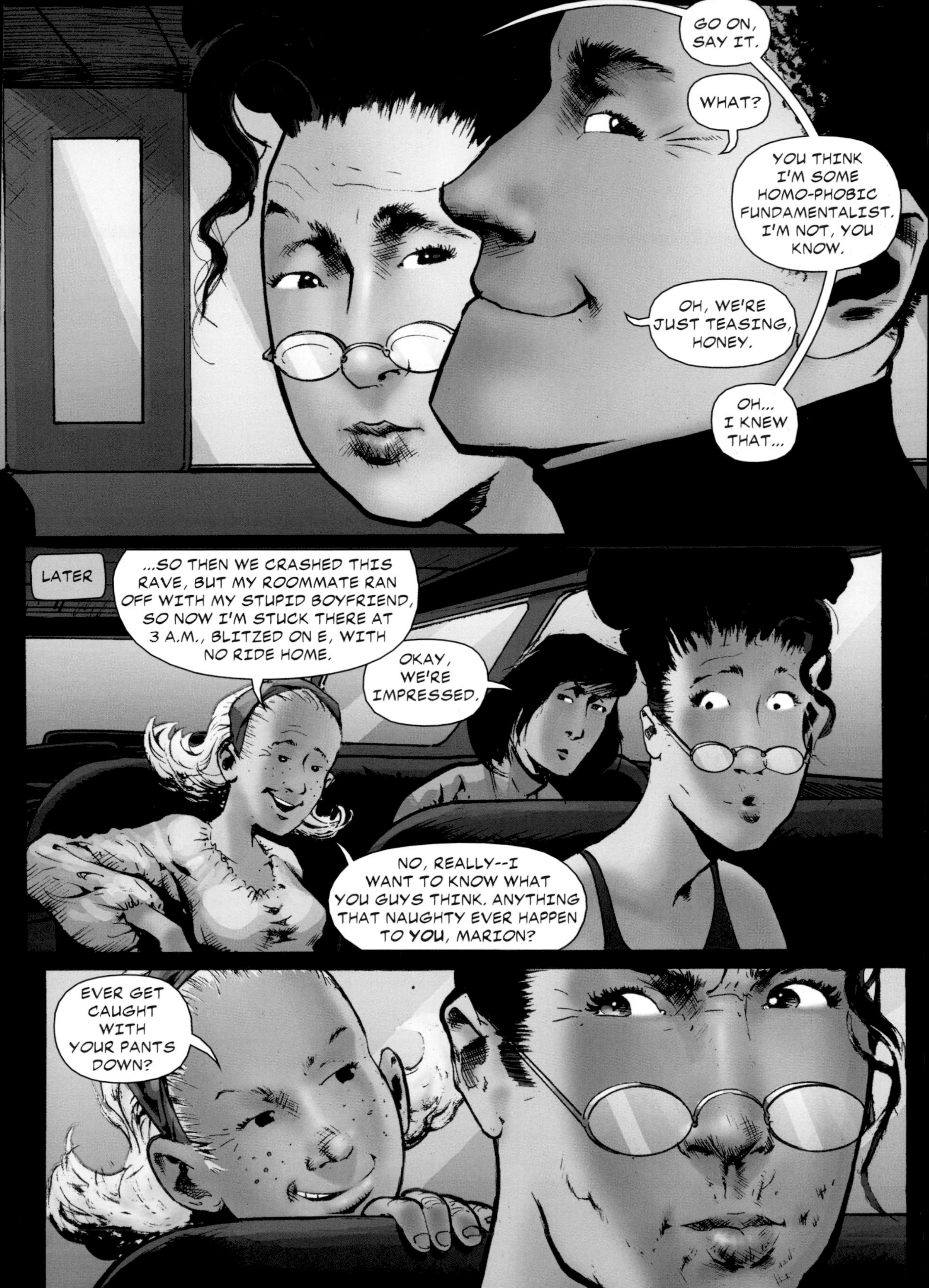
GO ON, SAY IT.
WHAT?
YOU THINK I'M SOME HOMO-PHOBIC FUNDAMENTALIST. I'M NOT, YOU KNOW.
OH, WE'RE JUST TEASING, HONEY.
OH... I KNEW THAT...
LATER
...SO THEN WE CRASHED THIS RAVE, BUT MY ROOMMATE RAN OFF WITH MY STUPID BOYFRIEND, SO NOW I'M STUCK THERE AT 3 A.M., BLITZED ON E, WITH NO RIDE HOME.
OKAY, WE'RE IMPRESSED.
NO, REALLY--I WANT TO KNOW WHAT YOU GUYS THINK. ANYTHING THAT NAUGHTY EVER HAPPEN TO YOU, MARION?
EVER GET CAUGHT WITH YOUR PANTS DOWN?

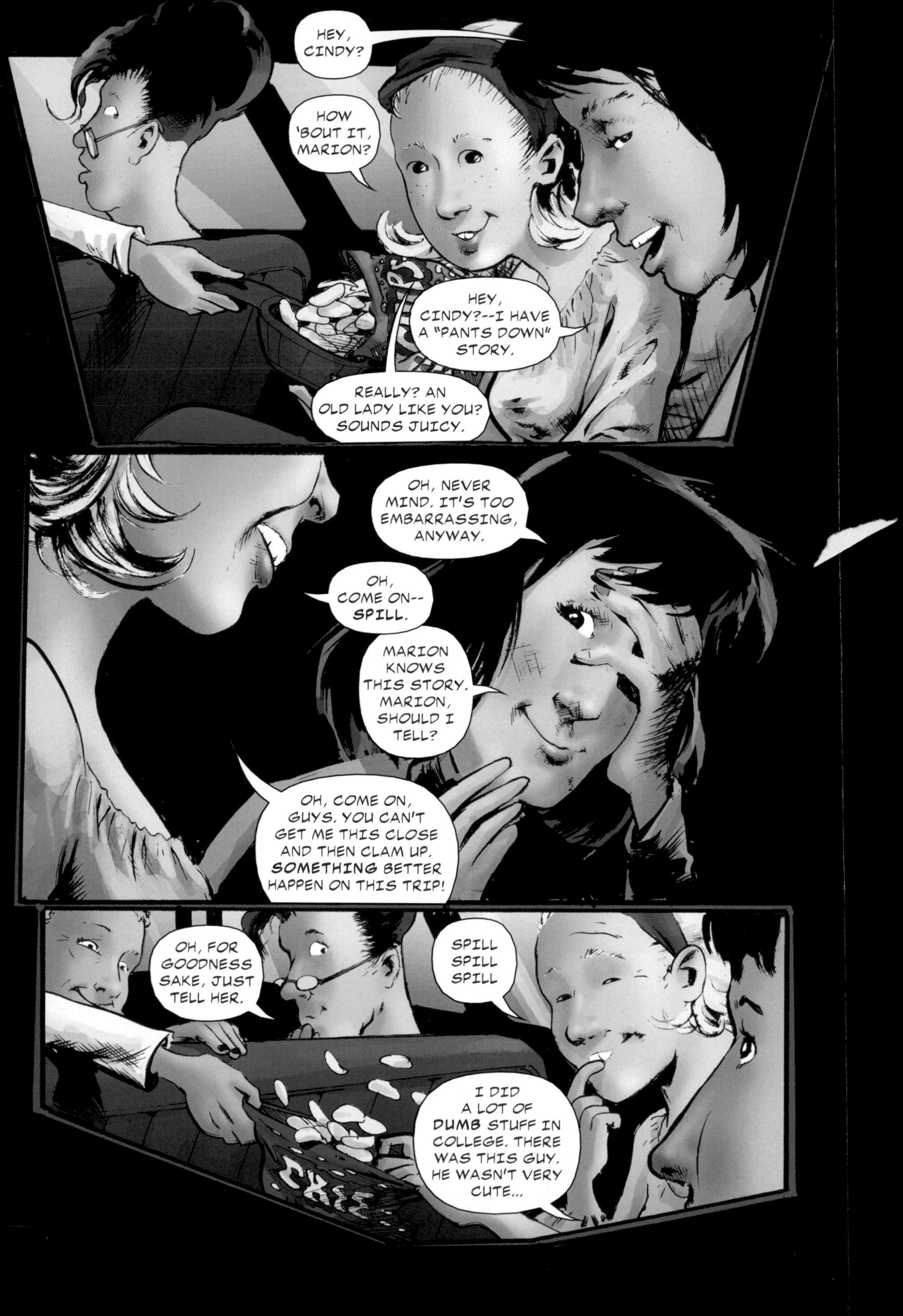
HEY, CINDY?
HOW 'BOUT IT, MARION?
HEY, CINDY?--I HAVE A "PANTS DOWN" STORY.
REALLY? AN OLD LADY LIKE YOU? SOUNDS JUICY.
OH, NEVER MIND. IT'S TOO EMBARRASSING, ANYWAY.
OH, COME ON-- SPILL.
MARION KNOWS THIS STORY. MARION, SHOULD I TELL?
OH, COME ON, GUYS. YOU CAN'T GET ME THIS CLOSE AND THEN CLAM UP. SOMETHING BETTER HAPPEN ON THIS TRIP!
OH, FOR GOODNESS SAKE, JUST TELL HER.
SPILL SPILL SPILL
I DID A LOT OF DUMB STUFF IN COLLEGE. THERE WAS THIS GUY. HE WASN'T VERY CUTE...

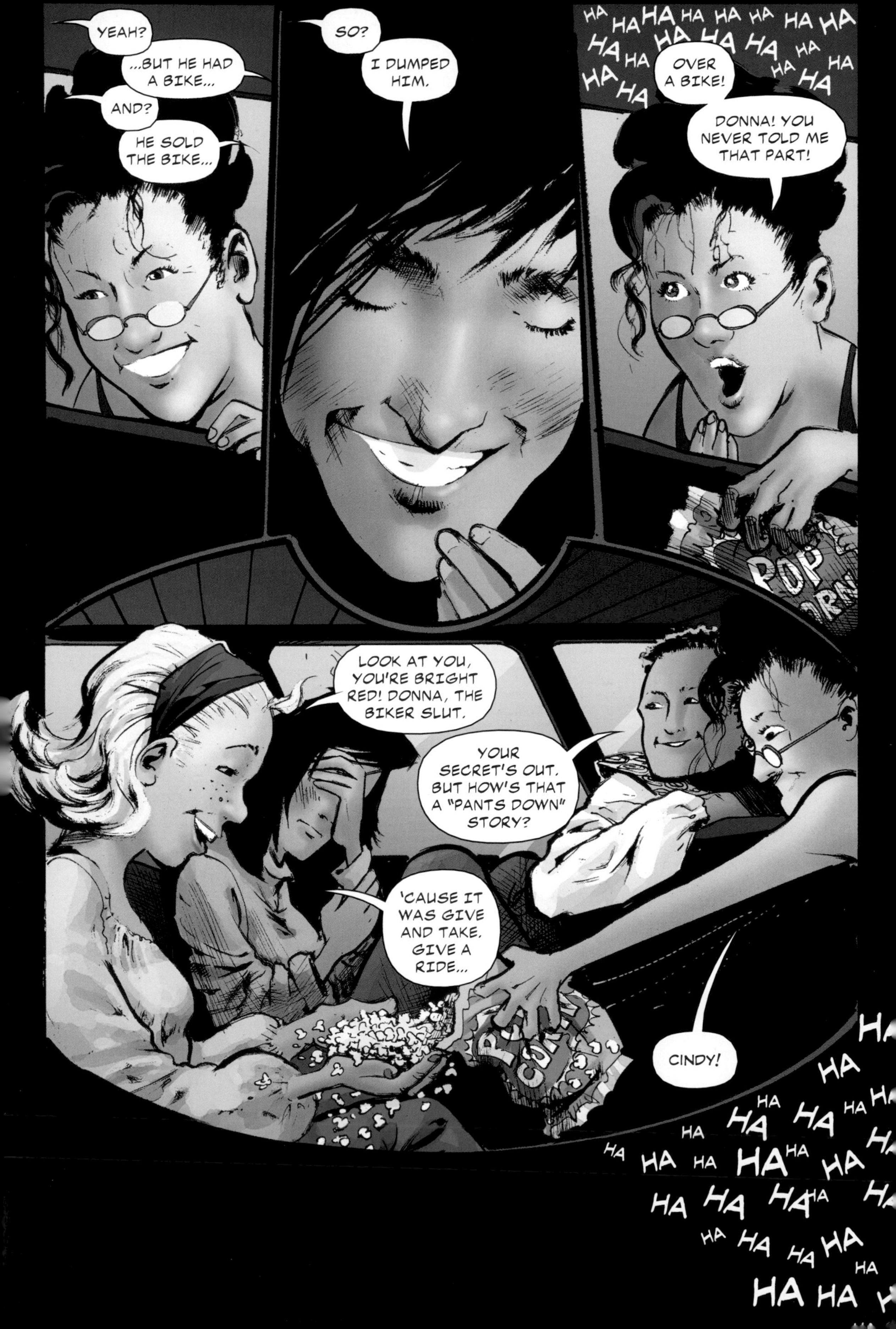
YEAH?
...BUT HE HAD A BIKE...
AND?
HE SOLD THE BIKE...
SO?
I DUMPED HIM.
HA HA HA HA HA HA HA HA HA HA HA HA HA HA HA HA HA HA HA
OVER A BIKE!
DONNA! YOU NEVER TOLD ME THAT PART!
LOOK AT YOU, YOU'RE BRIGHT RED! DONNA, THE BIKER SLUT.
YOUR SECRET'S OUT. BUT HOW'S THAT A "PANTS DOWN" STORY?
'CAUSE IT WAS GIVE AND TAKE. GIVE A RIDE...
CINDY!
HA HA HA HA HA HA HA HA HA HA HA HA HA HA HA HA HA HA HA HA HA HA HA HA

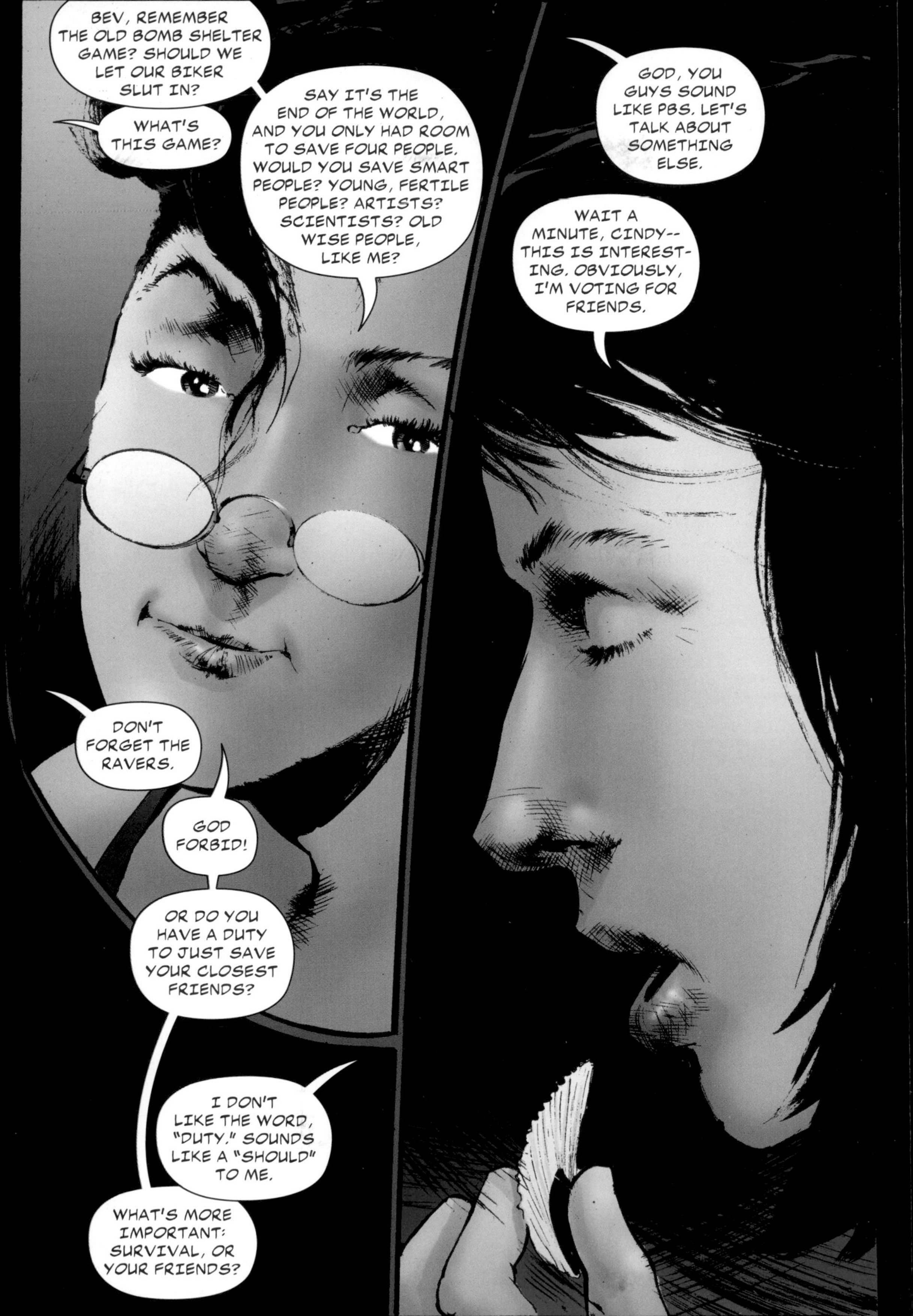
BEV, REMEMBER THE OLD BOMB SHELTER GAME? SHOULD WE LET OUR BIKER SLUT IN?
WHAT'S THIS GAME?
SAY IT'S THE END OF THE WORLD, AND YOU ONLY HAD ROOM TO SAVE FOUR PEOPLE. WOULD YOU SAVE SMART PEOPLE? YOUNG, FERTILE PEOPLE? ARTISTS? SCIENTISTS? OLD WISE PEOPLE, LIKE ME?
GOD, YOU GUYS SOUND LIKE PBS. LET'S TALK ABOUT SOMETHING ELSE.
WAIT A MINUTE, CINDY-- THIS IS INTEREST-ING. OBVIOUSLY, I'M VOTING FOR FRIENDS.
DON'T FORGET THE RAVERS.
GOD FORBID!
OR DO YOU HAVE A DUTY TO JUST SAVE YOUR CLOSEST FRIENDS?
I DON'T LIKE THE WORD, "DUTY." SOUNDS LIKE A "SHOULD" TO ME.
WHAT'S MORE IMPORTANT: SURVIVAL, OR YOUR FRIENDS?

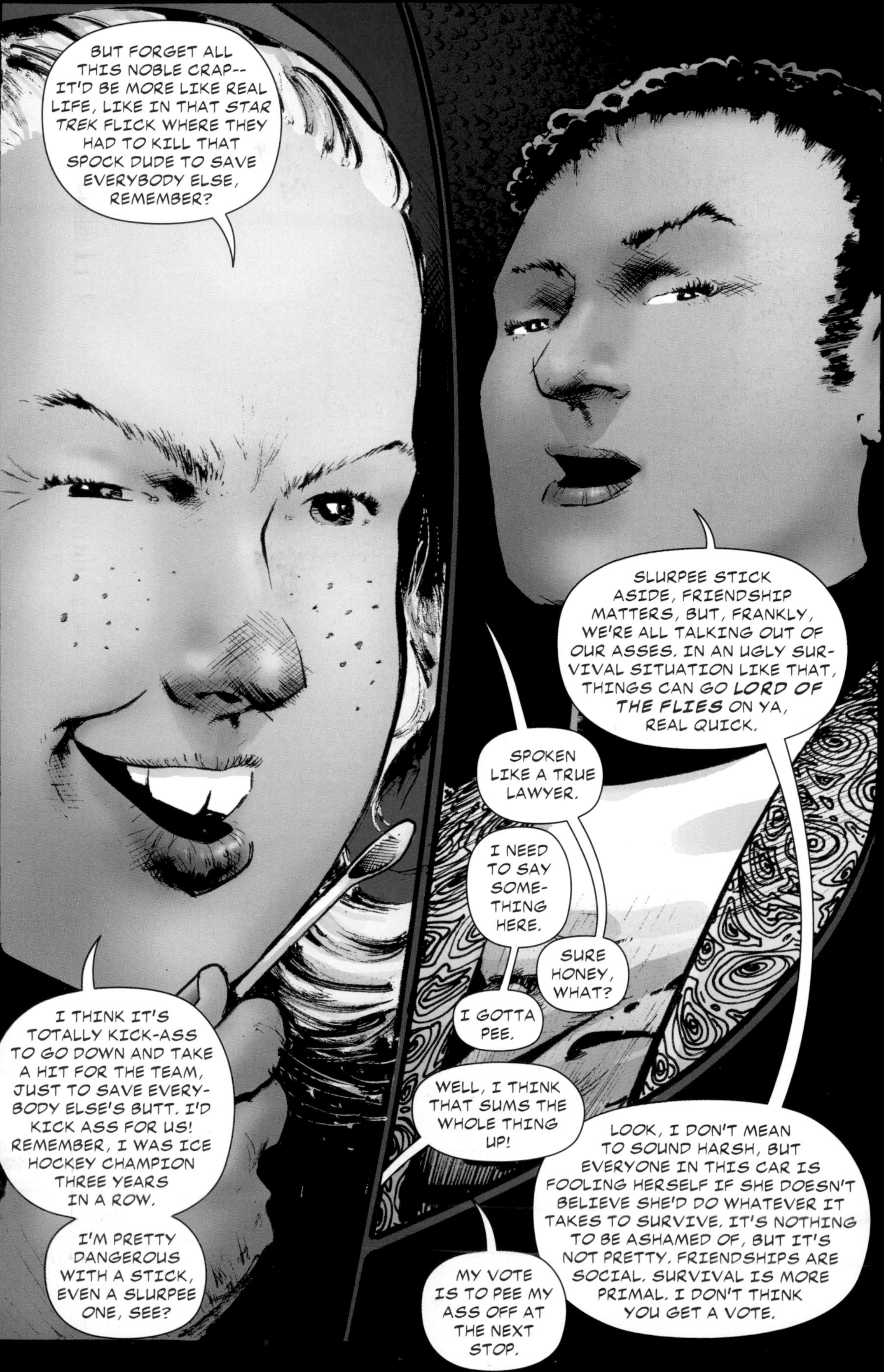

BUT FORGET ALL THIS NOBLE CRAP-- IT'D BE MORE LIKE REAL LIFE, LIKE IN THAT STAR TREK FLICK WHERE THEY HAD TO KILL THAT SPOCK DUDE TO SAVE EVERYBODY ELSE, REMEMBER?
SLURPEE STICK ASIDE, FRIENDSHIP MATTERS, BUT, FRANKLY, WE'RE ALL TALKING OUT OF OUR ASSES. IN AN UGLY SURVIVAL SITUATION LIKE THAT, THINGS CAN GO LORD OF THE FLIES ON YA, REAL QUICK.
SPOKEN LIKE A TRUE LAWYER.
I NEED TO SAY SOMETHING HERE.
SURE HONEY, WHAT?
I GOTTA PEE.
I THINK IT'S TOTALLY KICK-ASS TO GO DOWN AND TAKE A HIT FOR THE TEAM, JUST TO SAVE EVERYBODY ELSE'S BUTT. I'D KICK ASS FOR US! REMEMBER, I WAS ICE HOCKEY CHAMPION THREE YEARS IN A ROW.
I'M PRETTY DANGEROUS WITH A STICK, EVEN A SLURPEE ONE, SEE?
WELL, I THINK THAT SUMS THE WHOLE THING UP!
LOOK, I DON'T MEAN TO SOUND HARSH, BUT EVERYONE IN THIS CAR IS FOOLING HERSELF IF SHE DOESN'T BELIEVE SHE'D DO WHATEVER IT TAKES TO SURVIVE. IT'S NOTHING TO BE ASHAMED OF, BUT IT'S NOT PRETTY. FRIENDSHIPS ARE SOCIAL. SURVIVAL IS MORE PRIMAL. I DON'T THINK YOU GET A VOTE.
MY VOTE IS TO PEE MY ASS OFF AT THE NEXT STOP.

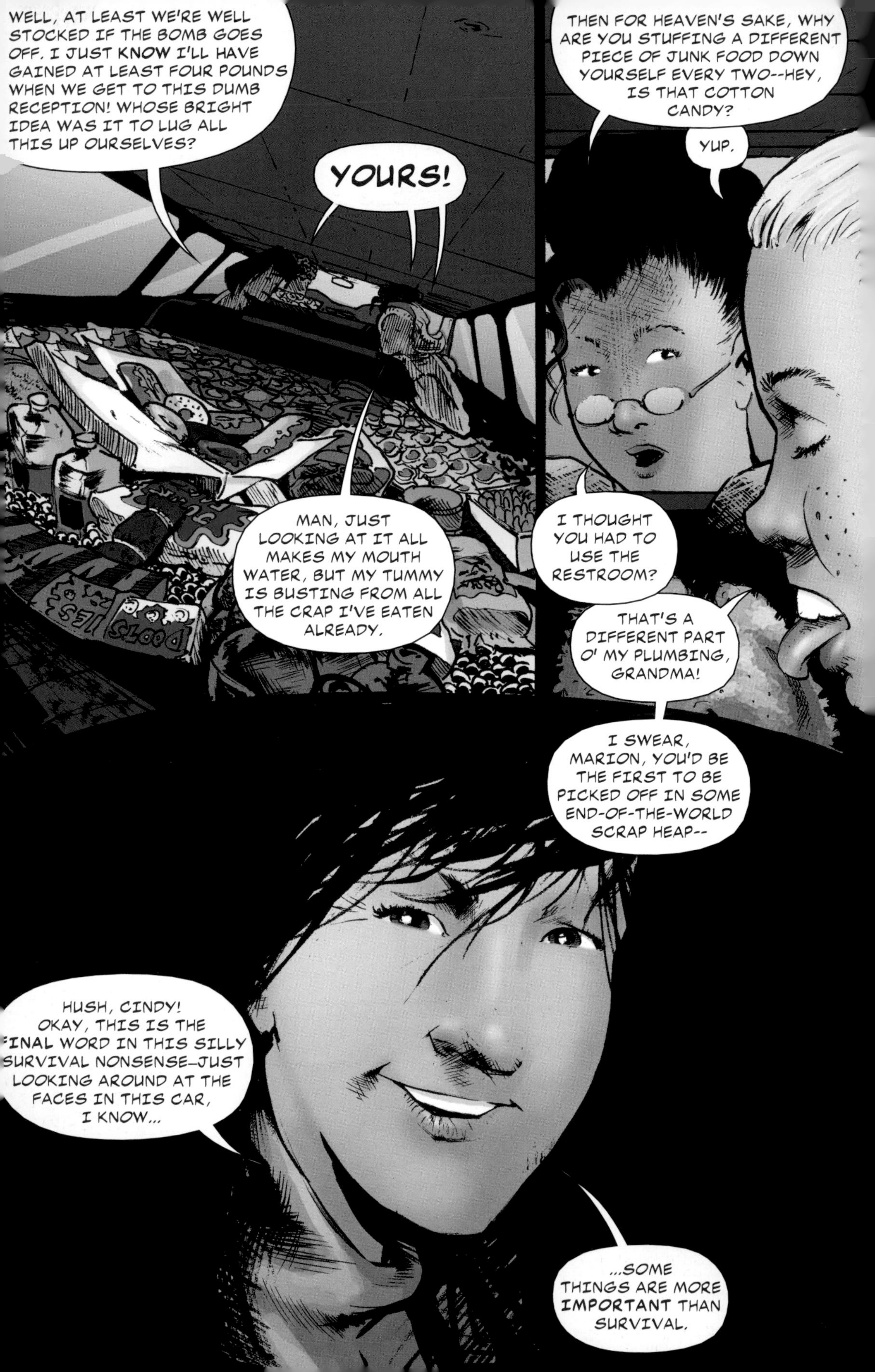
WELL, AT LEAST WE'RE WELL STOCKED IF THE BOMB GOES OFF. I JUST **KNOW** I'LL HAVE GAINED AT LEAST FOUR POUNDS WHEN WE GET TO THIS DUMB RECEPTION! WHOSE BRIGHT IDEA WAS IT TO LUG ALL THIS UP OURSELVES?
YOURS!
MAN, JUST LOOKING AT IT ALL MAKES MY MOUTH WATER, BUT MY TUMMY IS BUSTING FROM ALL THE CRAP I'VE EATEN ALREADY.
THEN FOR HEAVEN'S SAKE, WHY ARE YOU STUFFING A DIFFERENT PIECE OF JUNK FOOD DOWN YOURSELF EVERY TWO--HEY, IS THAT COTTON CANDY?
YUP.
I THOUGHT YOU HAD TO USE THE RESTROOM?
THAT'S A DIFFERENT PART O' MY PLUMBING, GRANDMA!
I SWEAR, MARION, YOU'D BE THE FIRST TO BE PICKED OFF IN SOME END-OF-THE-WORLD SCRAP HEAP--
HUSH, CINDY! OKAY, THIS IS THE **FINAL** WORD IN THIS SILLY SURVIVAL NONSENSE–JUST LOOKING AROUND AT THE FACES IN THIS CAR, I KNOW...
...SOME THINGS ARE MORE **IMPORTANT** THAN SURVIVAL.

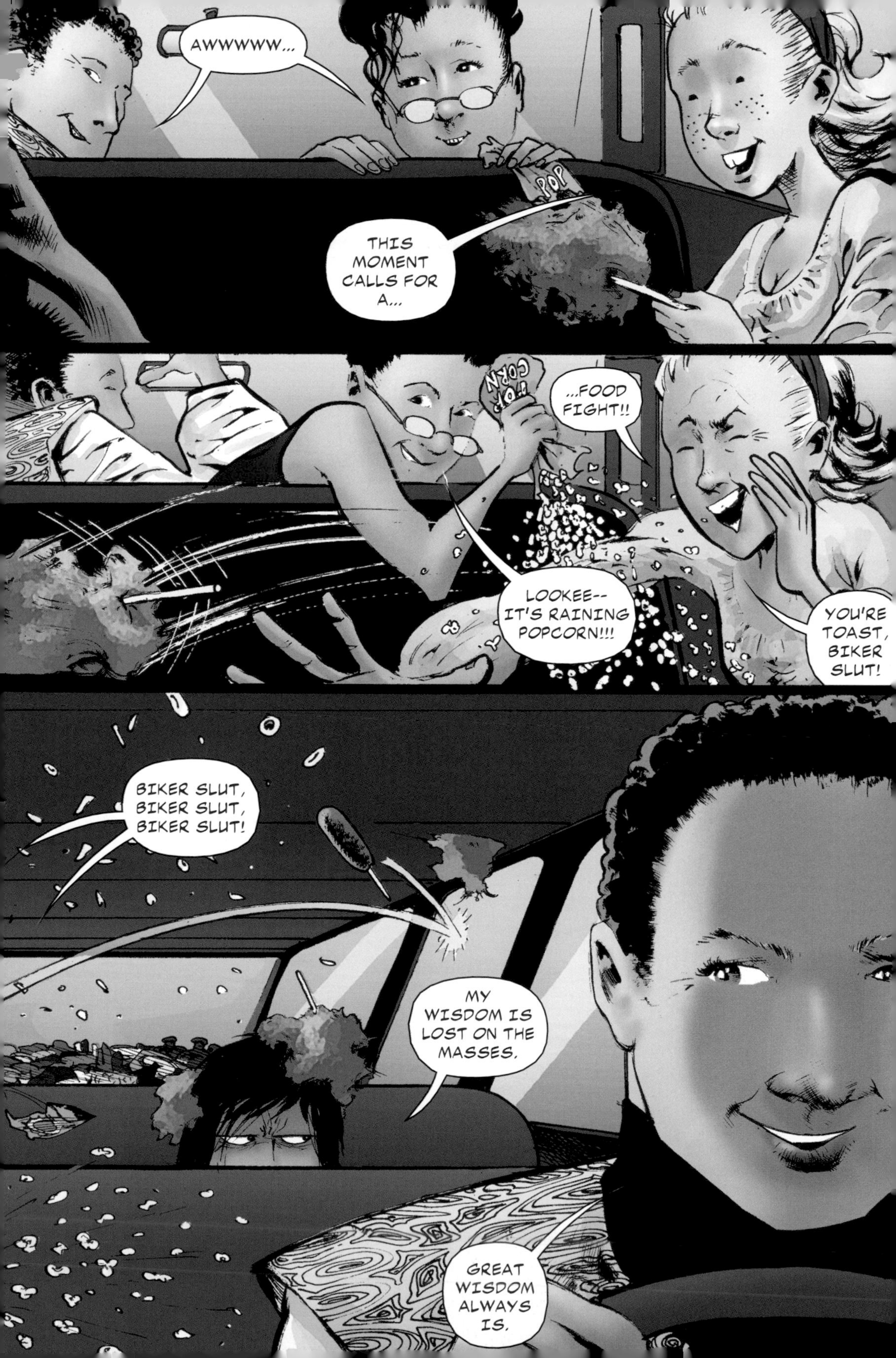
AWWWWW...
THIS MOMENT CALLS FOR A...
POP
...FOOD FIGHT!!
POP CORN
LOOKEE-- IT'S RAINING POPCORN!!!
YOU'RE TOAST, BIKER SLUT!
BIKER SLUT, BIKER SLUT, BIKER SLUT!
MY WISDOM IS LOST ON THE MASSES.
GREAT WISDOM ALWAYS IS.

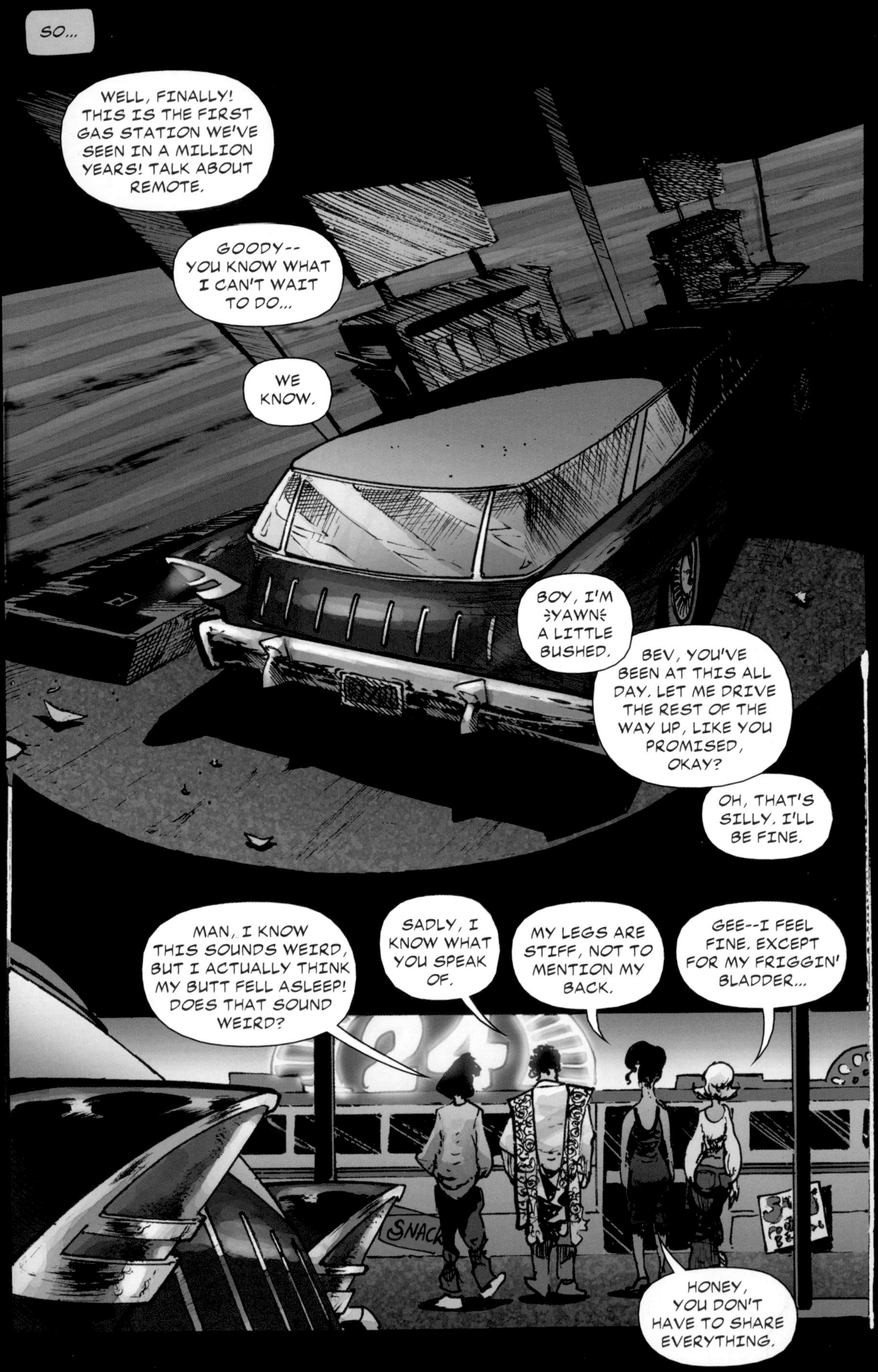
SO...
WELL, FINALLY! THIS IS THE FIRST GAS STATION WE'VE SEEN IN A MILLION YEARS! TALK ABOUT REMOTE.
GOODY-- YOU KNOW WHAT I CAN'T WAIT TO DO...
WE KNOW.
BOY, I'M ≶YAWN≶ A LITTLE BUSHED.
BEV, YOU'VE BEEN AT THIS ALL DAY. LET ME DRIVE THE REST OF THE WAY UP, LIKE YOU PROMISED, OKAY?
OH, THAT'S SILLY. I'LL BE FINE.
MAN, I KNOW THIS SOUNDS WEIRD, BUT I ACTUALLY THINK MY BUTT FELL ASLEEP! DOES THAT SOUND WEIRD?
SADLY, I KNOW WHAT YOU SPEAK OF.
MY LEGS ARE STIFF, NOT TO MENTION MY BACK.
GEE--I FEEL FINE. EXCEPT FOR MY FRIGGIN' BLADDER...
HONEY, YOU DON'T HAVE TO SHARE EVERYTHING.

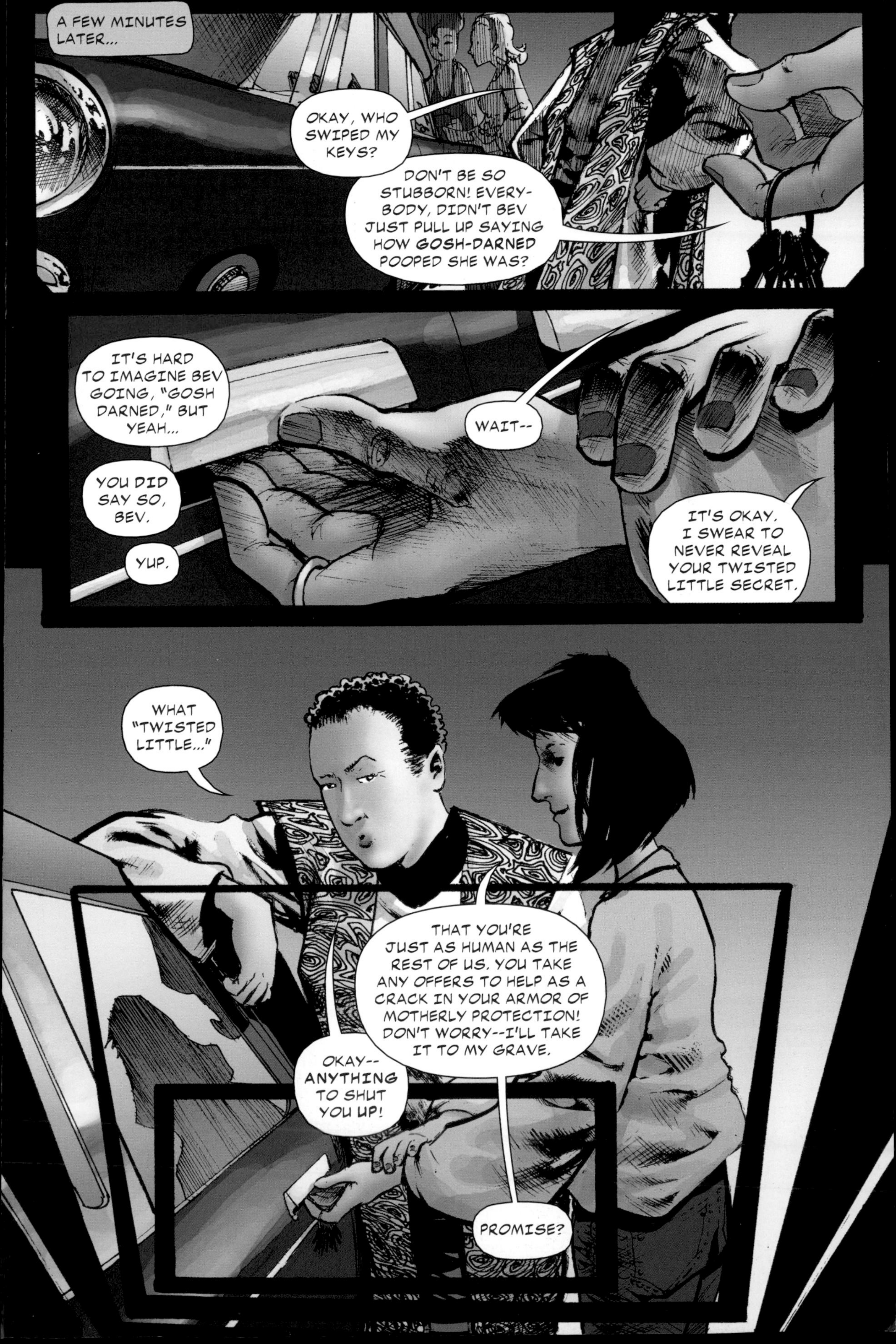
A FEW MINUTES LATER...
OKAY, WHO SWIPED MY KEYS?
DON'T BE SO STUBBORN! EVERY-BODY, DIDN'T BEV JUST PULL UP SAYING HOW GOSH-DARNED POOPED SHE WAS?
IT'S HARD TO IMAGINE BEV GOING, "GOSH DARNED," BUT YEAH...
YOU DID SAY SO, BEV.
YUP.
WAIT--
IT'S OKAY. I SWEAR TO NEVER REVEAL YOUR TWISTED LITTLE SECRET.
WHAT "TWISTED LITTLE..."
THAT YOU'RE JUST AS HUMAN AS THE REST OF US. YOU TAKE ANY OFFERS TO HELP AS A CRACK IN YOUR ARMOR OF MOTHERLY PROTECTION! DON'T WORRY--I'LL TAKE IT TO MY GRAVE.
OKAY-- ANYTHING TO SHUT YOU UP!
PROMISE?

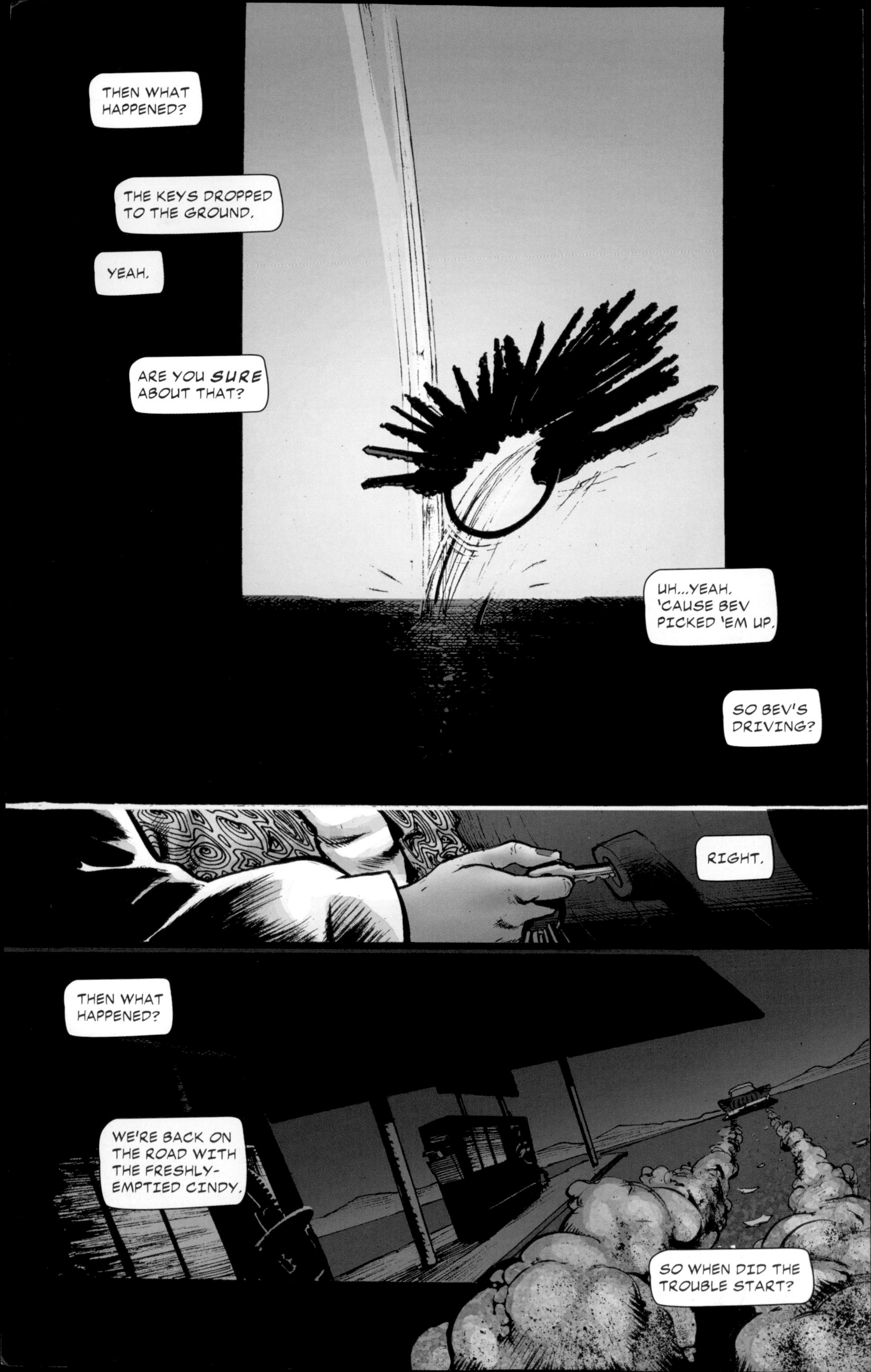
THEN WHAT HAPPENED?
THE KEYS DROPPED TO THE GROUND.
YEAH.
ARE YOU SURE ABOUT THAT?
UH...YEAH. 'CAUSE BEV PICKED 'EM UP.
SO BEV'S DRIVING?
RIGHT.
THEN WHAT HAPPENED?
WE'RE BACK ON THE ROAD WITH THE FRESHLY-EMPTIED CINDY.
SO WHEN DID THE TROUBLE START?

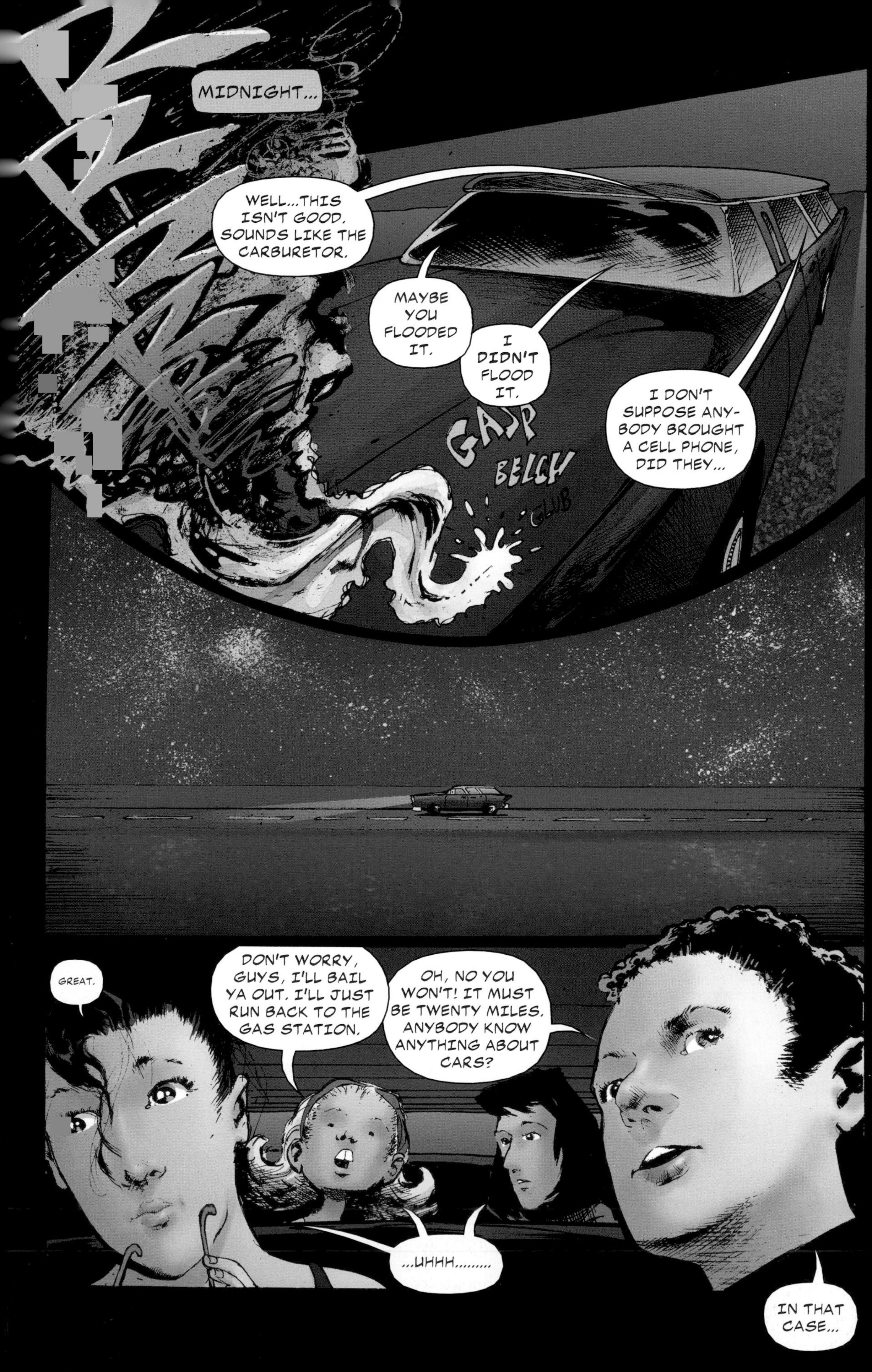
MIDNIGHT...
WELL...THIS ISN'T GOOD. SOUNDS LIKE THE CARBURETOR.
MAYBE YOU FLOODED IT.
I DIDN'T FLOOD IT.
I DON'T SUPPOSE ANYBODY BROUGHT A CELL PHONE, DID THEY...
GASP
BELCH
GLUB
GREAT.
DON'T WORRY, GUYS, I'LL BAIL YA OUT. I'LL JUST RUN BACK TO THE GAS STATION.
OH, NO YOU WON'T! IT MUST BE TWENTY MILES. ANYBODY KNOW ANYTHING ABOUT CARS?
...UHHH.........
IN THAT CASE...

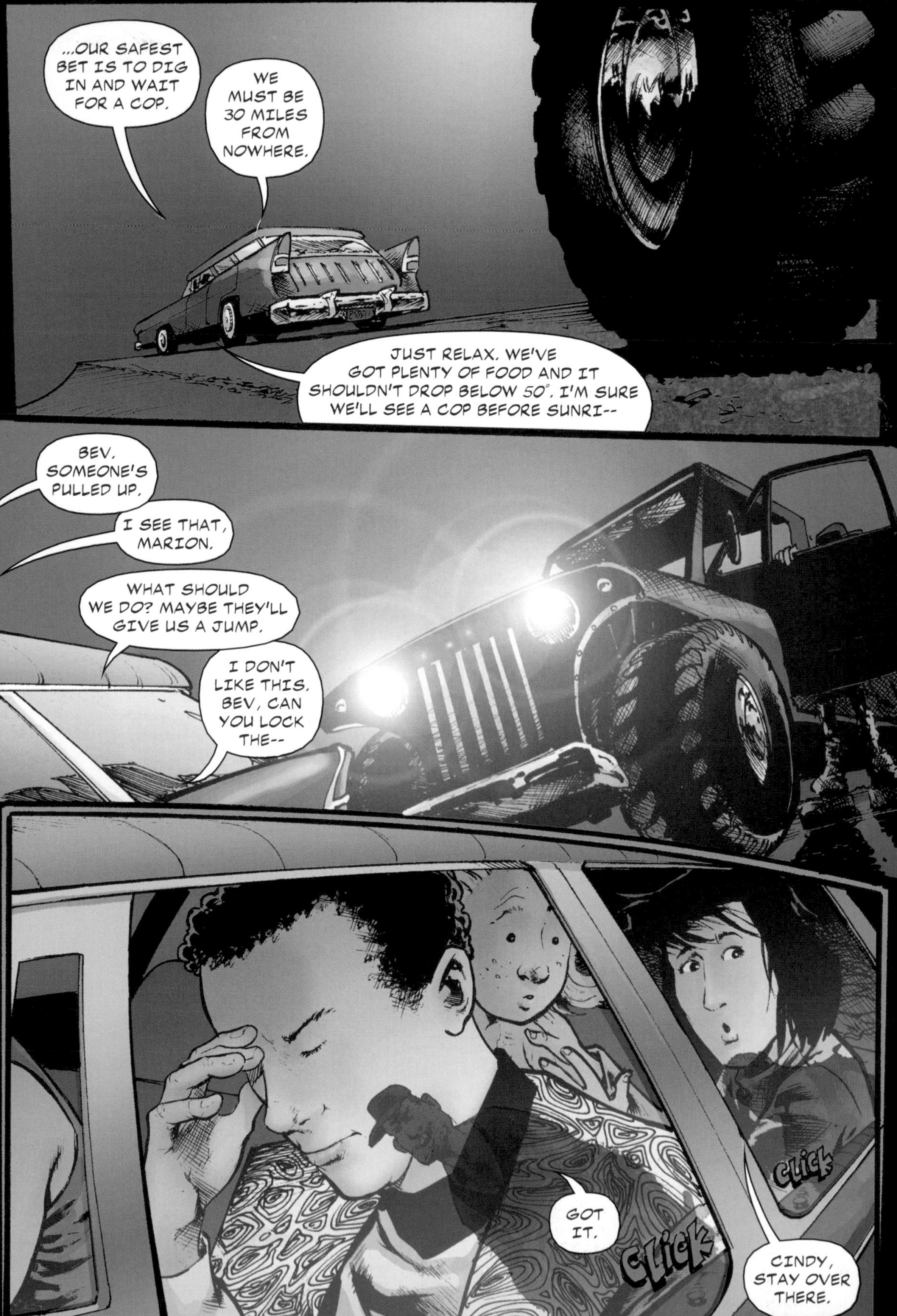
...OUR SAFEST BET IS TO DIG IN AND WAIT FOR A COP.
WE MUST BE 30 MILES FROM NOWHERE.
JUST RELAX. WE'VE GOT PLENTY OF FOOD AND IT SHOULDN'T DROP BELOW 50°. I'M SURE WE'LL SEE A COP BEFORE SUNRI--
BEV. SOMEONE'S PULLED UP.
I SEE THAT, MARION.
WHAT SHOULD WE DO? MAYBE THEY'LL GIVE US A JUMP.
I DON'T LIKE THIS. BEV, CAN YOU LOCK THE--
CLICK
GOT IT.
CLICK
CINDY, STAY OVER THERE.

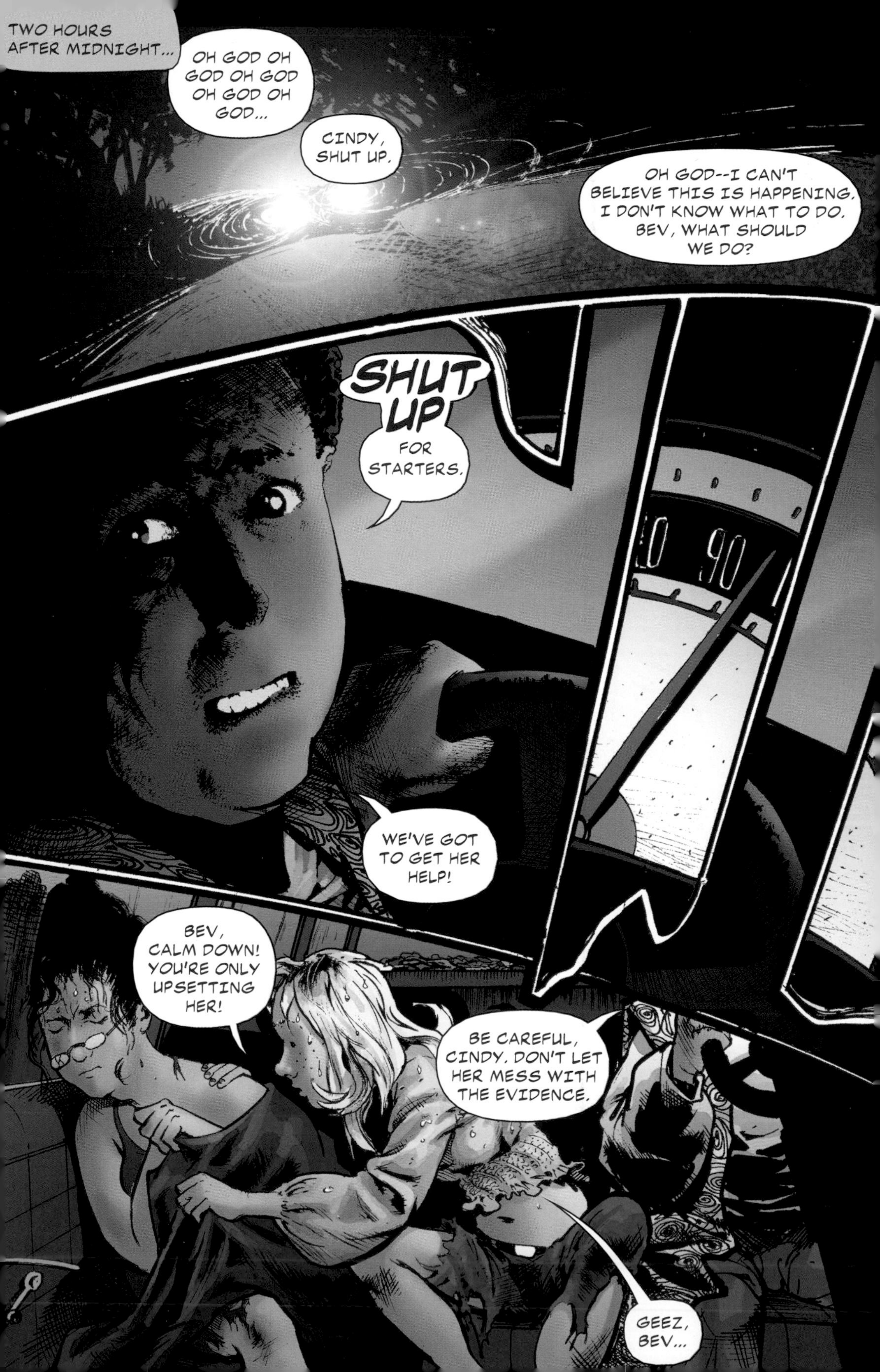
TWO HOURS AFTER MIDNIGHT...
OH GOD OH GOD OH GOD OH GOD OH GOD...
CINDY, SHUT UP.
OH GOD--I CAN'T BELIEVE THIS IS HAPPENING. I DON'T KNOW WHAT TO DO. BEV, WHAT SHOULD WE DO?
SHUT UP
FOR STARTERS.
WE'VE GOT TO GET HER HELP!
BEV, CALM DOWN! YOU'RE ONLY UPSETTING HER!
BE CAREFUL, CINDY. DON'T LET HER MESS WITH THE EVIDENCE.
GEEZ, BEV...

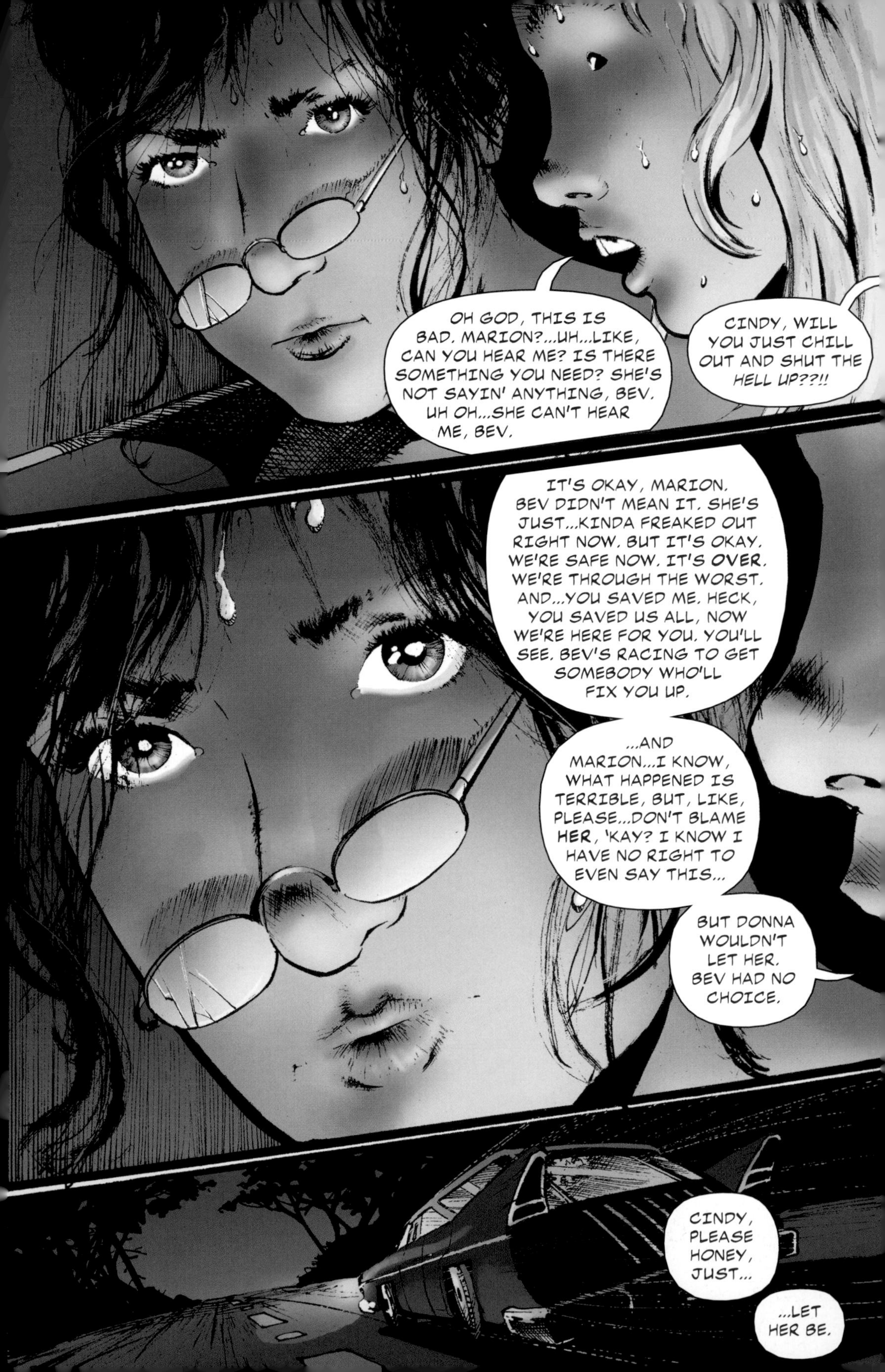
OH GOD, THIS IS BAD. MARION?...UH...LIKE, CAN YOU HEAR ME? IS THERE SOMETHING YOU NEED? SHE'S NOT SAYIN' ANYTHING, BEV. UH OH...SHE CAN'T HEAR ME, BEV.
CINDY, WILL YOU JUST CHILL OUT AND SHUT THE HELL UP??!!
IT'S OKAY, MARION. BEV DIDN'T MEAN IT. SHE'S JUST...KINDA FREAKED OUT RIGHT NOW. BUT IT'S OKAY. WE'RE SAFE NOW. IT'S OVER. WE'RE THROUGH THE WORST. AND...YOU SAVED ME. HECK, YOU SAVED US ALL, NOW WE'RE HERE FOR YOU. YOU'LL SEE. BEV'S RACING TO GET SOMEBODY WHO'LL FIX YOU UP.
...AND MARION...I KNOW, WHAT HAPPENED IS TERRIBLE, BUT, LIKE, PLEASE...DON'T BLAME HER, 'KAY? I KNOW I HAVE NO RIGHT TO EVEN SAY THIS...
BUT DONNA WOULDN'T LET HER. BEV HAD NO CHOICE.
CINDY, PLEASE HONEY, JUST...
...LET HER BE.

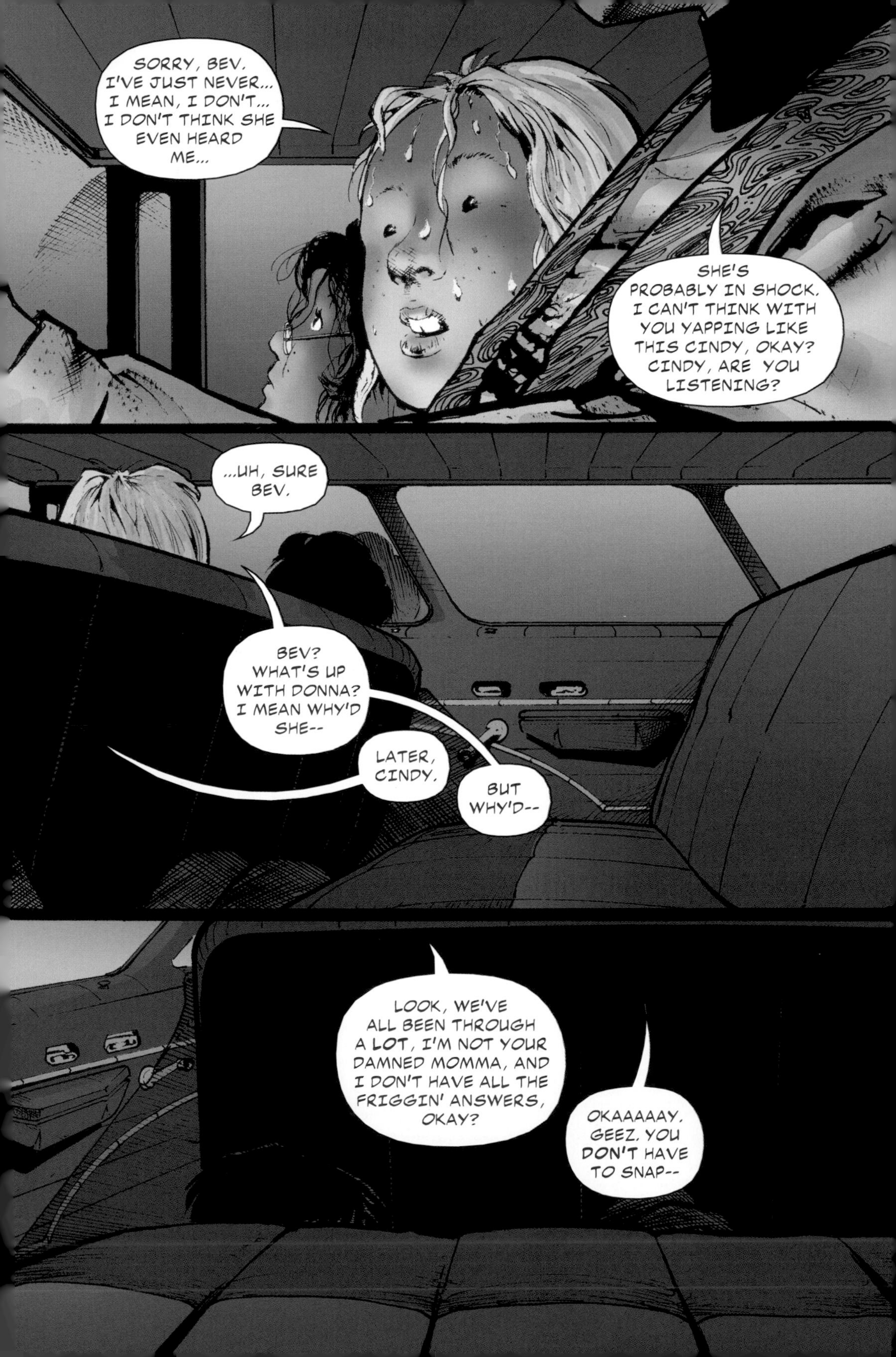
SORRY, BEV. I'VE JUST NEVER... I MEAN, I DON'T... I DON'T THINK SHE EVEN HEARD ME...
SHE'S PROBABLY IN SHOCK. I CAN'T THINK WITH YOU YAPPING LIKE THIS CINDY, OKAY? CINDY, ARE YOU LISTENING?
...UH, SURE BEV.
BEV? WHAT'S UP WITH DONNA? I MEAN WHY'D SHE--
LATER, CINDY.
BUT WHY'D--
LOOK, WE'VE ALL BEEN THROUGH A **LOT**, I'M NOT YOUR DAMNED MOMMA, AND I DON'T HAVE ALL THE FRIGGIN' ANSWERS, OKAY?
OKAAAAAY. GEEZ. YOU **DON'T** HAVE TO SNAP--

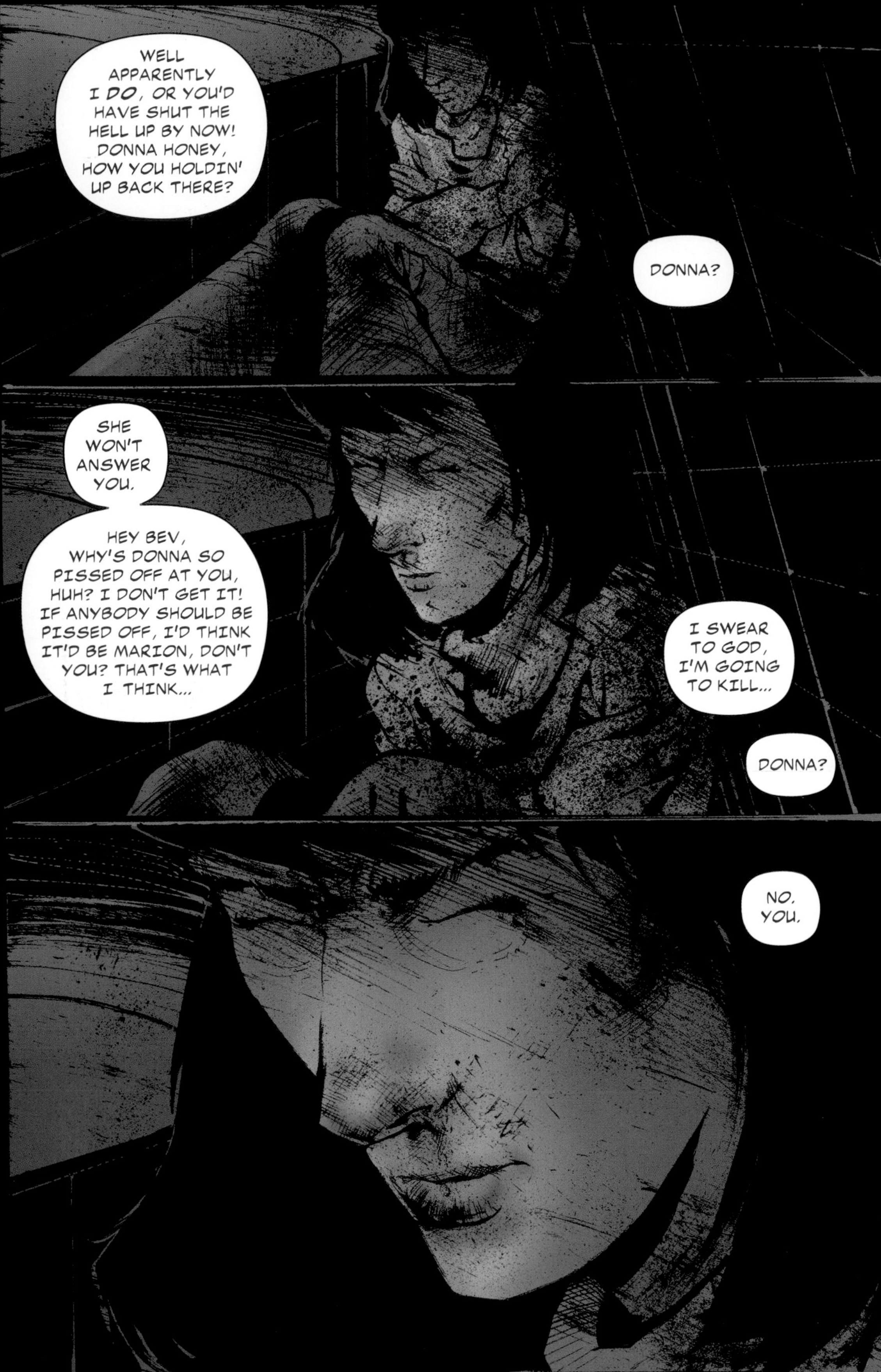
WELL APPARENTLY I DO, OR YOU'D HAVE SHUT THE HELL UP BY NOW! DONNA HONEY, HOW YOU HOLDIN' UP BACK THERE?
DONNA?
SHE WON'T ANSWER YOU.
HEY BEV, WHY'S DONNA SO PISSED OFF AT YOU, HUH? I DON'T GET IT! IF ANYBODY SHOULD BE PISSED OFF, I'D THINK IT'D BE MARION, DON'T YOU? THAT'S WHAT I THINK...
I SWEAR TO GOD, I'M GOING TO KILL...
DONNA?
NO. YOU.

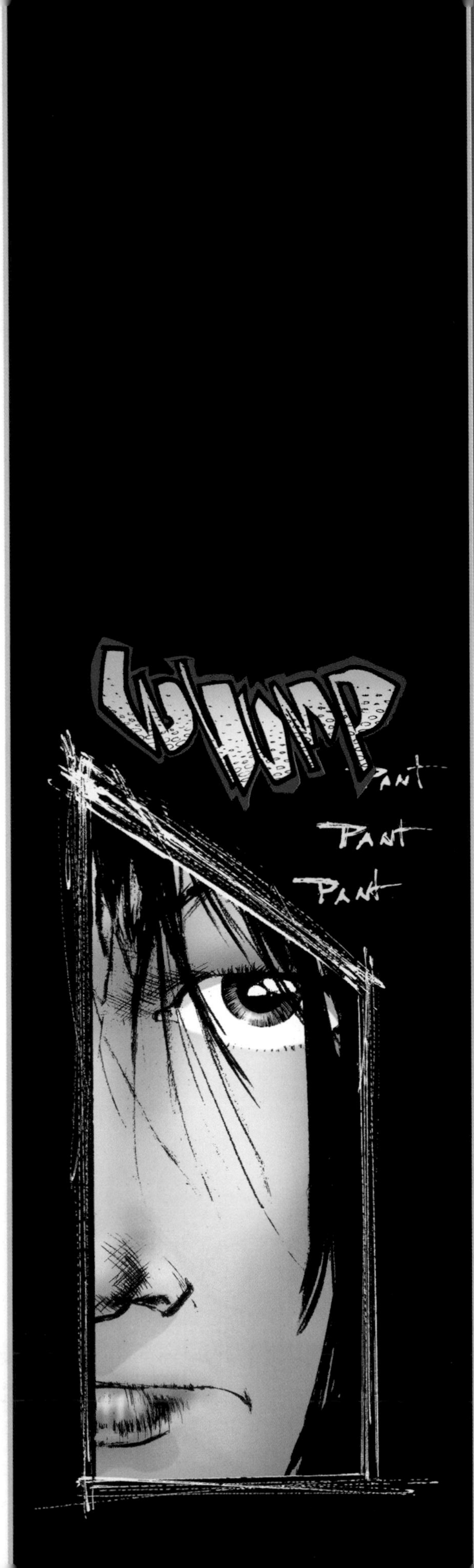
WHOMP
PANT
PANT
PANT

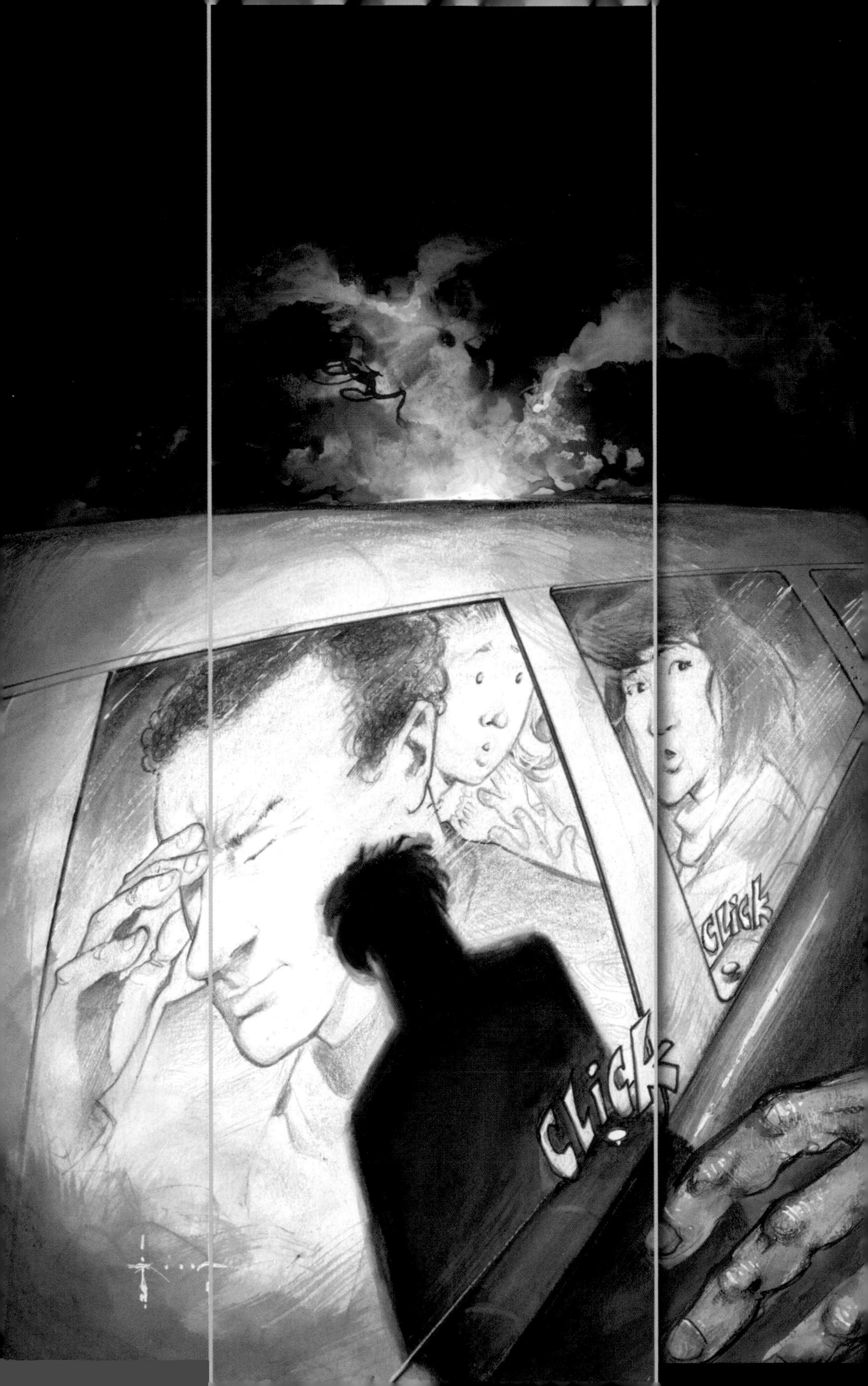
CLICK
CLICK

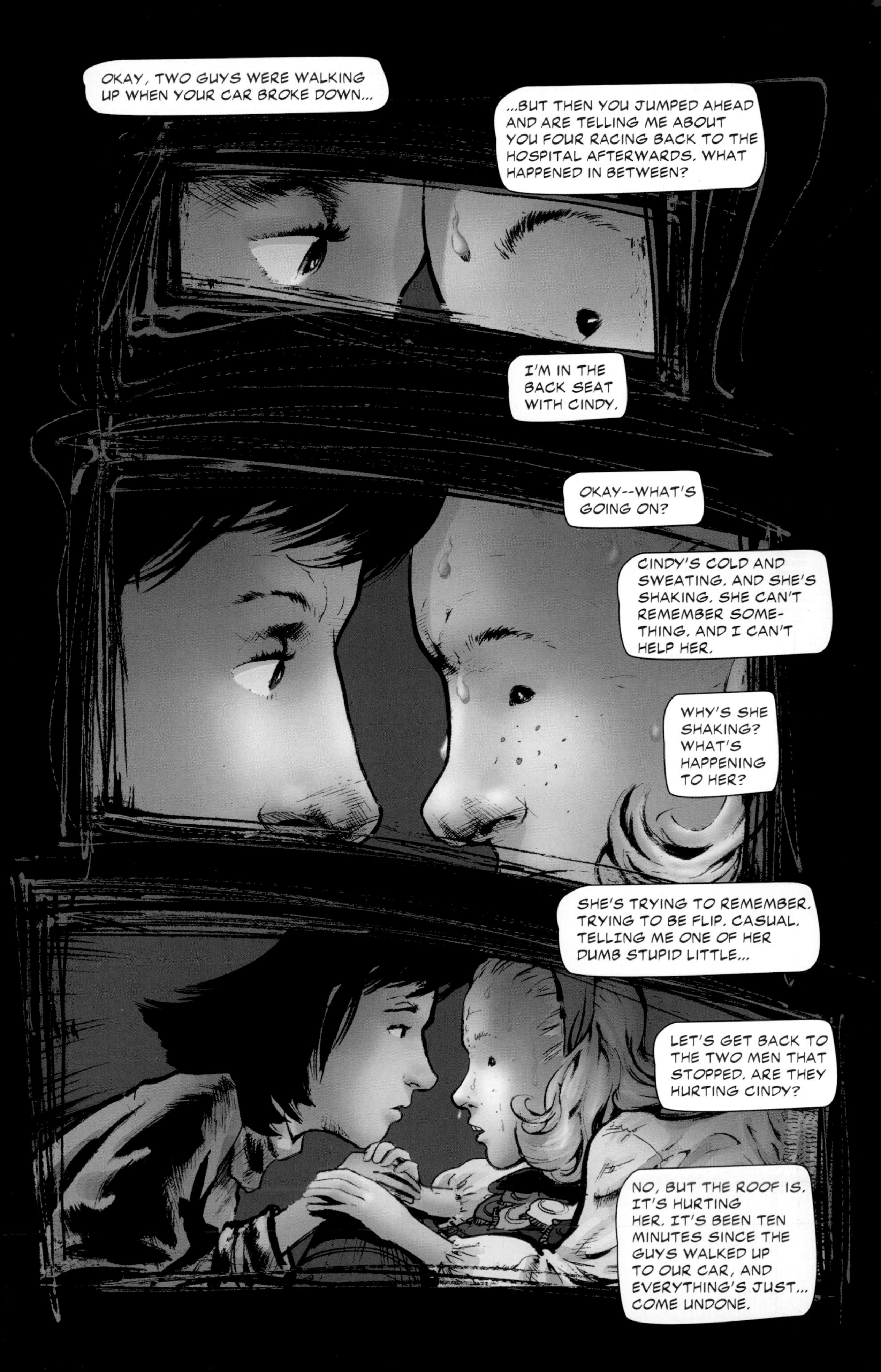
OKAY, TWO GUYS WERE WALKING UP WHEN YOUR CAR BROKE DOWN...
...BUT THEN YOU JUMPED AHEAD AND ARE TELLING ME ABOUT YOU FOUR RACING BACK TO THE HOSPITAL AFTERWARDS. WHAT HAPPENED IN BETWEEN?
I'M IN THE BACK SEAT WITH CINDY.
OKAY--WHAT'S GOING ON?
CINDY'S COLD AND SWEATING. AND SHE'S SHAKING. SHE CAN'T REMEMBER SOME-THING. AND I CAN'T HELP HER.
WHY'S SHE SHAKING? WHAT'S HAPPENING TO HER?
SHE'S TRYING TO REMEMBER. TRYING TO BE FLIP. CASUAL. TELLING ME ONE OF HER DUMB STUPID LITTLE...
LET'S GET BACK TO THE TWO MEN THAT STOPPED. ARE THEY HURTING CINDY?
NO, BUT THE ROOF IS. IT'S HURTING HER. IT'S BEEN TEN MINUTES SINCE THE GUYS WALKED UP TO OUR CAR, AND EVERYTHING'S JUST... COME UNDONE.

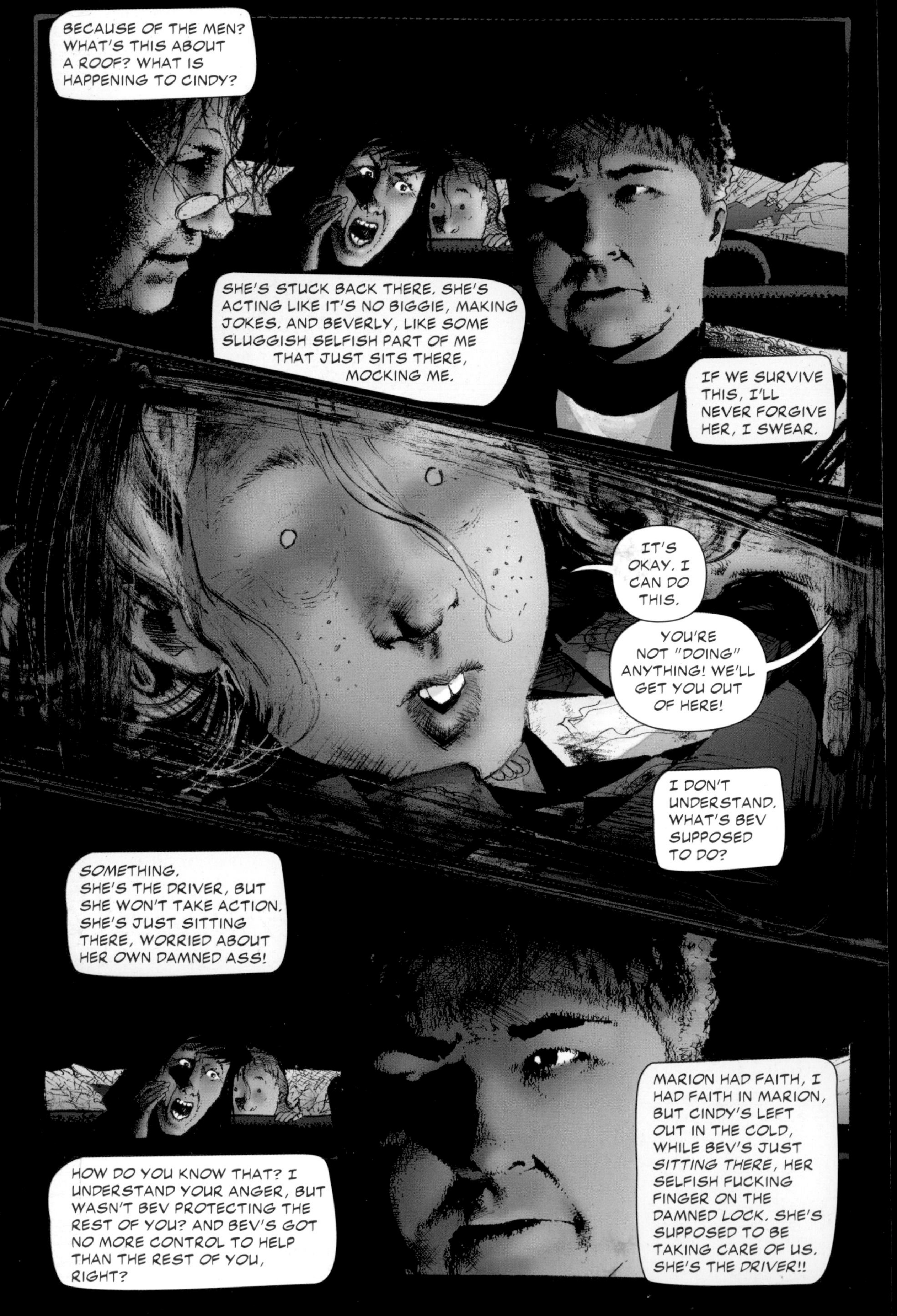
BECAUSE OF THE MEN? WHAT'S THIS ABOUT A ROOF? WHAT IS HAPPENING TO CINDY?
SHE'S STUCK BACK THERE. SHE'S ACTING LIKE IT'S NO BIGGIE, MAKING JOKES. AND BEVERLY, LIKE SOME SLUGGISH SELFISH PART OF ME THAT JUST SITS THERE, MOCKING ME.
IF WE SURVIVE THIS, I'LL NEVER FORGIVE HER, I SWEAR.
IT'S OKAY. I CAN DO THIS.
YOU'RE NOT "DOING" ANYTHING! WE'LL GET YOU OUT OF HERE!
I DON'T UNDERSTAND. WHAT'S BEV SUPPOSED TO DO?
SOMETHING. SHE'S THE DRIVER, BUT SHE WON'T TAKE ACTION. SHE'S JUST SITTING THERE, WORRIED ABOUT HER OWN DAMNED ASS!
MARION HAD FAITH, I HAD FAITH IN MARION, BUT CINDY'S LEFT OUT IN THE COLD, WHILE BEV'S JUST *SITTING THERE*, HER SELFISH FUCKING FINGER ON THE DAMNED *LOCK*. SHE'S SUPPOSED TO BE TAKING CARE OF US. SHE'S THE *DRIVER*!!
HOW DO YOU KNOW THAT? I UNDERSTAND YOUR ANGER, BUT WASN'T BEV PROTECTING THE REST OF YOU? AND BEV'S GOT NO MORE CONTROL TO HELP THAN THE REST OF YOU, RIGHT?

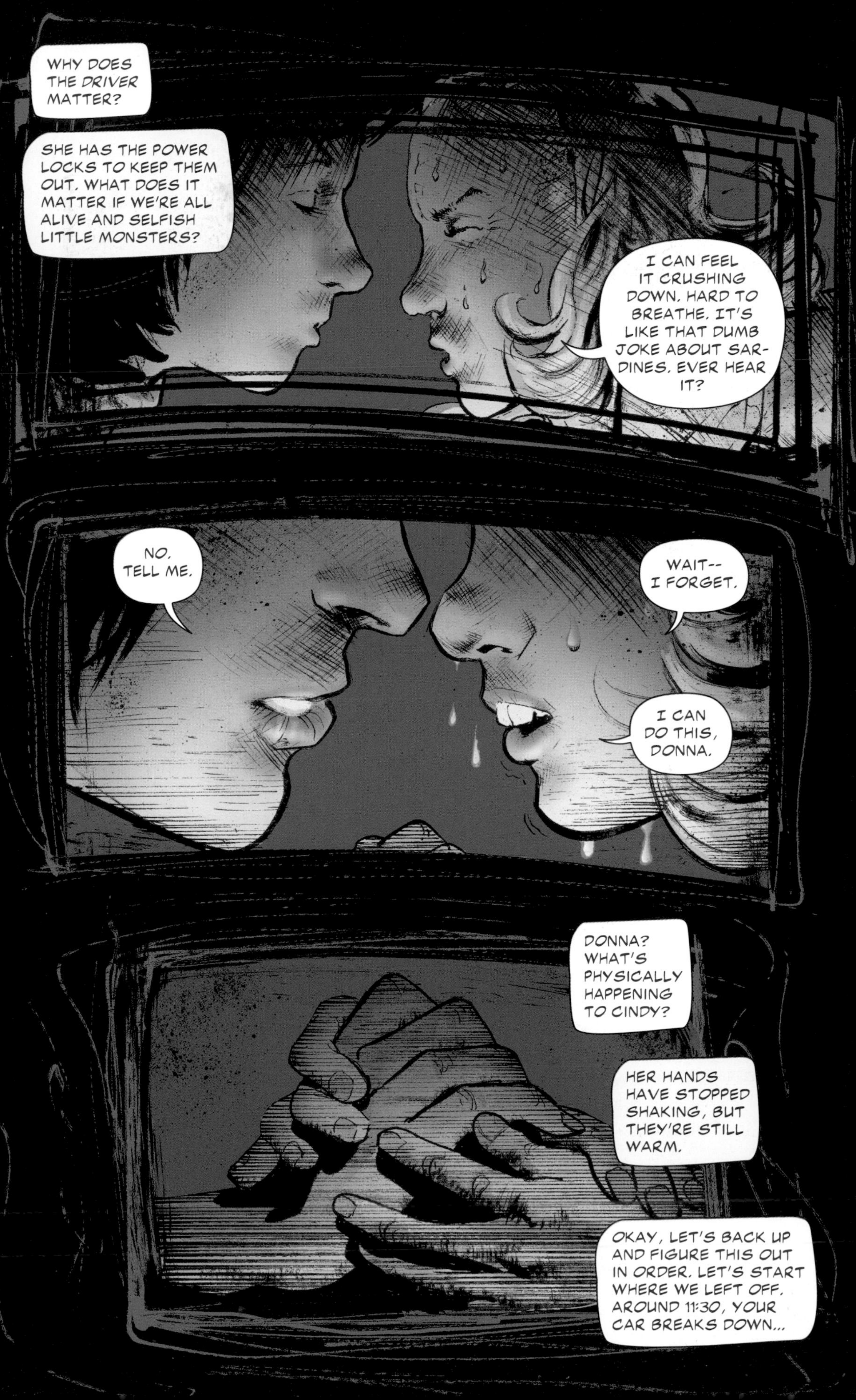
WHY DOES THE *DRIVER* MATTER?
SHE HAS THE POWER LOCKS TO KEEP THEM OUT. WHAT DOES IT MATTER IF WE'RE ALL ALIVE AND SELFISH LITTLE MONSTERS?
I CAN FEEL IT CRUSHING DOWN. HARD TO BREATHE. IT'S LIKE THAT DUMB JOKE ABOUT SAR-DINES. EVER HEAR IT?
NO. TELL ME.
WAIT-- I FORGET.
I CAN DO THIS, DONNA.
DONNA? WHAT'S PHYSICALLY HAPPENING TO CINDY?
HER HANDS HAVE STOPPED SHAKING, BUT THEY'RE STILL WARM.
OKAY, LET'S BACK UP AND FIGURE THIS OUT IN ORDER. LET'S START WHERE WE LEFT OFF. AROUND 11:30, YOUR CAR BREAKS DOWN...

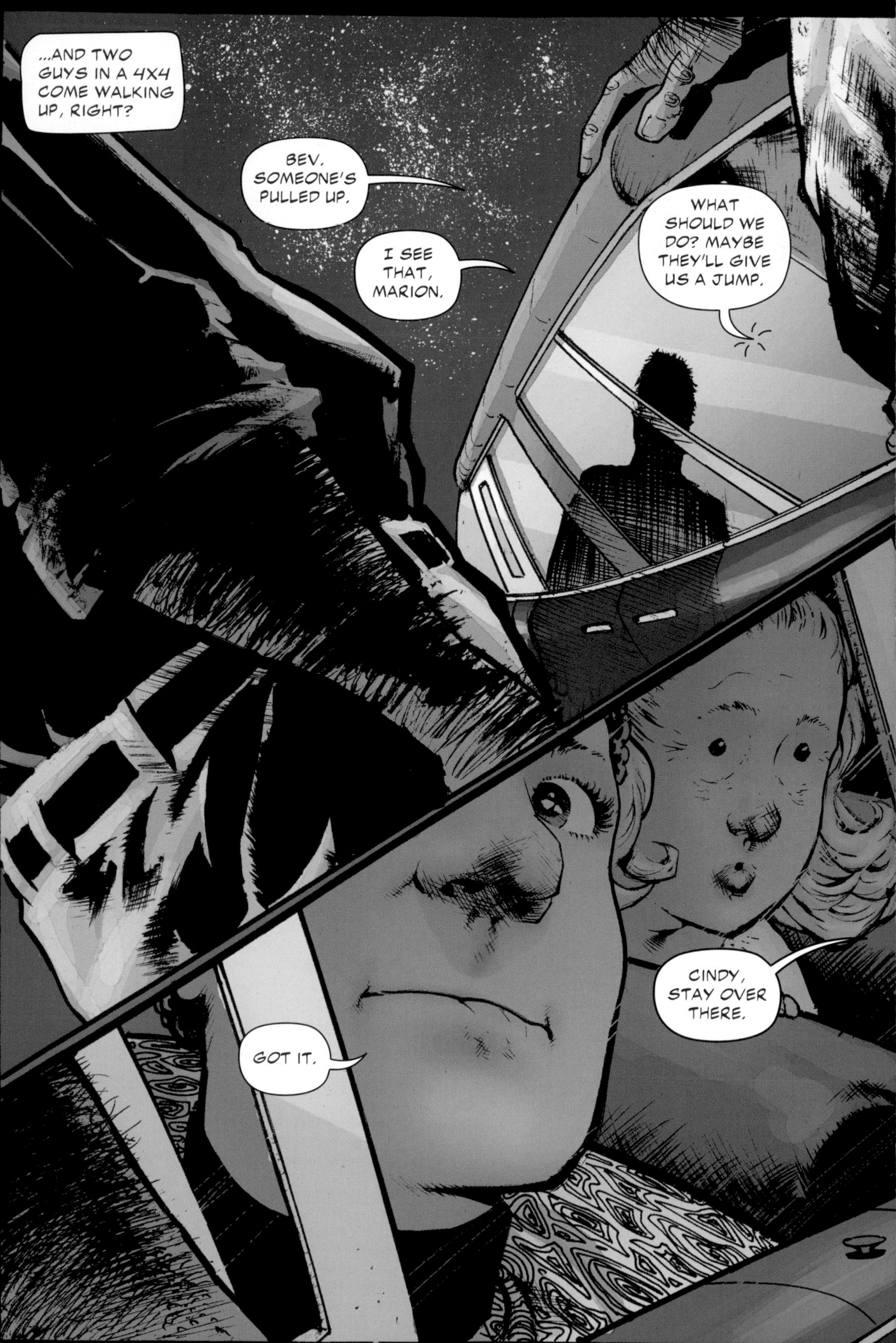
...AND TWO GUYS IN A 4X4 COME WALKING UP, RIGHT?
BEV. SOMEONE'S PULLED UP.
I SEE THAT, MARION.
WHAT SHOULD WE DO? MAYBE THEY'LL GIVE US A JUMP.
CINDY, STAY OVER THERE.
GOT IT.

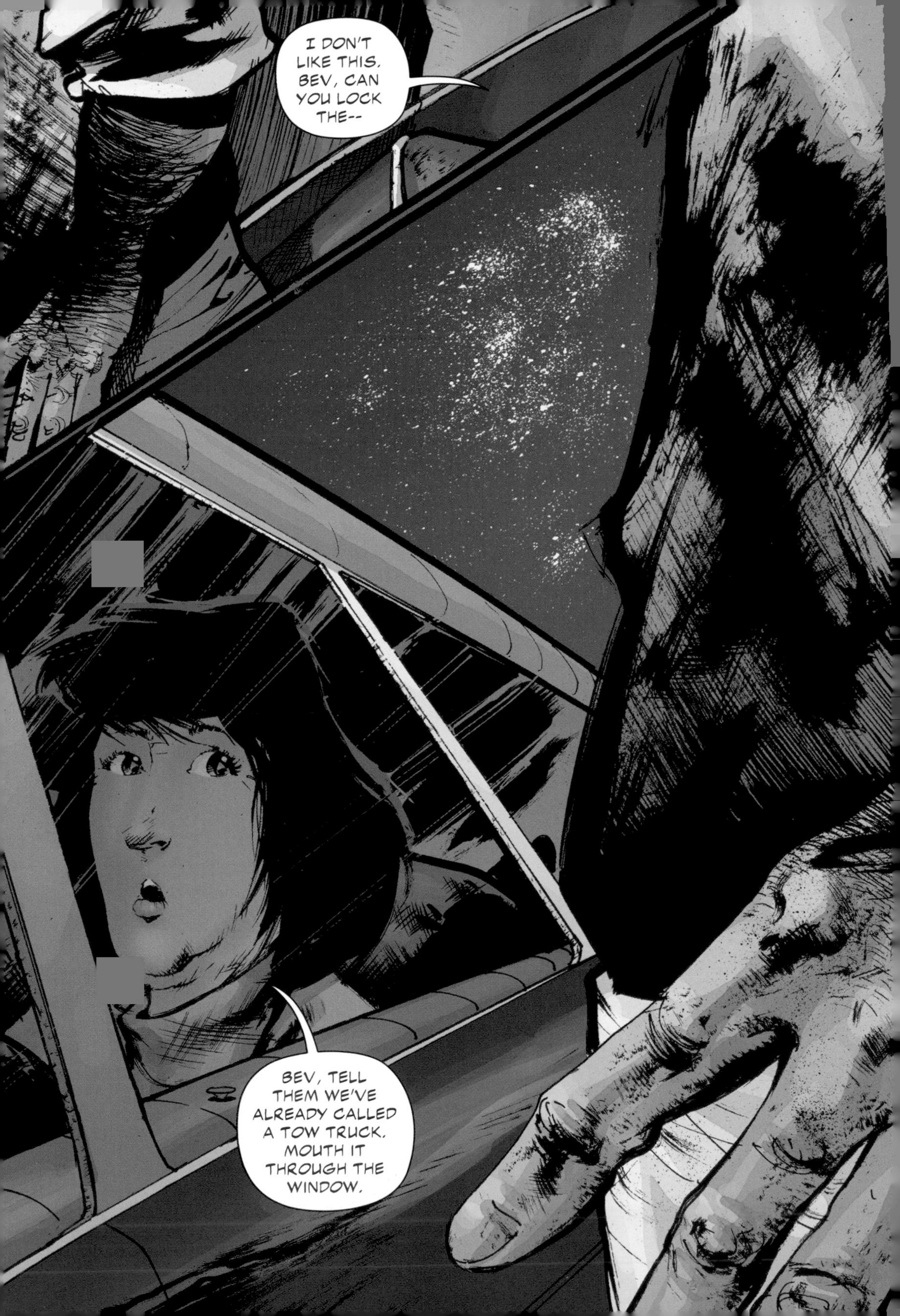
I DON'T LIKE THIS, BEV, CAN YOU LOCK THE--
BEV, TELL THEM WE'VE ALREADY CALLED A TOW TRUCK. MOUTH IT THROUGH THE WINDOW.

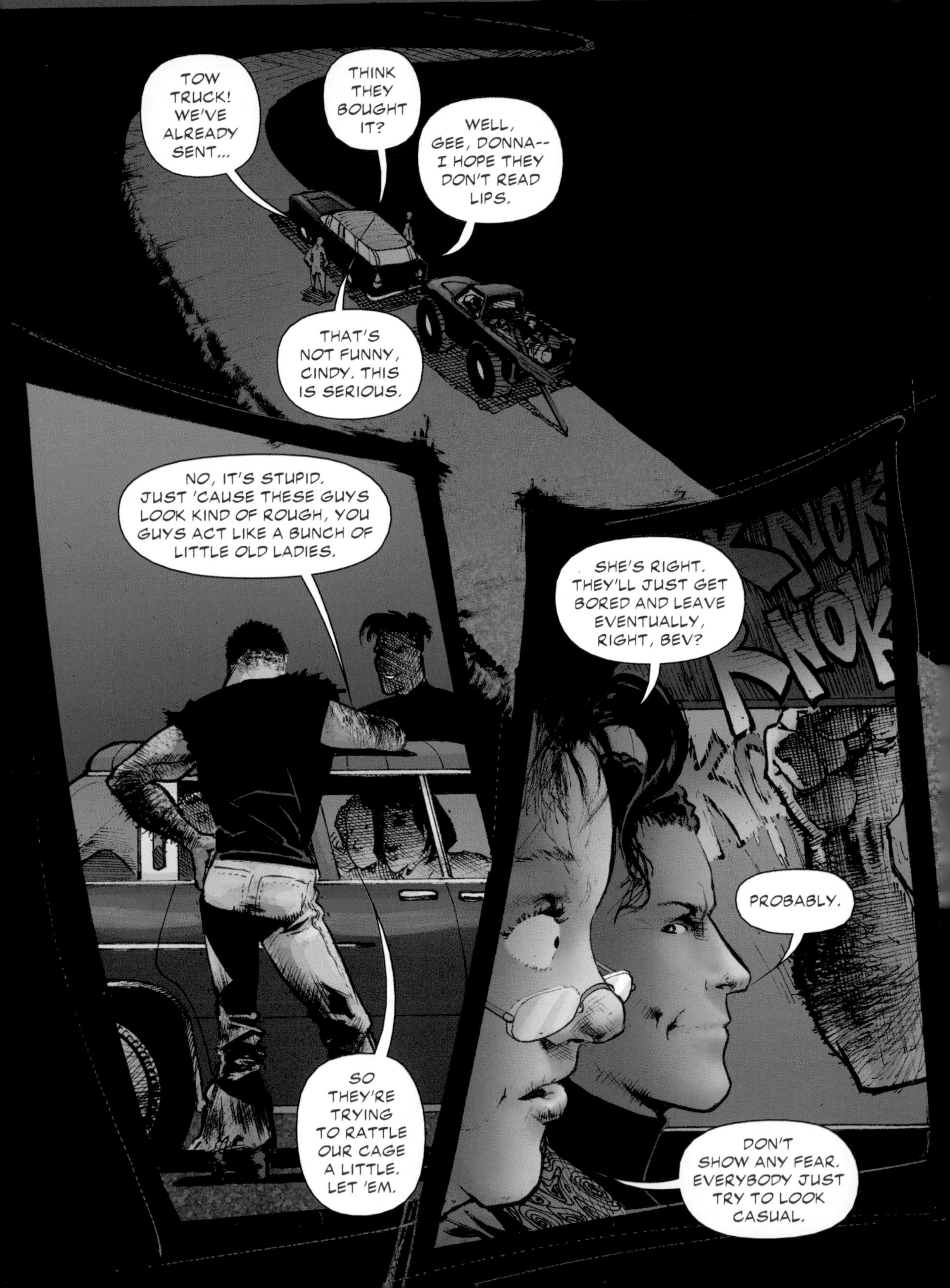
TOW TRUCK! WE'VE ALREADY SENT...
THINK THEY BOUGHT IT?
WELL, GEE, DONNA-- I HOPE THEY DON'T READ LIPS.
THAT'S NOT FUNNY, CINDY. THIS IS SERIOUS.
NO, IT'S STUPID. JUST 'CAUSE THESE GUYS LOOK KIND OF ROUGH, YOU GUYS ACT LIKE A BUNCH OF LITTLE OLD LADIES.
SO THEY'RE TRYING TO RATTLE OUR CAGE A LITTLE. LET 'EM.
SHE'S RIGHT. THEY'LL JUST GET BORED AND LEAVE EVENTUALLY, RIGHT, BEV?
PROBABLY.
DON'T SHOW ANY FEAR. EVERYBODY JUST TRY TO LOOK CASUAL.

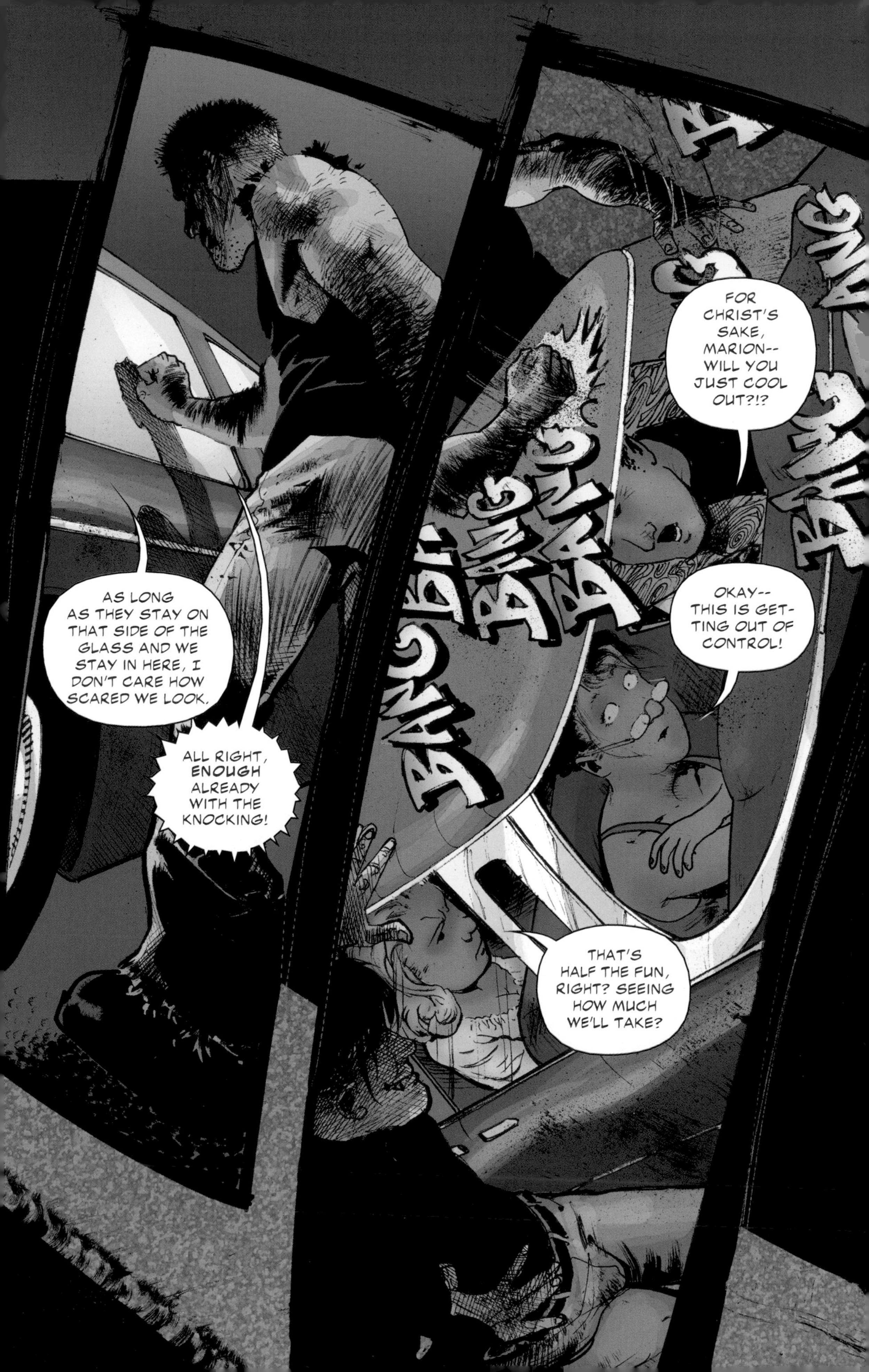
AS LONG AS THEY STAY ON THAT SIDE OF THE GLASS AND WE STAY IN HERE, I DON'T CARE HOW SCARED WE LOOK.
ALL RIGHT, ENOUGH ALREADY WITH THE KNOCKING!
BANG BANG BANG BANG
FOR CHRIST'S SAKE, MARION-- WILL YOU JUST COOL OUT?!?
OKAY-- THIS IS GETTING OUT OF CONTROL!
THAT'S HALF THE FUN, RIGHT? SEEING HOW MUCH WE'LL TAKE?

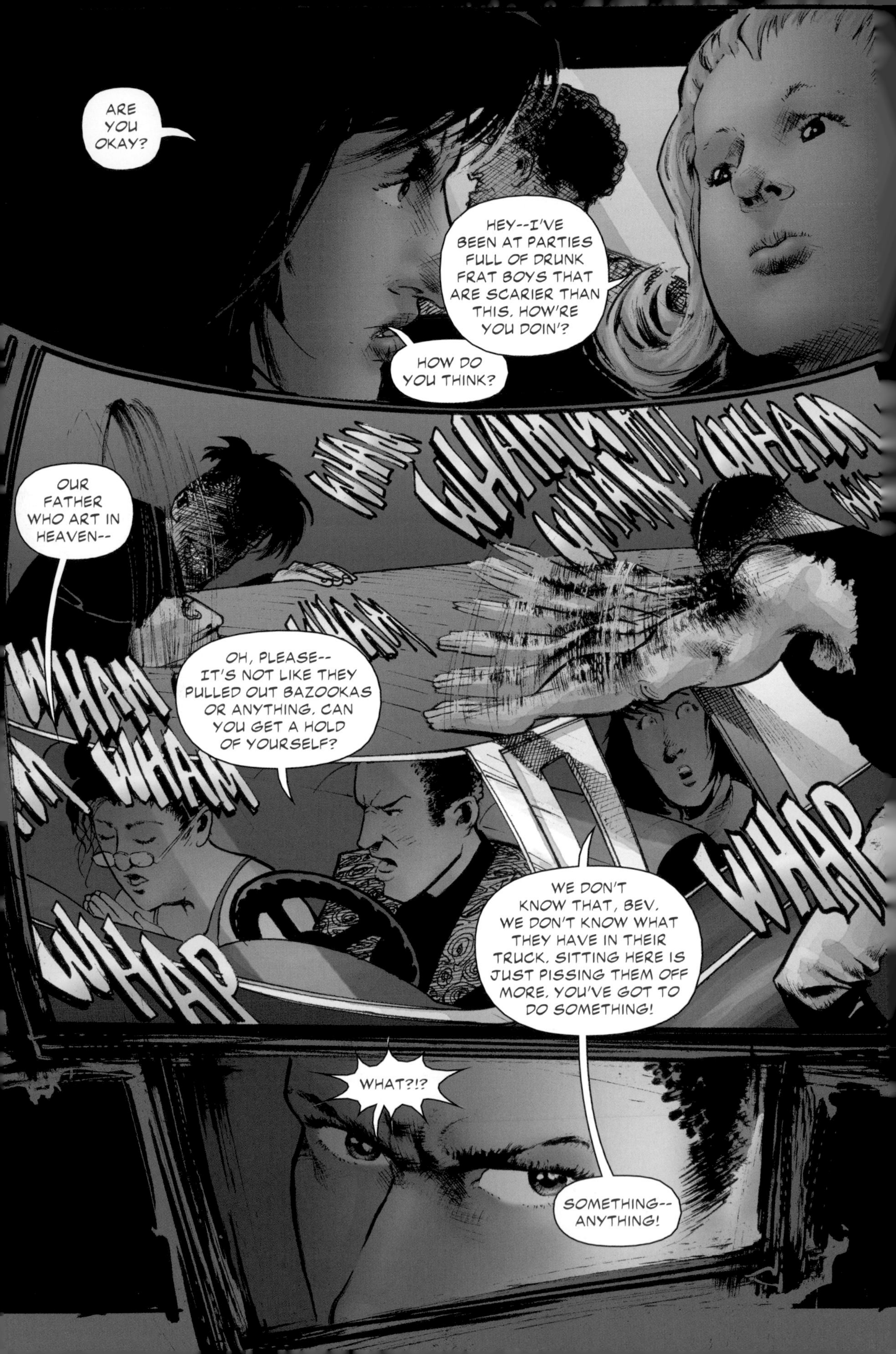
ARE YOU OKAY?
HEY--I'VE BEEN AT PARTIES FULL OF DRUNK FRAT BOYS THAT ARE SCARIER THAN THIS. HOW'RE YOU DOIN'?
HOW DO YOU THINK?
OUR FATHER WHO ART IN HEAVEN--
WHAM
WHAM
WHAM
WHAM
WHAM
OH, PLEASE-- IT'S NOT LIKE THEY PULLED OUT BAZOOKAS OR ANYTHING. CAN YOU GET A HOLD OF YOURSELF?
WHAP
WHAP
WE DON'T KNOW THAT, BEV. WE DON'T KNOW WHAT THEY HAVE IN THEIR TRUCK. SITTING HERE IS JUST PISSING THEM OFF MORE. YOU'VE GOT TO DO SOMETHING!
WHAT?!?
SOMETHING-- ANYTHING!

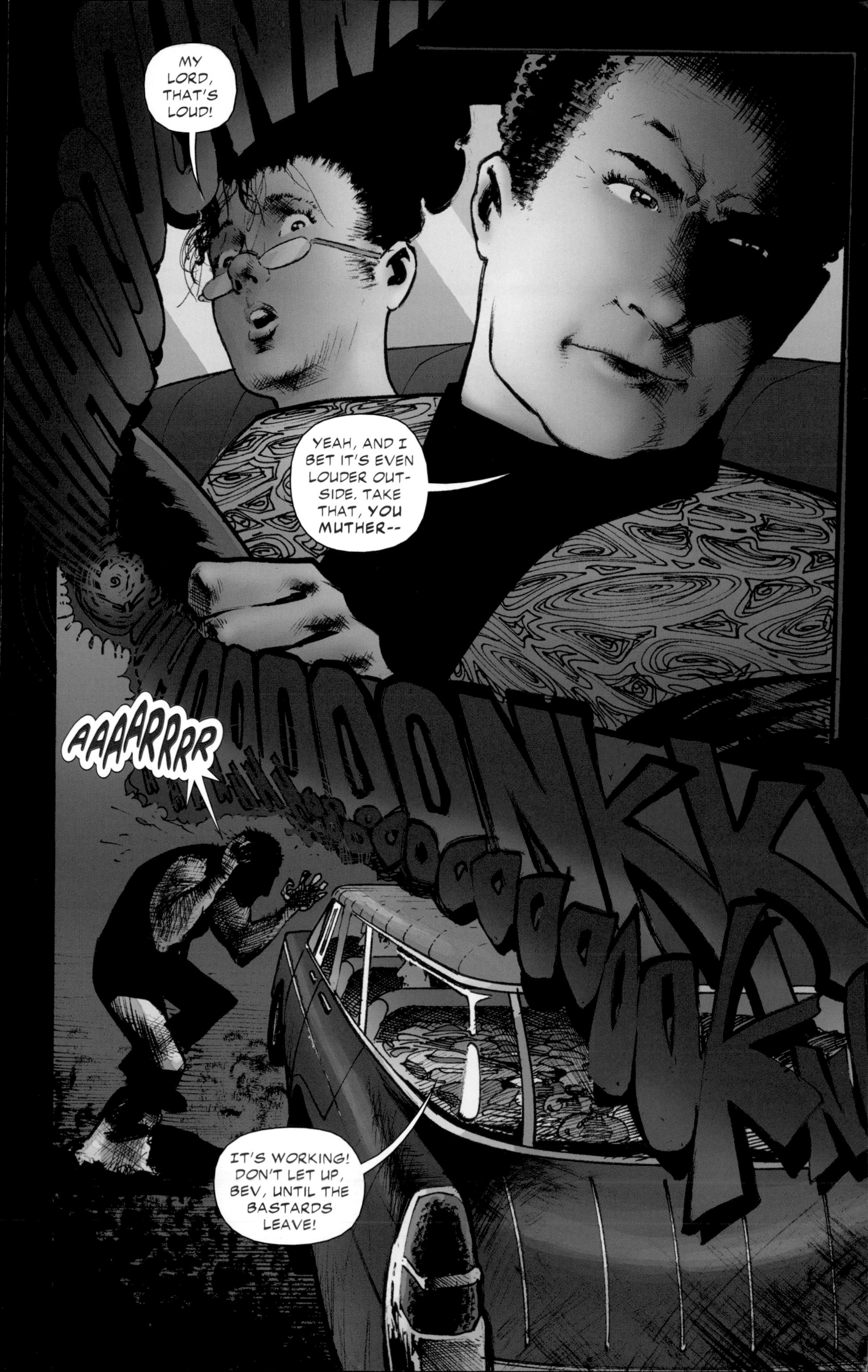
MY LORD, THAT'S LOUD!
YEAH, AND I BET IT'S EVEN LOUDER OUT-SIDE. TAKE THAT, YOU MUTHER--
AAAARRRR
IT'S WORKING! DON'T LET UP, BEV, UNTIL THE BASTARDS LEAVE!

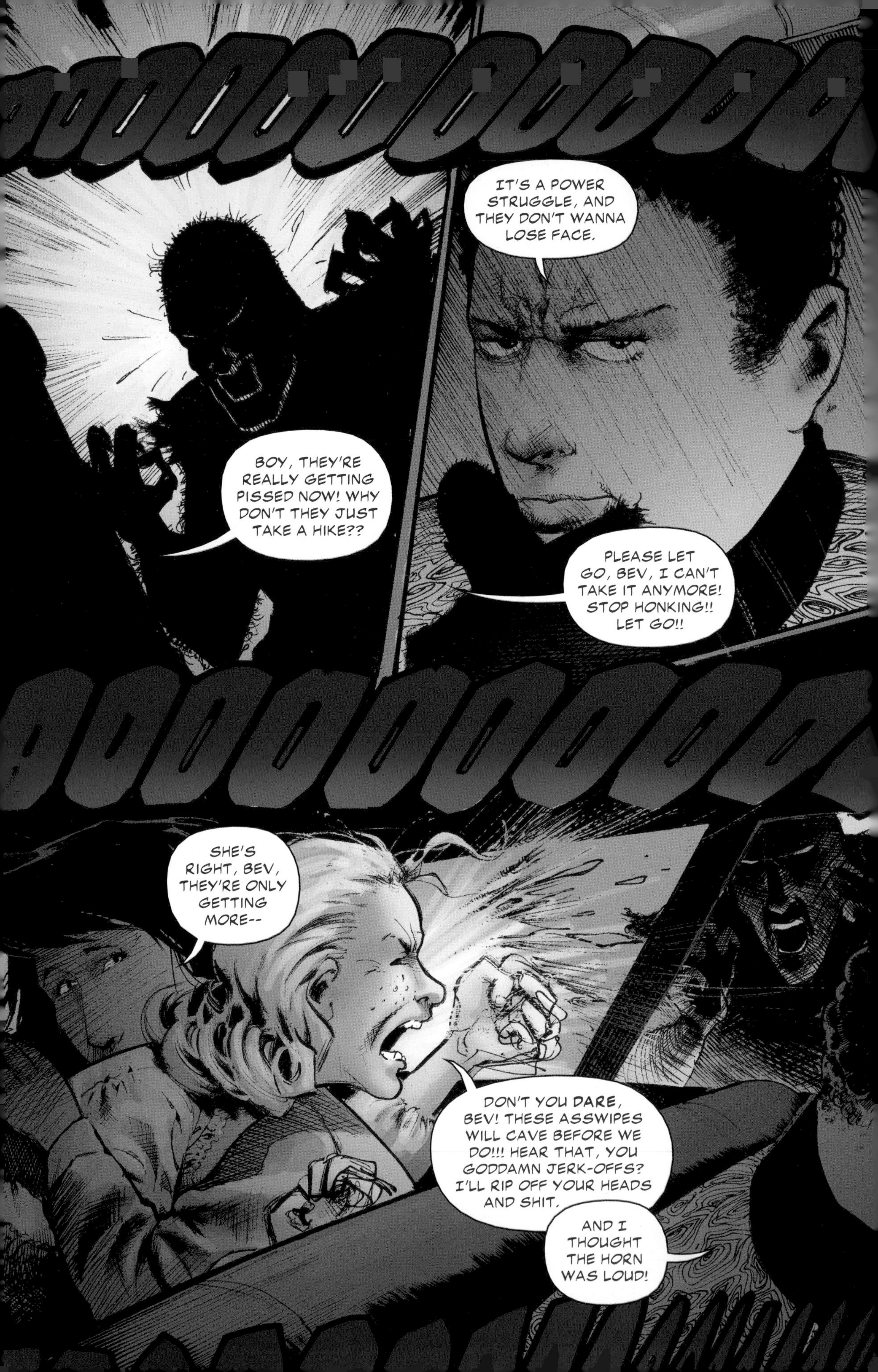
BOY, THEY'RE REALLY GETTING PISSED NOW! WHY DON'T THEY JUST TAKE A HIKE??
IT'S A POWER STRUGGLE, AND THEY DON'T WANNA LOSE FACE.
PLEASE LET GO, BEV, I CAN'T TAKE IT ANYMORE! STOP HONKING!! LET GO!!
SHE'S RIGHT, BEV, THEY'RE ONLY GETTING MORE--
DON'T YOU DARE, BEV! THESE ASSWIPES WILL CAVE BEFORE WE DO!!! HEAR THAT, YOU GODDAMN JERK-OFFS? I'LL RIP OFF YOUR HEADS AND SHIT.
AND I THOUGHT THE HORN WAS LOUD!

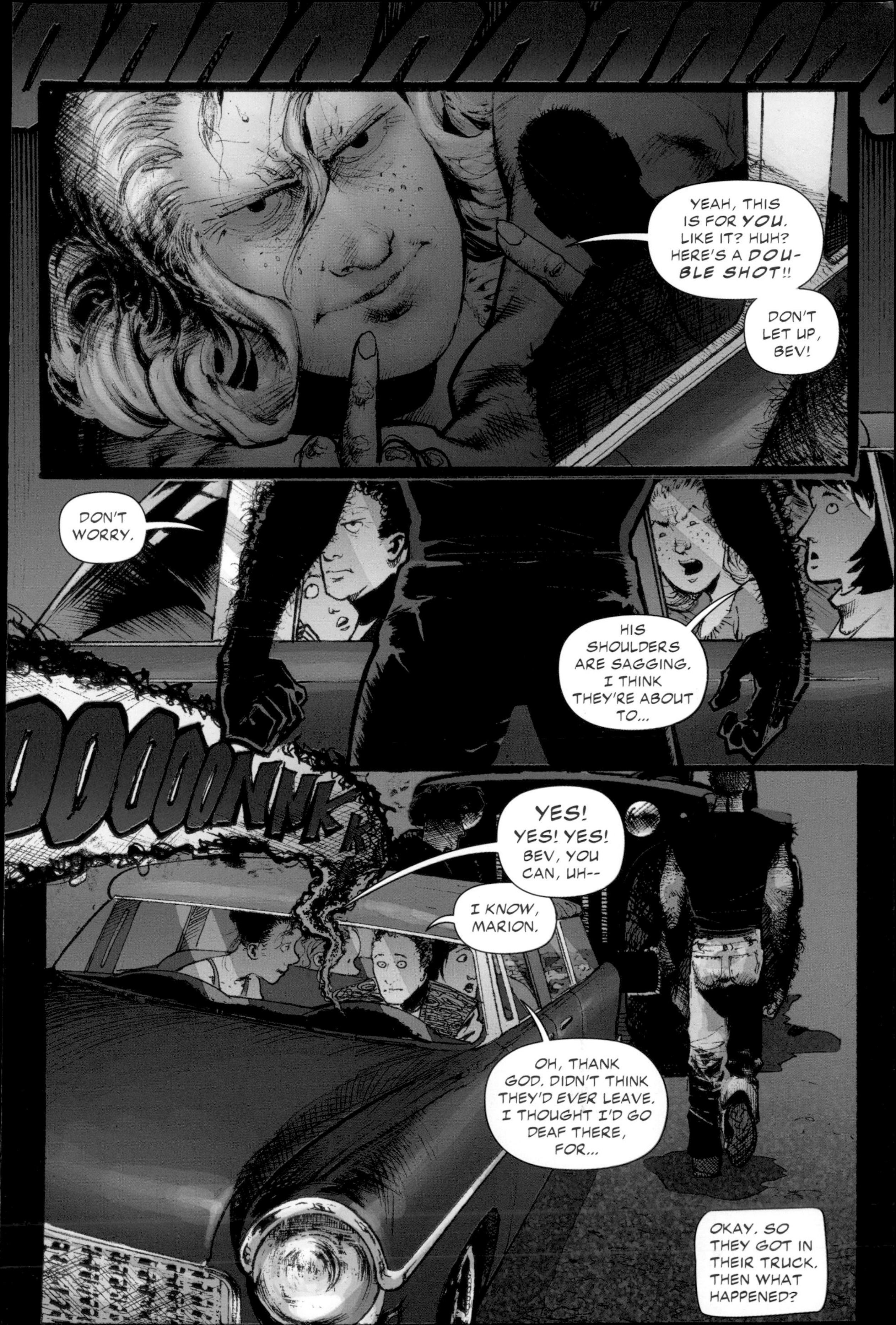
YEAH, THIS IS FOR YOU. LIKE IT? HUH? HERE'S A DOUBLE SHOT!!
DON'T LET UP, BEV!
DON'T WORRY.
HIS SHOULDERS ARE SAGGING. I THINK THEY'RE ABOUT TO...
DOOOONNK
YES! YES! YES! BEV, YOU CAN, UH--
I KNOW, MARION.
OH, THANK GOD. DIDN'T THINK THEY'D EVER LEAVE. I THOUGHT I'D GO DEAF THERE, FOR...
OKAY. SO THEY GOT IN THEIR TRUCK. THEN WHAT HAPPENED?

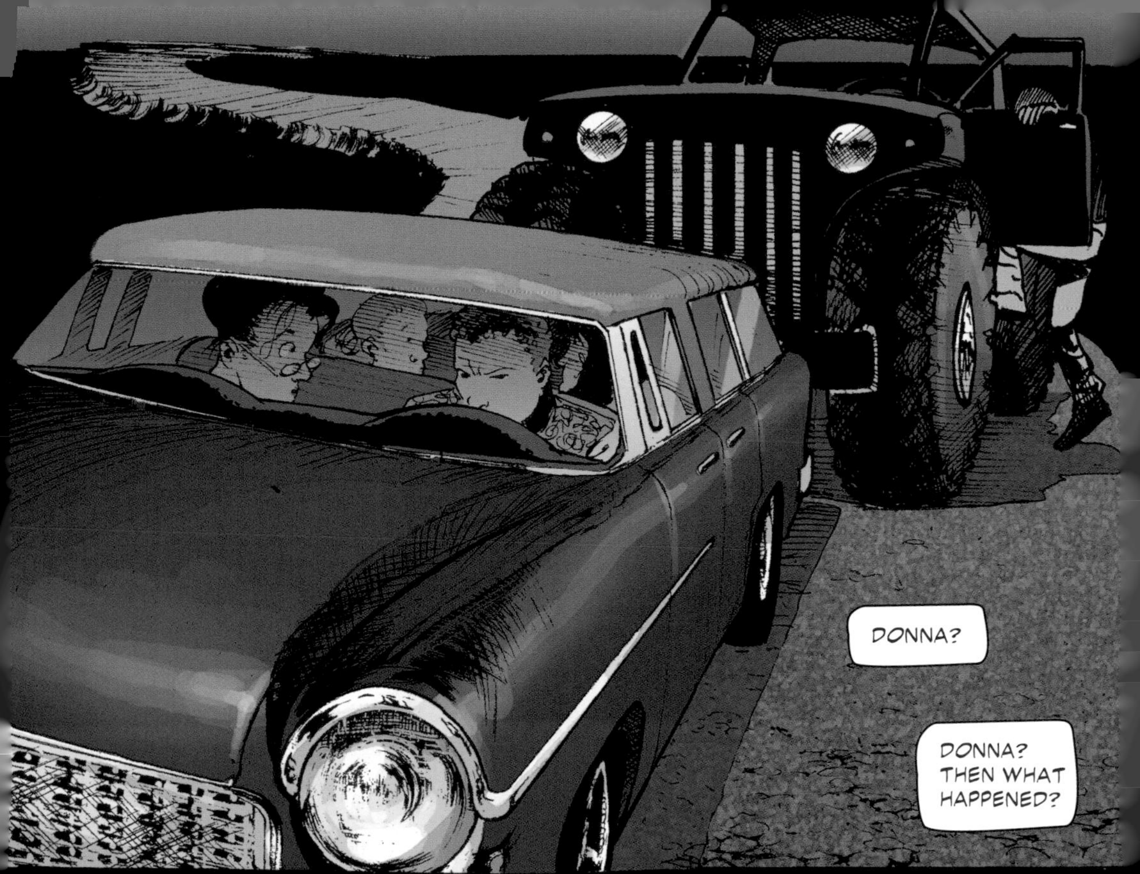
DONNA?
DONNA? THEN WHAT HAPPENED?
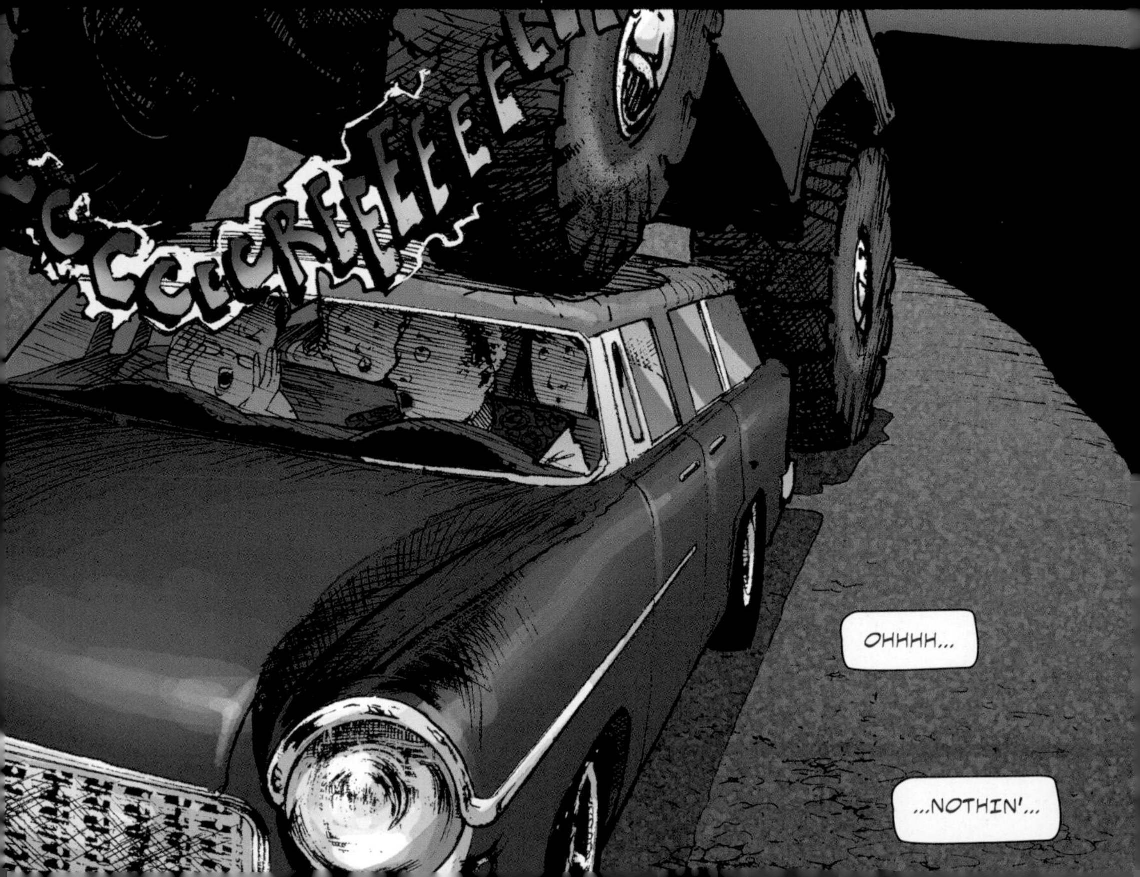
CCCCREEEEEE
OHHHH...
...NOTHIN'...

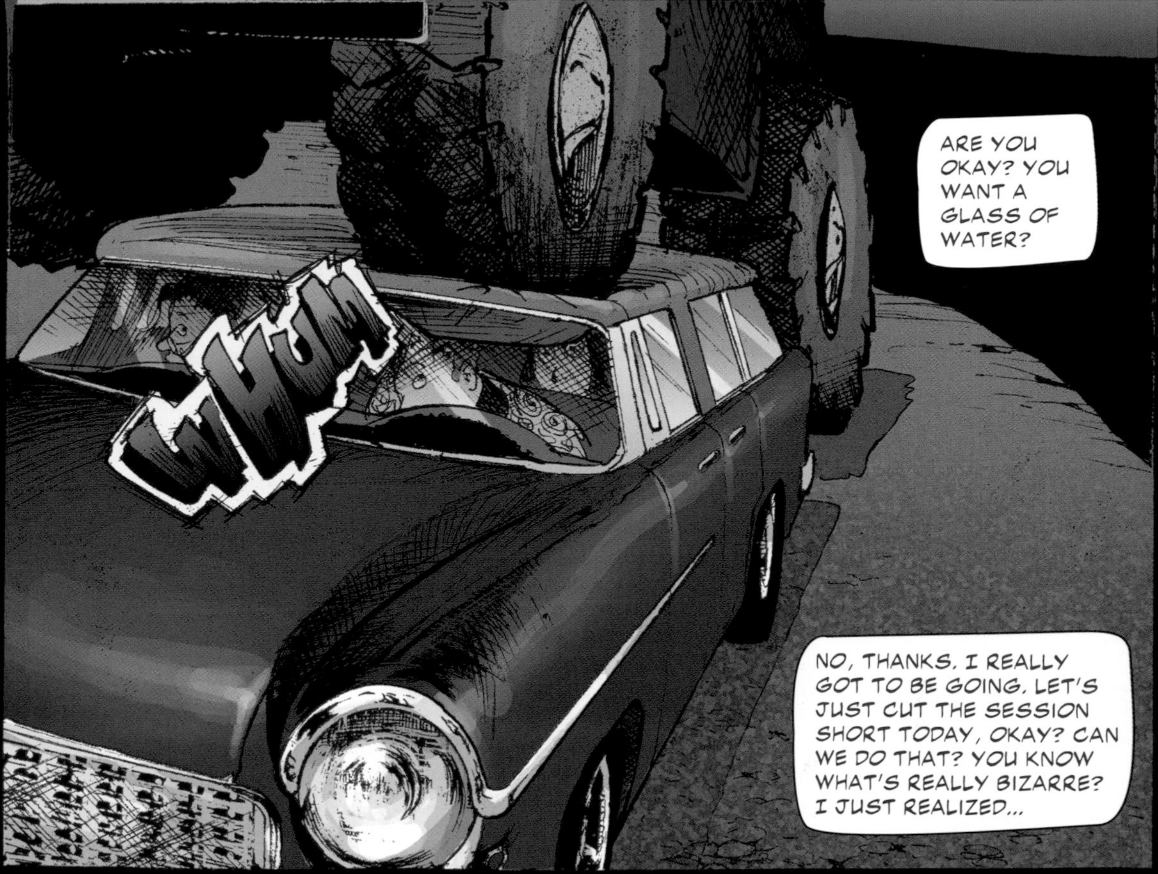
ARE YOU OKAY? YOU WANT A GLASS OF WATER?
WHUNG
NO, THANKS. I REALLY GOT TO BE GOING. LET'S JUST CUT THE SESSION SHORT TODAY, OKAY? CAN WE DO THAT? YOU KNOW WHAT'S REALLY BIZARRE? I JUST REALIZED...

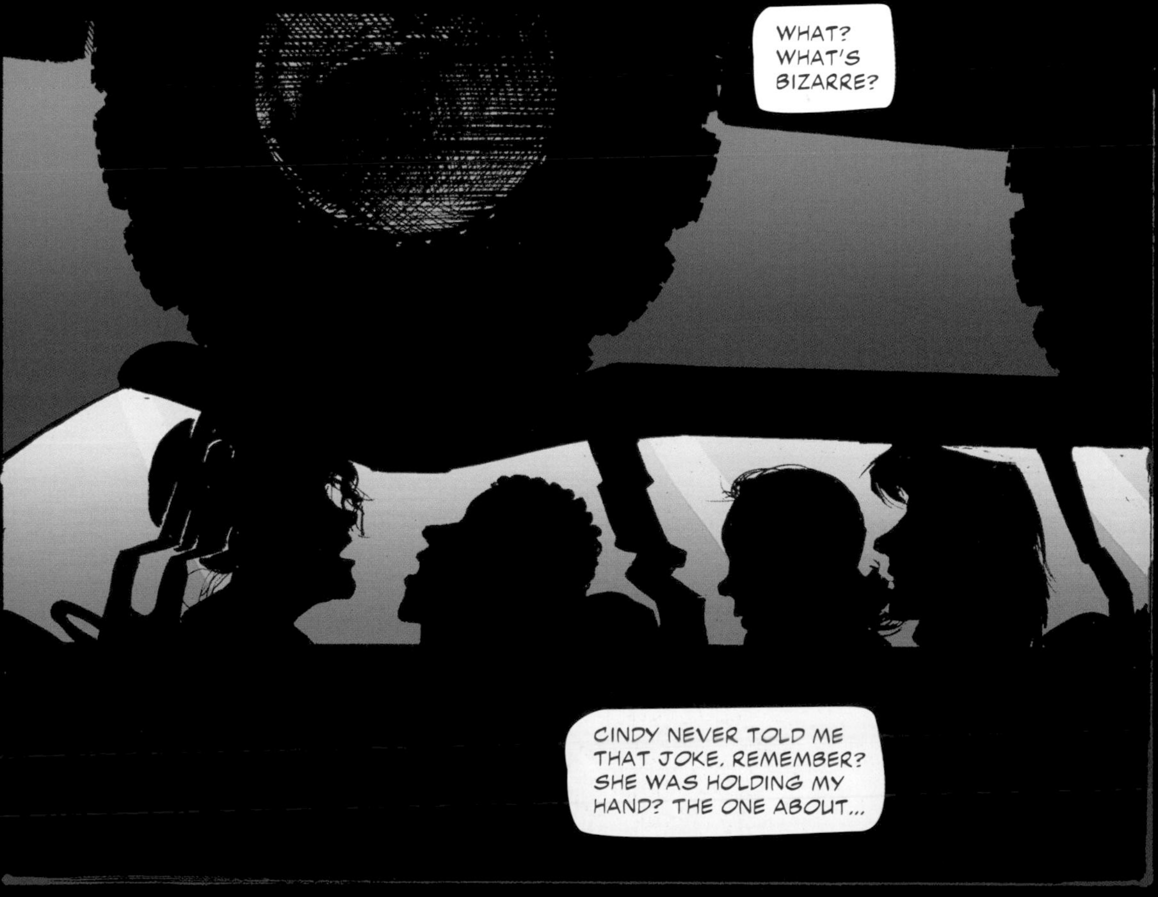
WHAT? WHAT'S BIZARRE?
CINDY NEVER TOLD ME THAT JOKE. REMEMBER? SHE WAS HOLDING MY HAND? THE ONE ABOUT...

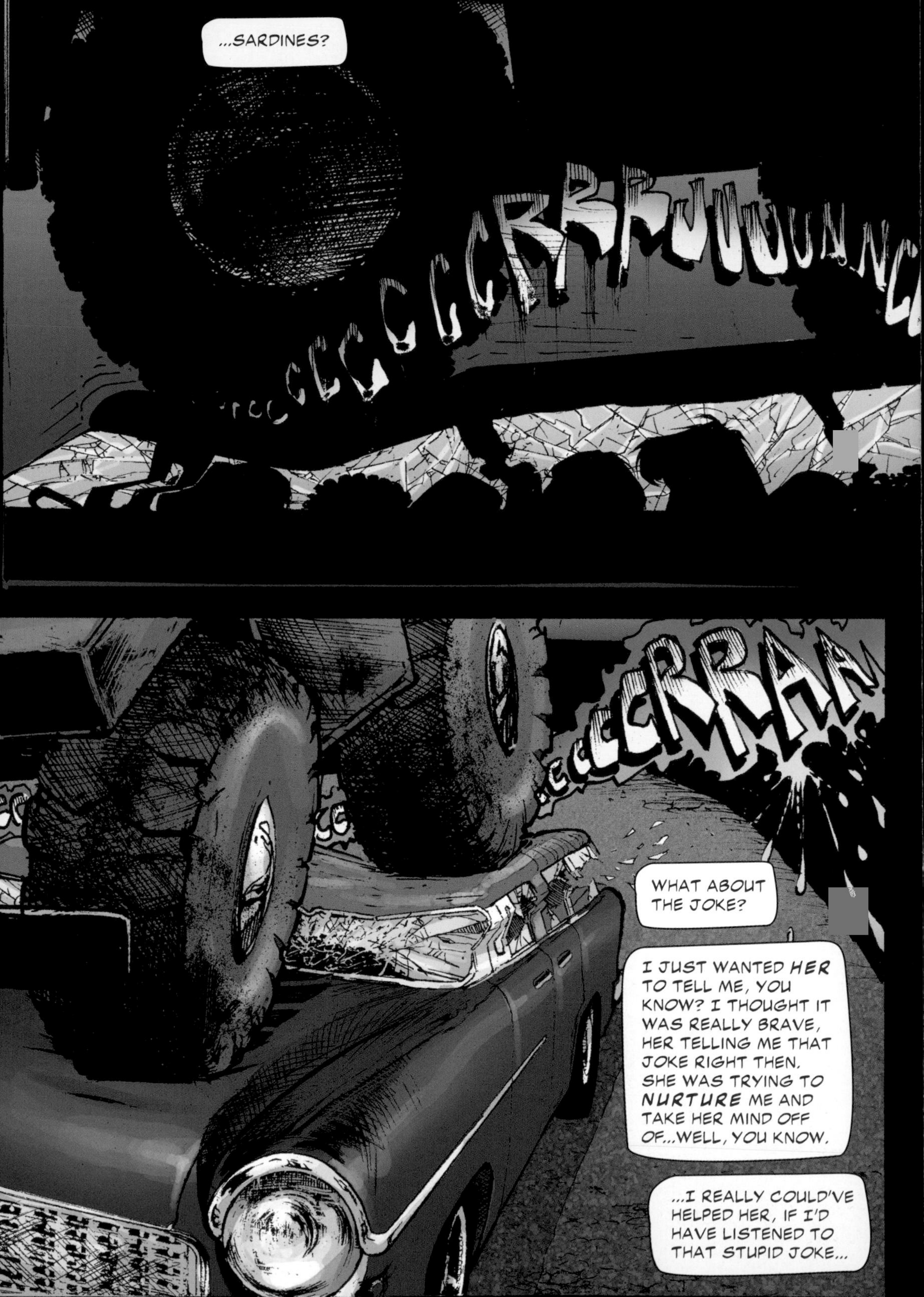
...SARDINES?
WHAT ABOUT THE JOKE?
I JUST WANTED HER TO TELL ME, YOU KNOW? I THOUGHT IT WAS REALLY BRAVE, HER TELLING ME THAT JOKE RIGHT THEN. SHE WAS TRYING TO NURTURE ME AND TAKE HER MIND OFF OF...WELL, YOU KNOW.
...I REALLY COULD'VE HELPED HER, IF I'D HAVE LISTENED TO THAT STUPID JOKE...

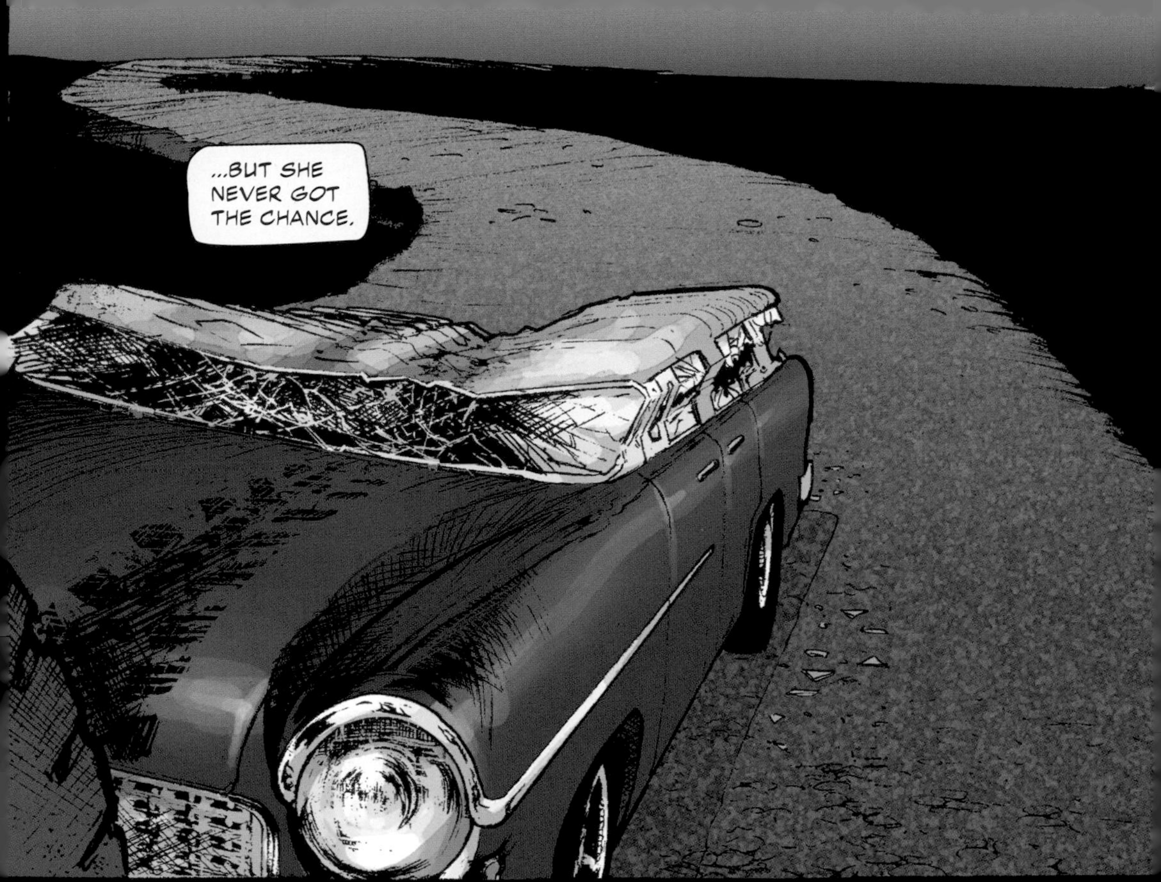
...BUT SHE NEVER GOT THE CHANCE.

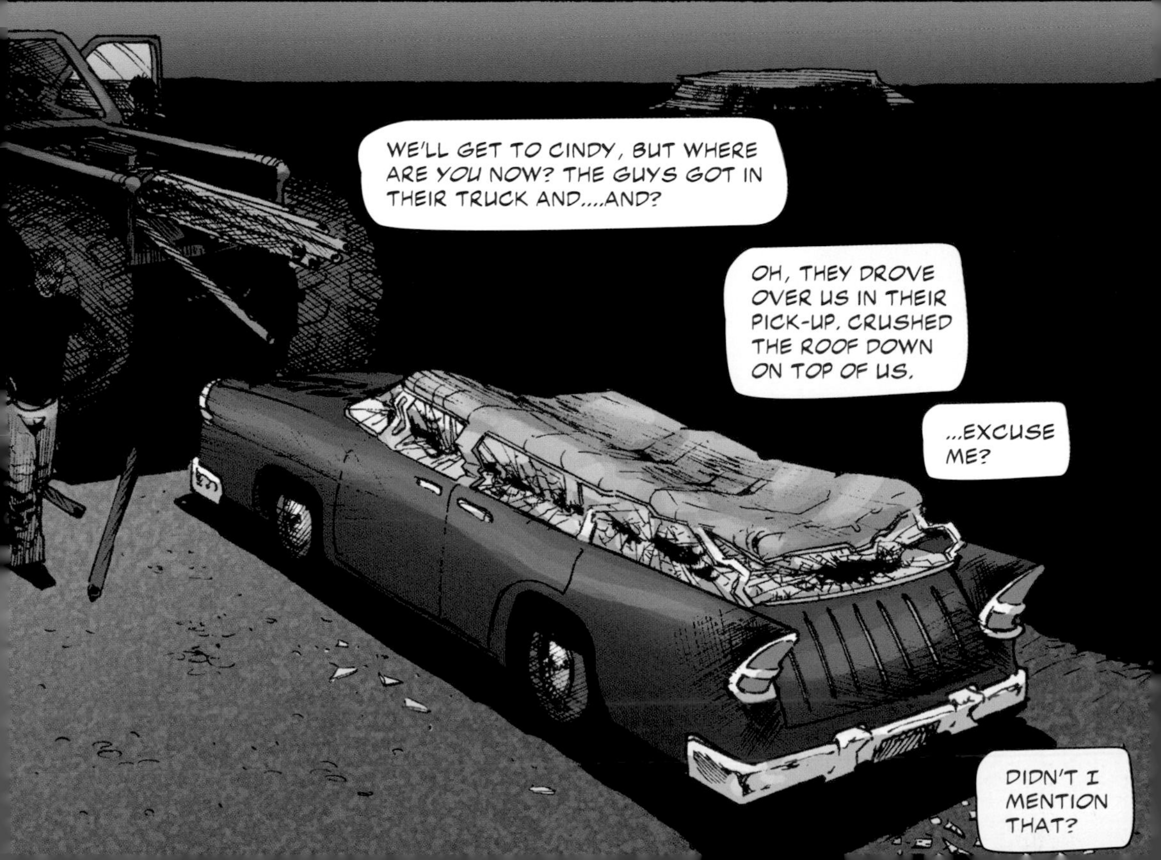
WE'LL GET TO CINDY, BUT WHERE ARE YOU NOW? THE GUYS GOT IN THEIR TRUCK AND....AND?
OH, THEY DROVE OVER US IN THEIR PICK-UP. CRUSHED THE ROOF DOWN ON TOP OF US.
...EXCUSE ME?
DIDN'T I MENTION THAT?

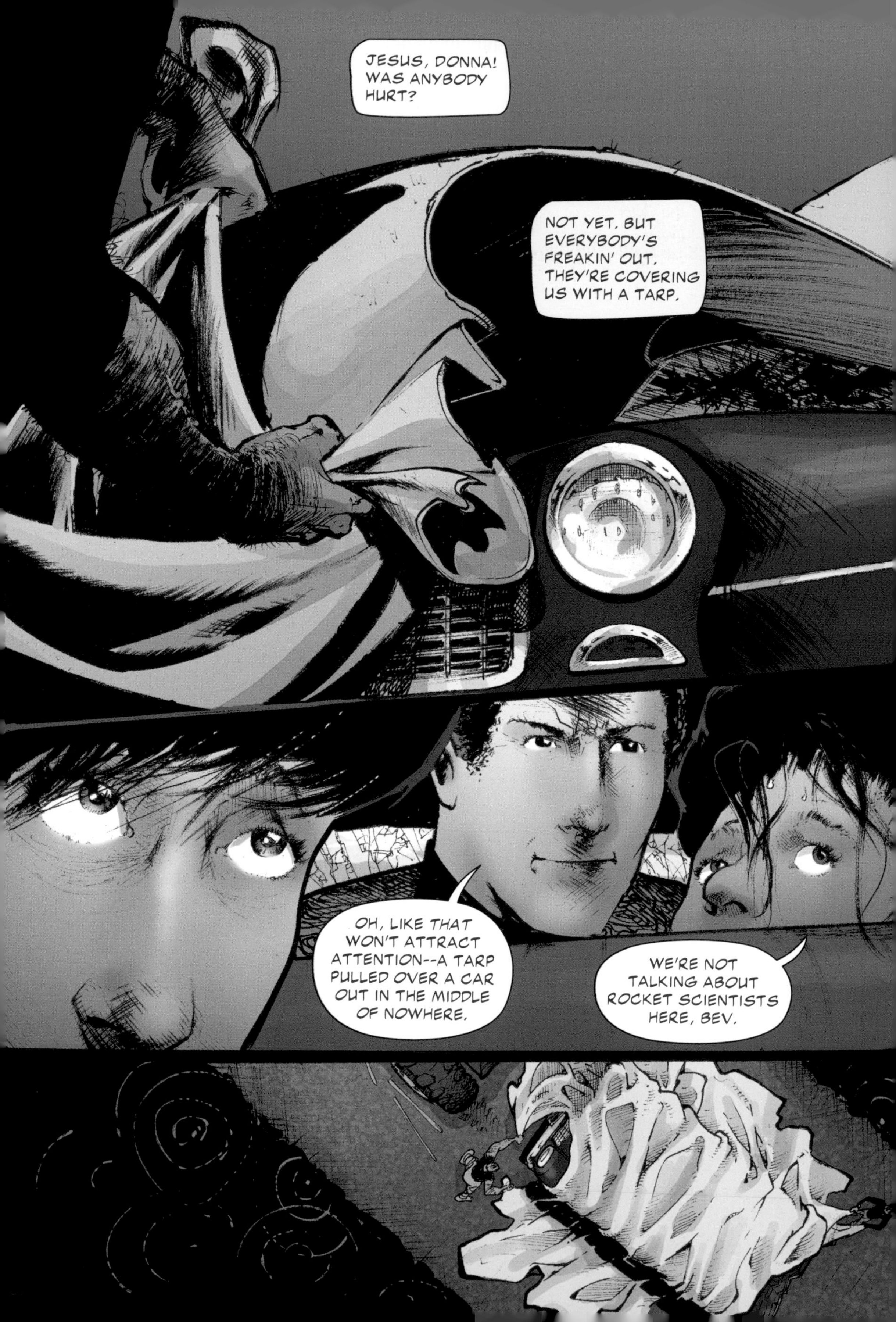
JESUS, DONNA! WAS ANYBODY HURT?
NOT YET. BUT EVERYBODY'S FREAKIN' OUT. THEY'RE COVERING US WITH A TARP.
OH, LIKE THAT WON'T ATTRACT ATTENTION--A TARP PULLED OVER A CAR OUT IN THE MIDDLE OF NOWHERE.
WE'RE NOT TALKING ABOUT ROCKET SCIENTISTS HERE, BEV.

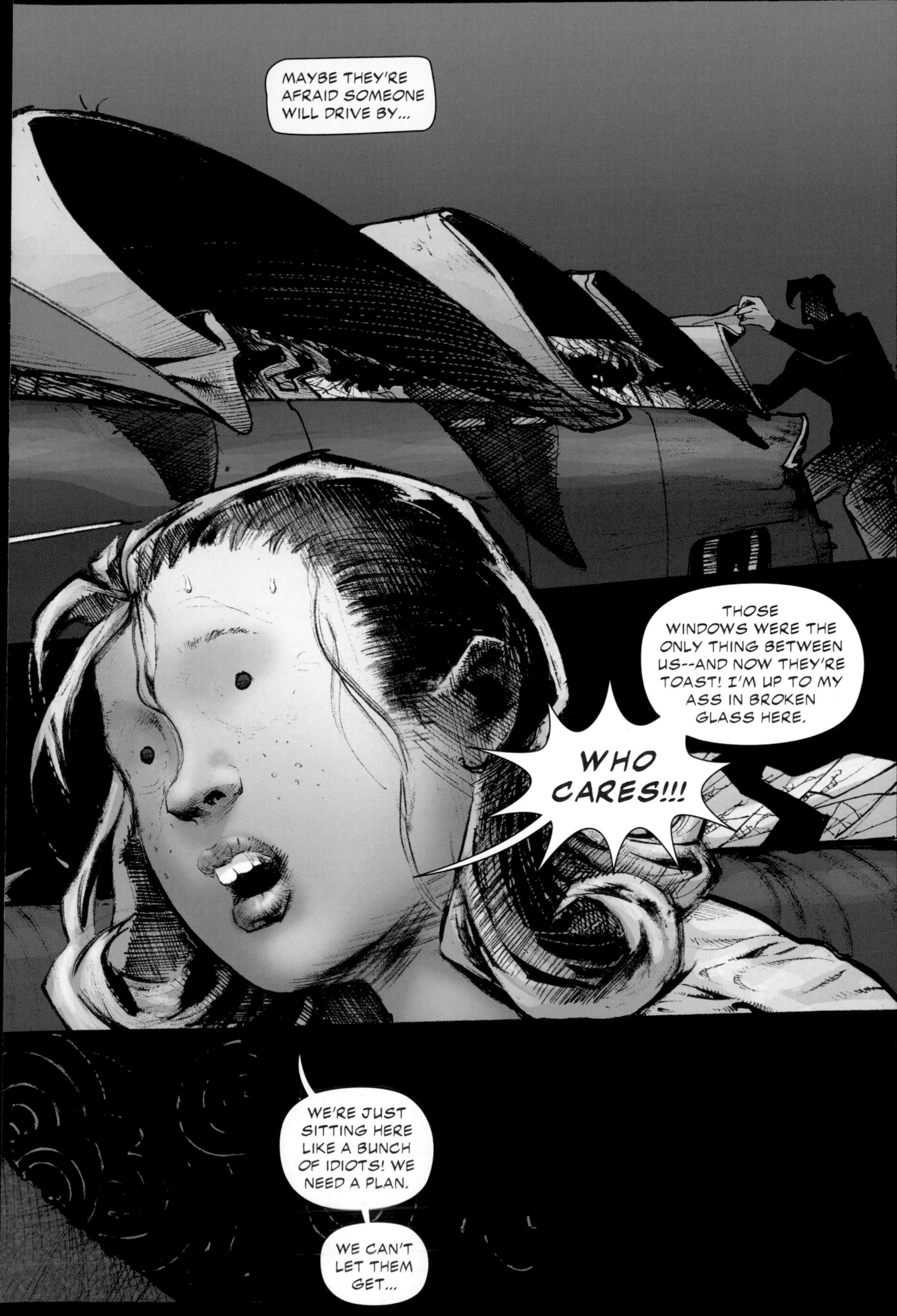
MAYBE THEY'RE AFRAID SOMEONE WILL DRIVE BY...
THOSE WINDOWS WERE THE ONLY THING BETWEEN US--AND NOW THEY'RE TOAST! I'M UP TO MY ASS IN BROKEN GLASS HERE.
WHO CARES!!!
WE'RE JUST SITTING HERE LIKE A BUNCH OF IDIOTS! WE NEED A PLAN.
WE CAN'T LET THEM GET...

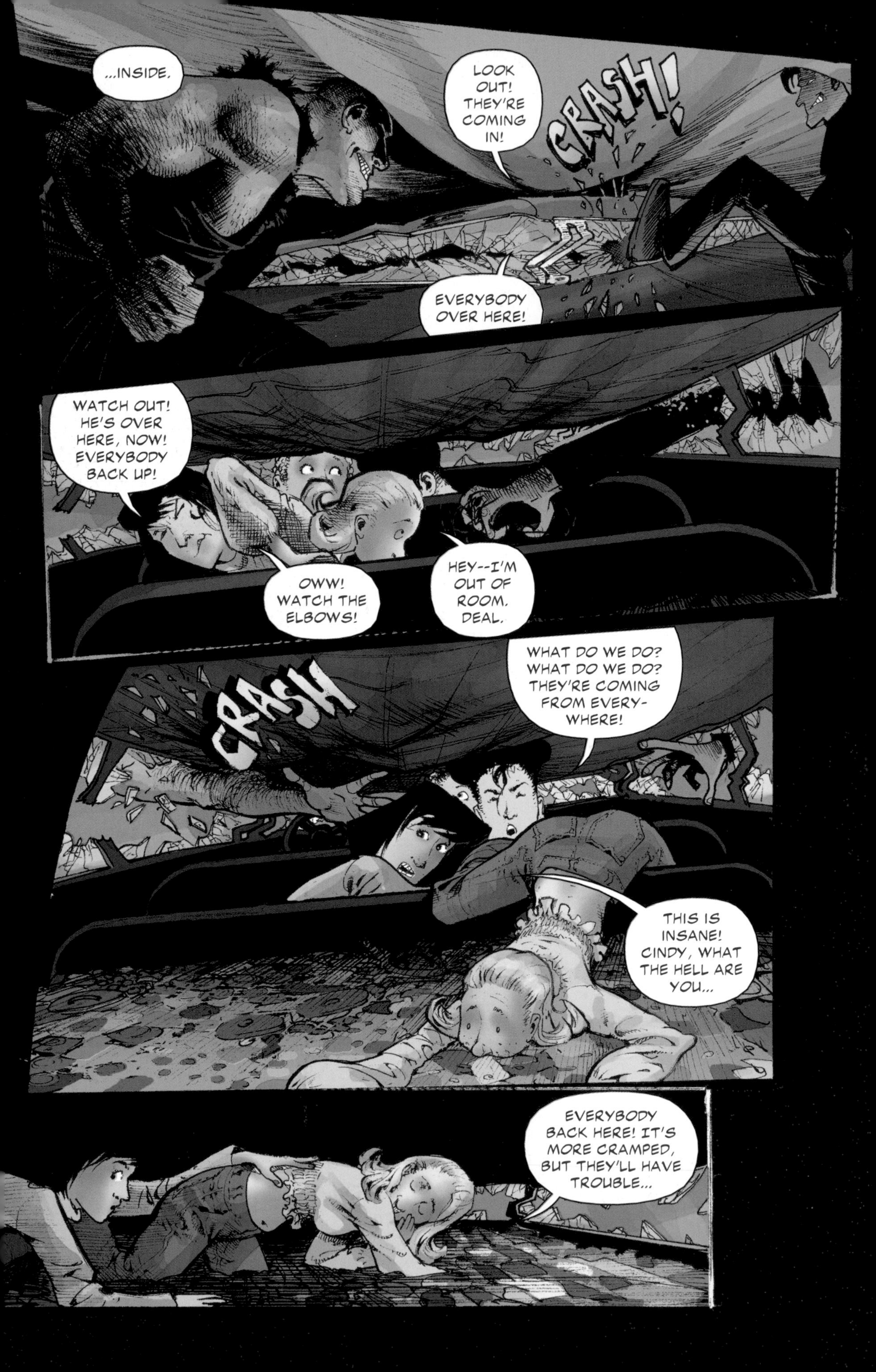
...INSIDE.
LOOK OUT! THEY'RE COMING IN!
CRASH!
EVERYBODY OVER HERE!
WATCH OUT! HE'S OVER HERE, NOW! EVERYBODY BACK UP!
OWW! WATCH THE ELBOWS!
HEY--I'M OUT OF ROOM. DEAL.
CRASH
WHAT DO WE DO? WHAT DO WE DO? THEY'RE COMING FROM EVERY-WHERE!
THIS IS INSANE! CINDY, WHAT THE HELL ARE YOU...
EVERYBODY BACK HERE! IT'S MORE CRAMPED, BUT THEY'LL HAVE TROUBLE...

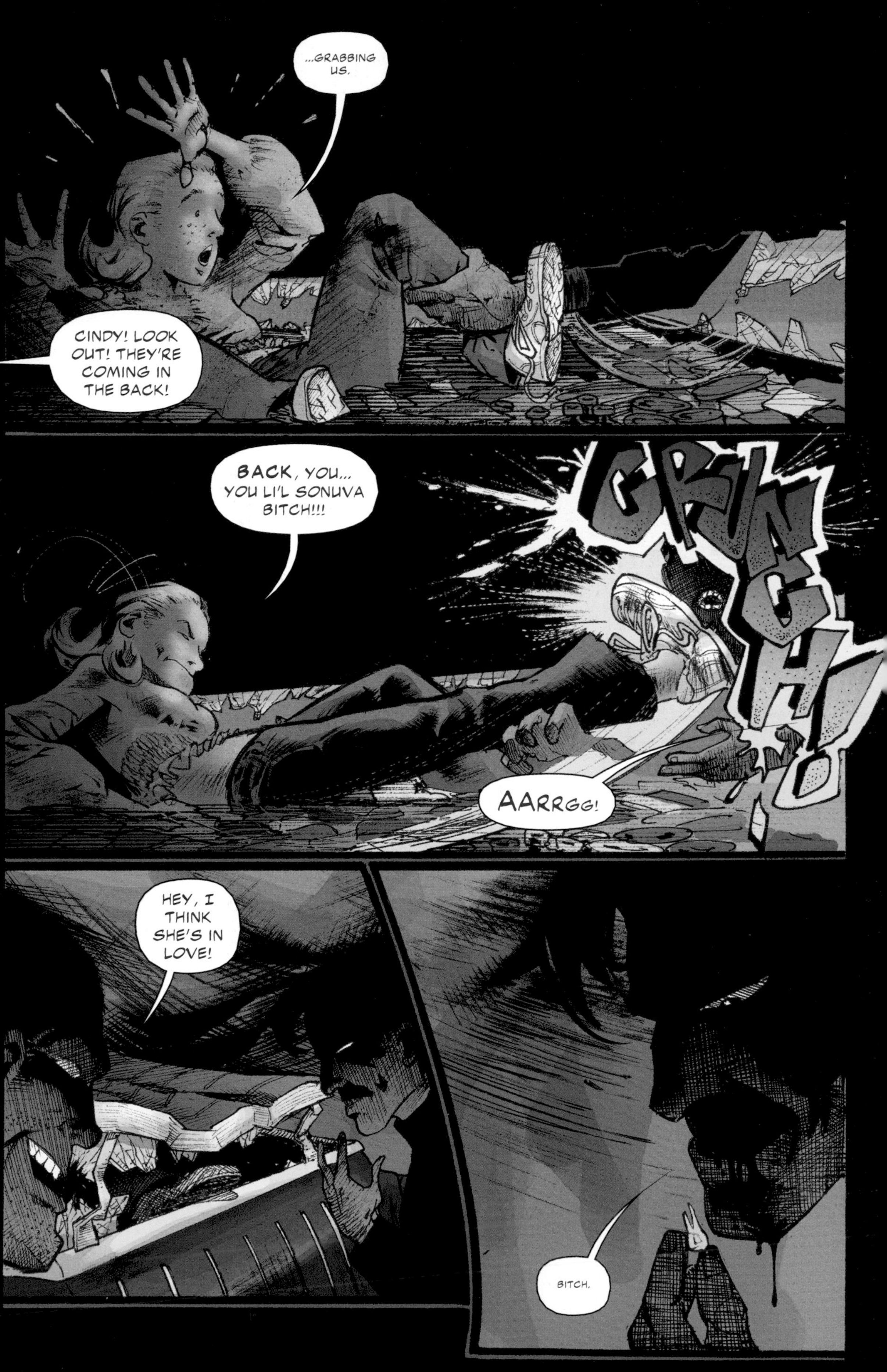
...GRABBING US.
CINDY! LOOK OUT! THEY'RE COMING IN THE BACK!
BACK, YOU... YOU LI'L SONUVA BITCH!!!
CRUNCH!
AARRGG!
HEY, I THINK SHE'S IN LOVE!
BITCH.

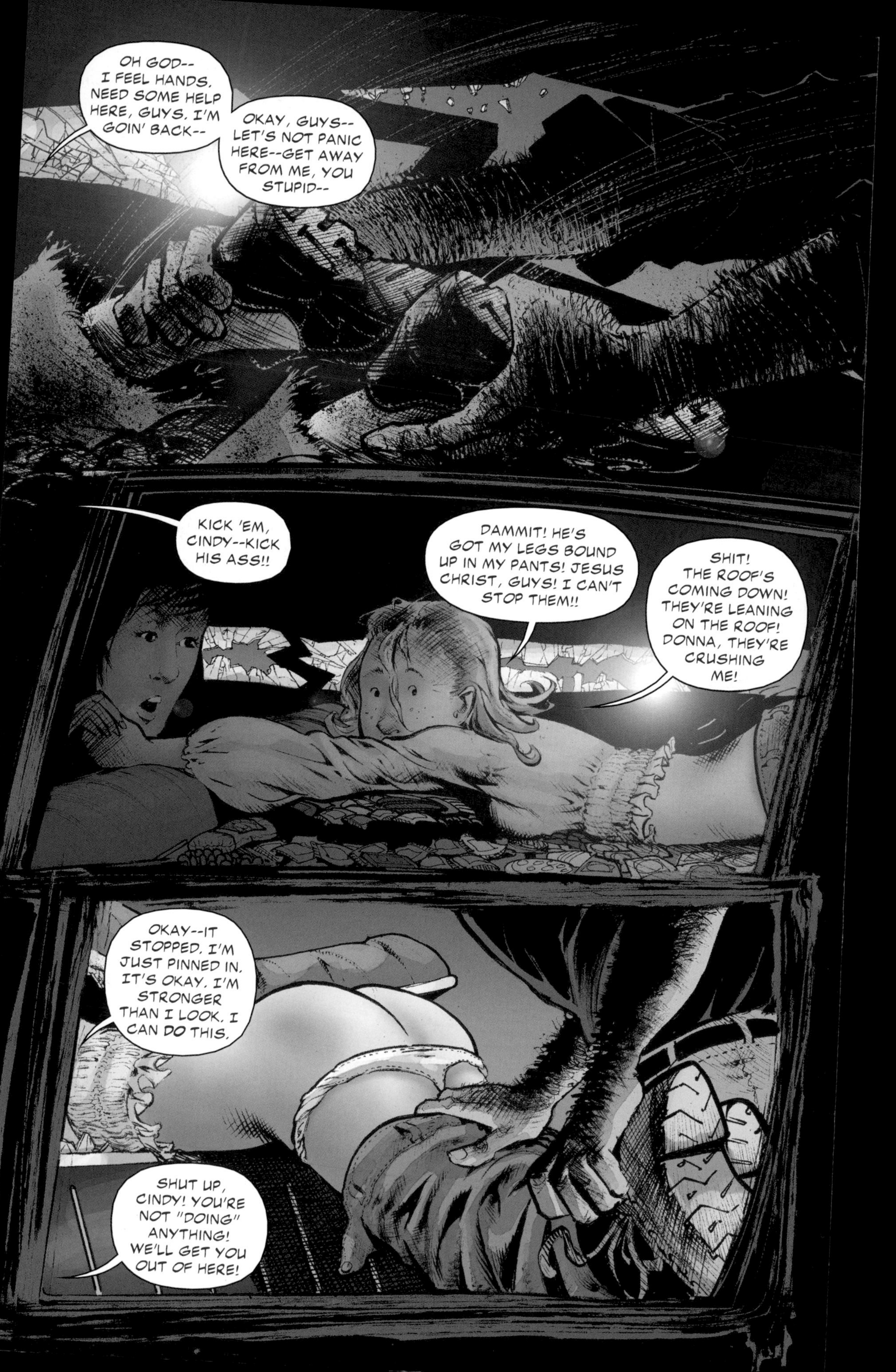
OH GOD-- I FEEL HANDS. NEED SOME HELP HERE, GUYS. I'M GOIN' BACK--
OKAY, GUYS-- LET'S NOT PANIC HERE--GET AWAY FROM ME, YOU STUPID--
KICK 'EM, CINDY--KICK HIS ASS!!
DAMMIT! HE'S GOT MY LEGS BOUND UP IN MY PANTS! JESUS CHRIST, GUYS! I CAN'T STOP THEM!!
SHIT! THE ROOF'S COMING DOWN! THEY'RE LEANING ON THE ROOF! DONNA, THEY'RE CRUSHING ME!
OKAY--IT STOPPED. I'M JUST PINNED IN. IT'S OKAY. I'M STRONGER THAN I LOOK. I CAN DO THIS.
SHUT UP, CINDY! YOU'RE NOT "DOING" ANYTHING! WE'LL GET YOU OUT OF HERE!

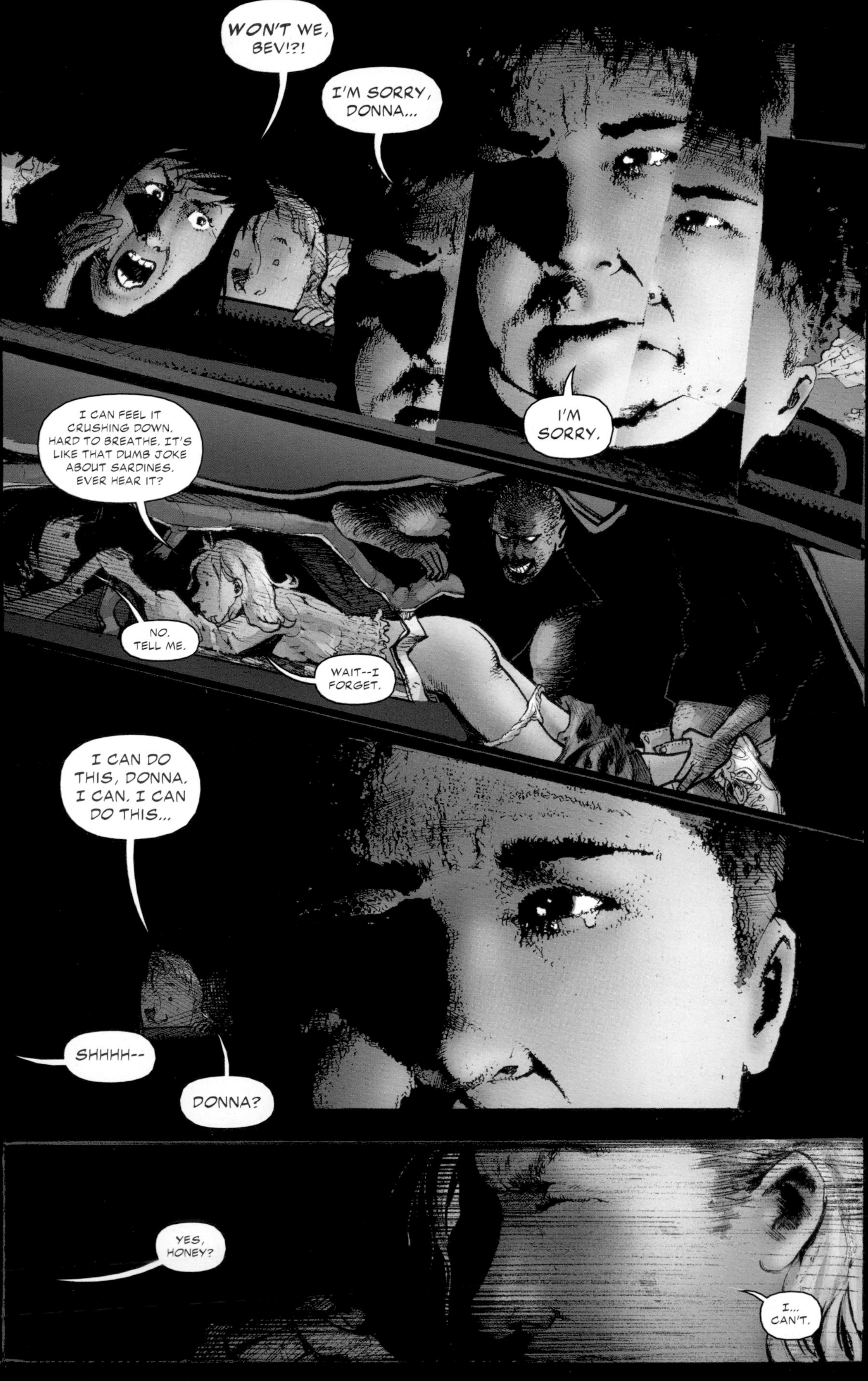
WON'T WE, BEV!?!
I'M SORRY, DONNA...
I'M SORRY.
I CAN FEEL IT CRUSHING DOWN. HARD TO BREATHE. IT'S LIKE THAT DUMB JOKE ABOUT SARDINES. EVER HEAR IT?
NO. TELL ME.
WAIT--I FORGET.
I CAN DO THIS, DONNA. I CAN. I CAN DO THIS...
SHHHH--
DONNA?
YES, HONEY?
I... CAN'T.

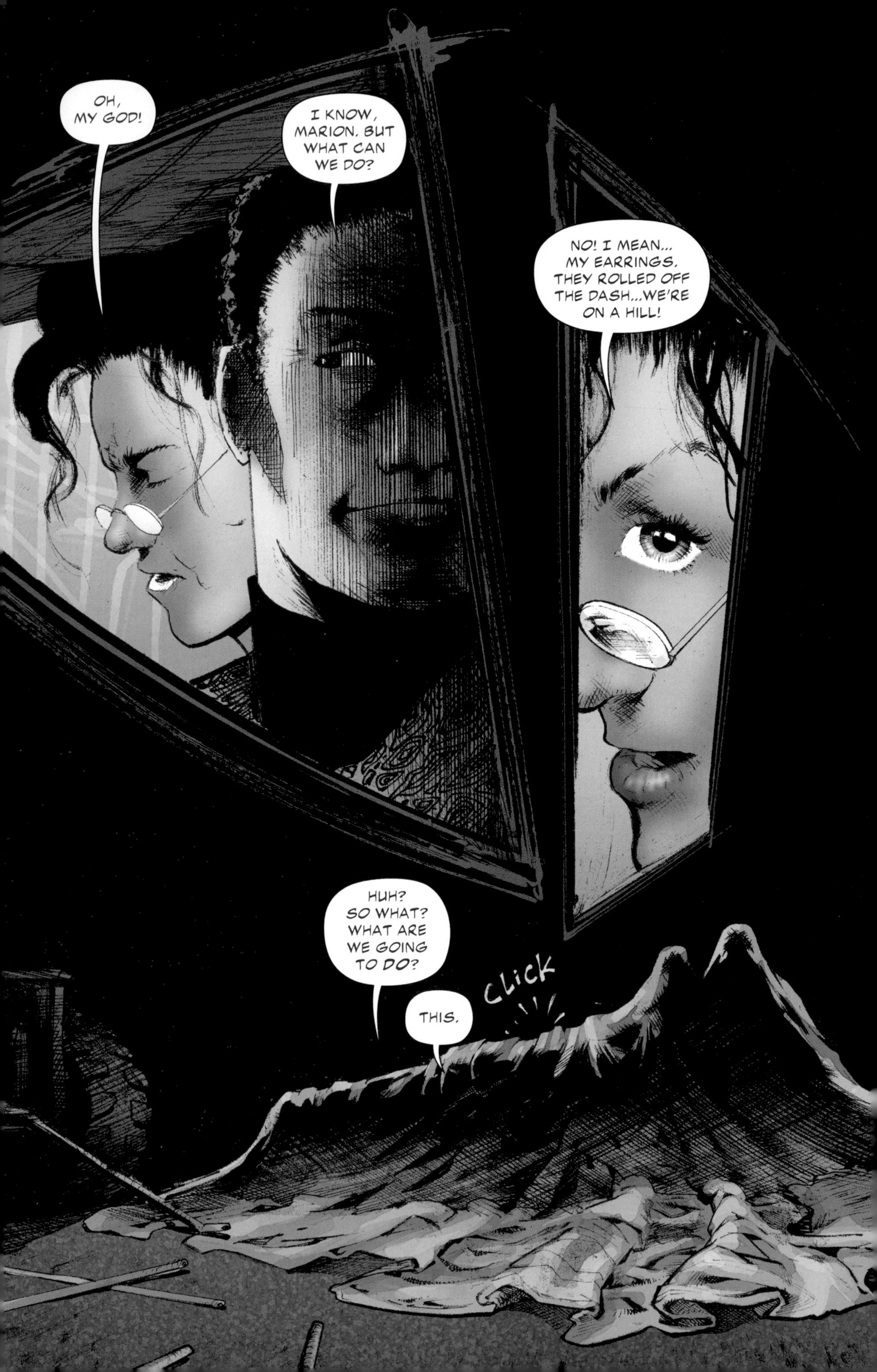
OH, MY GOD!
I KNOW, MARION. BUT WHAT CAN WE DO?
NO! I MEAN... MY EARRINGS. THEY ROLLED OFF THE DASH...WE'RE ON A HILL!
HUH? SO WHAT? WHAT ARE WE GOING TO DO?
THIS.
CLICK

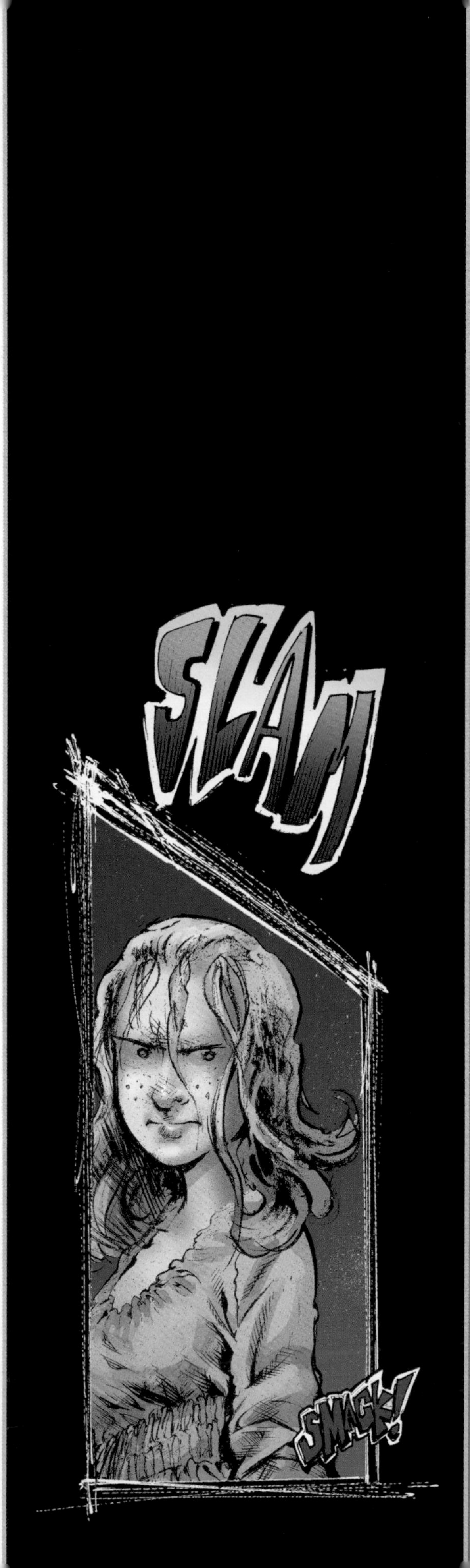
SLAM
SMACK!

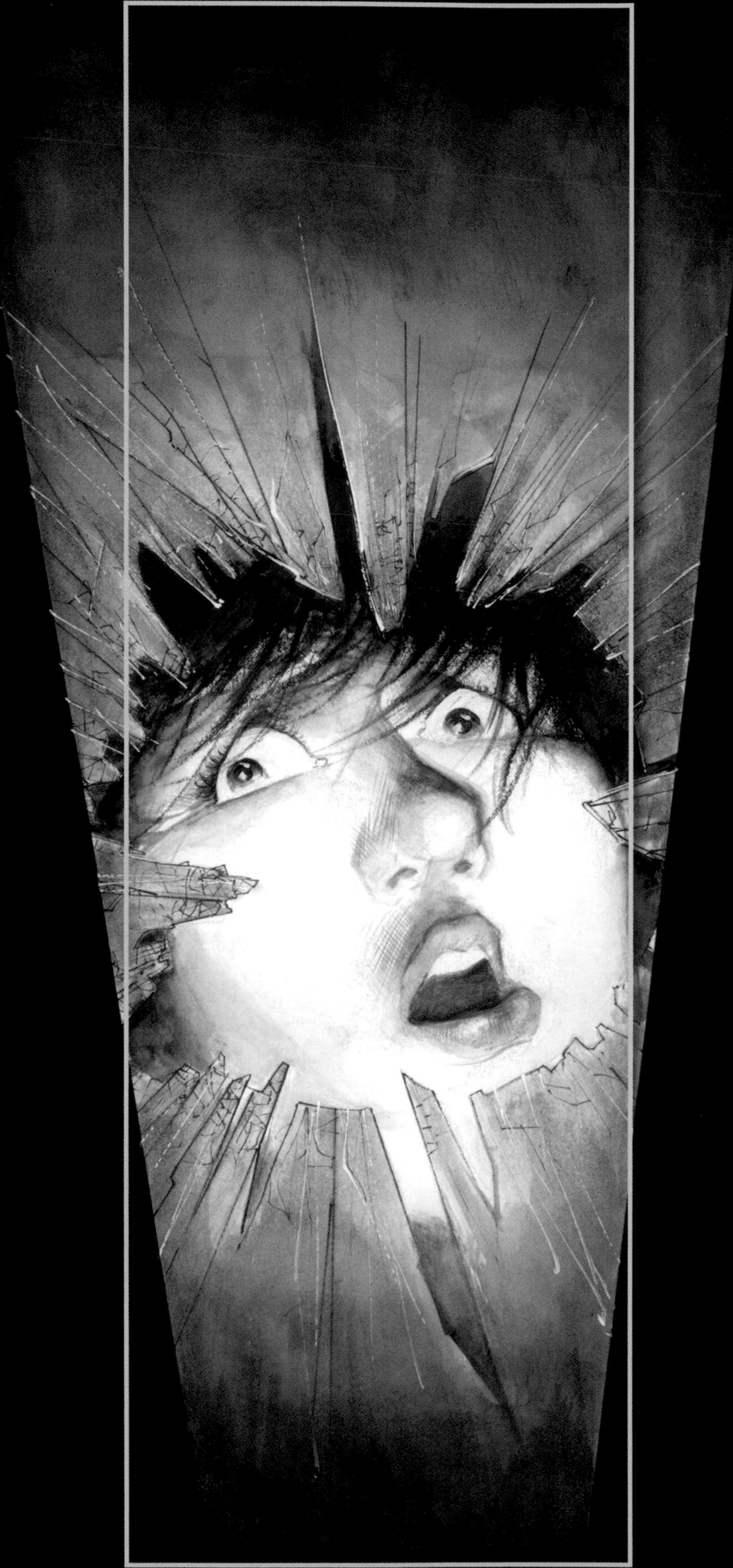

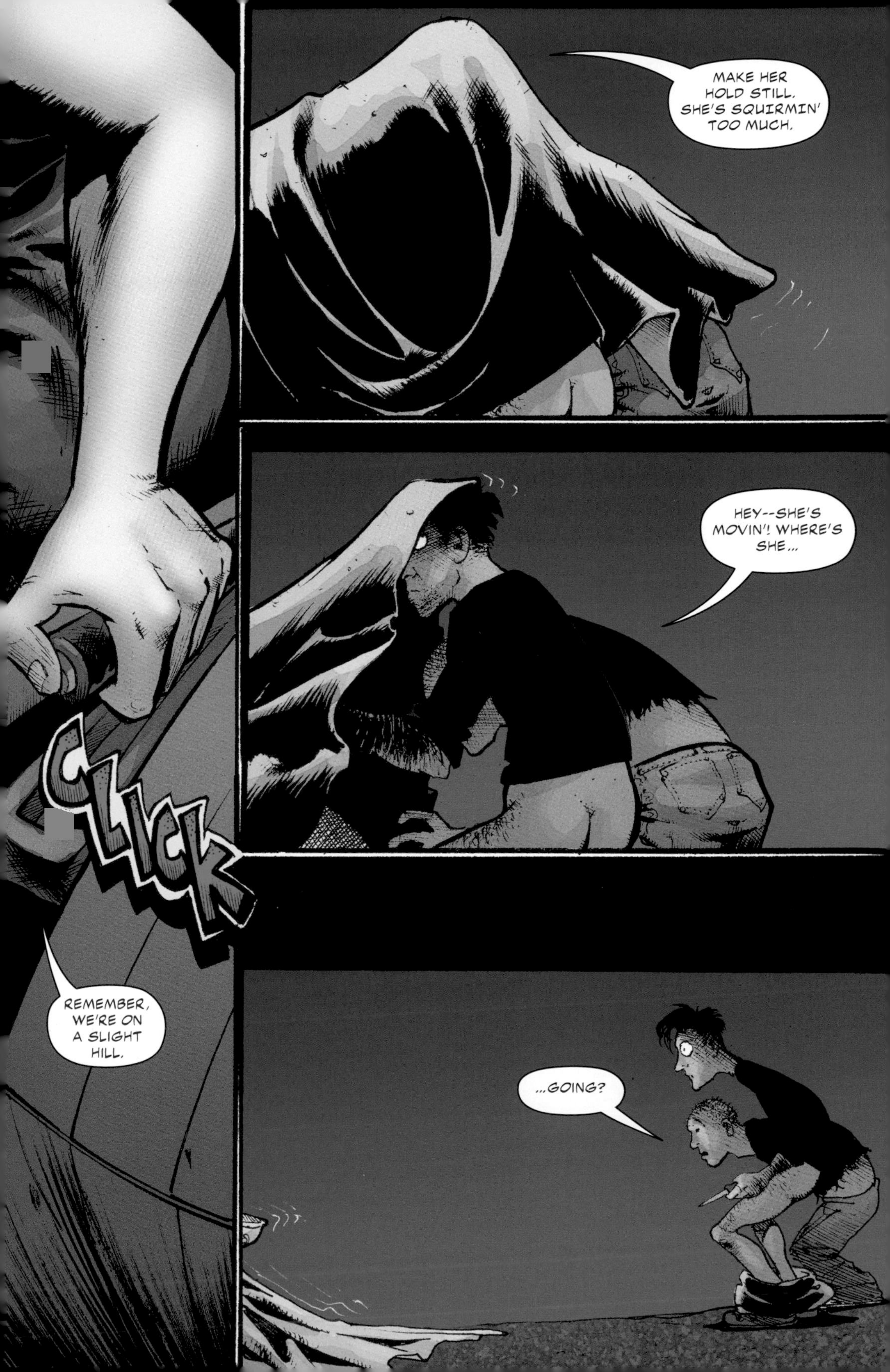
MAKE HER HOLD STILL. SHE'S SQUIRMIN' TOO MUCH.
HEY--SHE'S MOVIN'! WHERE'S SHE...
CLICK
REMEMBER, WE'RE ON A SLIGHT HILL.
...GOING?

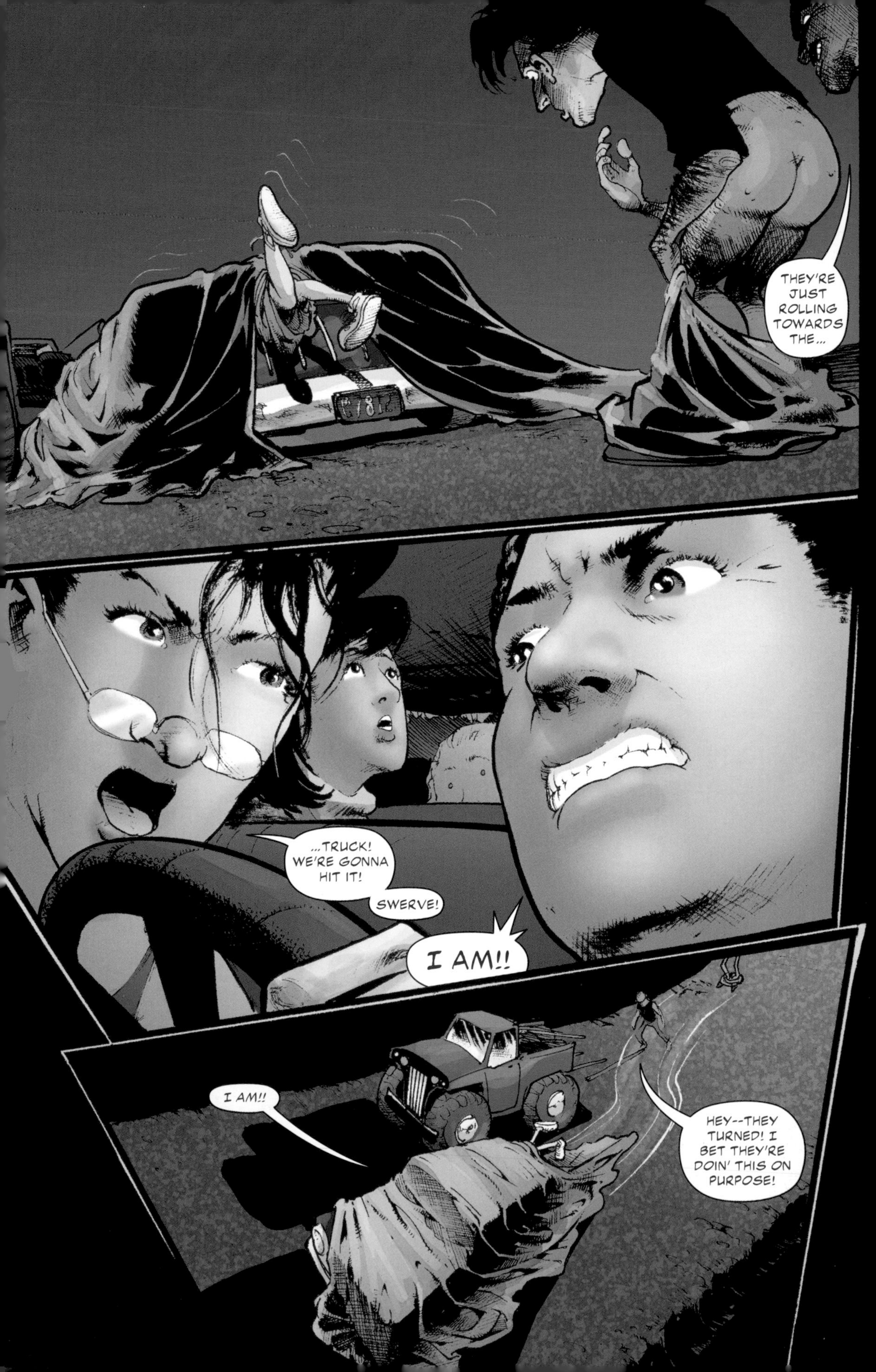
THEY'RE JUST ROLLING TOWARDS THE...
...TRUCK! WE'RE GONNA HIT IT!
SWERVE!
I AM!!
I AM!!
HEY--THEY TURNED! I BET THEY'RE DOIN' THIS ON PURPOSE!

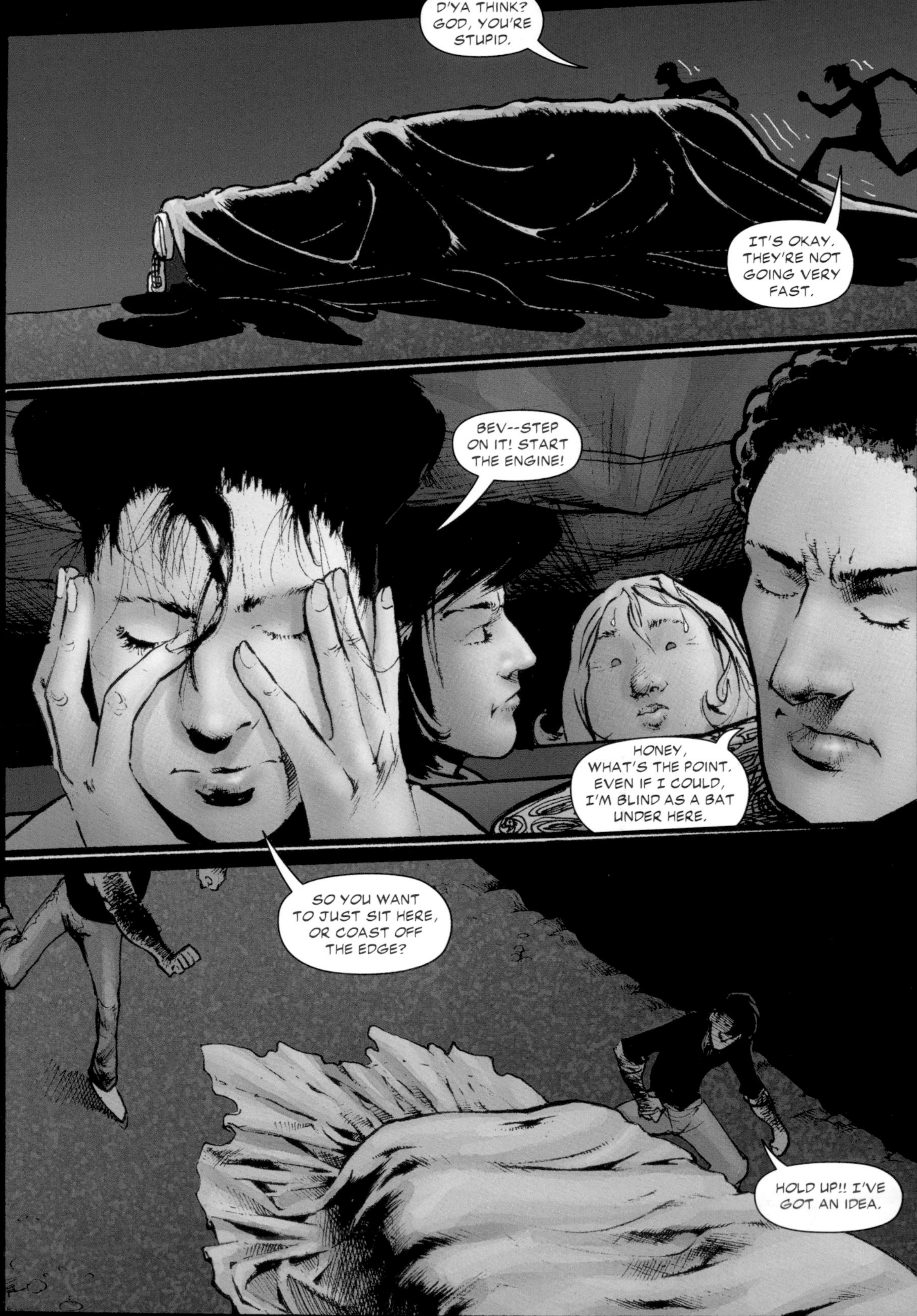
D'YA THINK? GOD, YOU'RE STUPID.
IT'S OKAY. THEY'RE NOT GOING VERY FAST.
BEV--STEP ON IT! START THE ENGINE!
HONEY, WHAT'S THE POINT. EVEN IF I COULD, I'M BLIND AS A BAT UNDER HERE.
SO YOU WANT TO JUST SIT HERE, OR COAST OFF THE EDGE?
HOLD UP!! I'VE GOT AN IDEA.

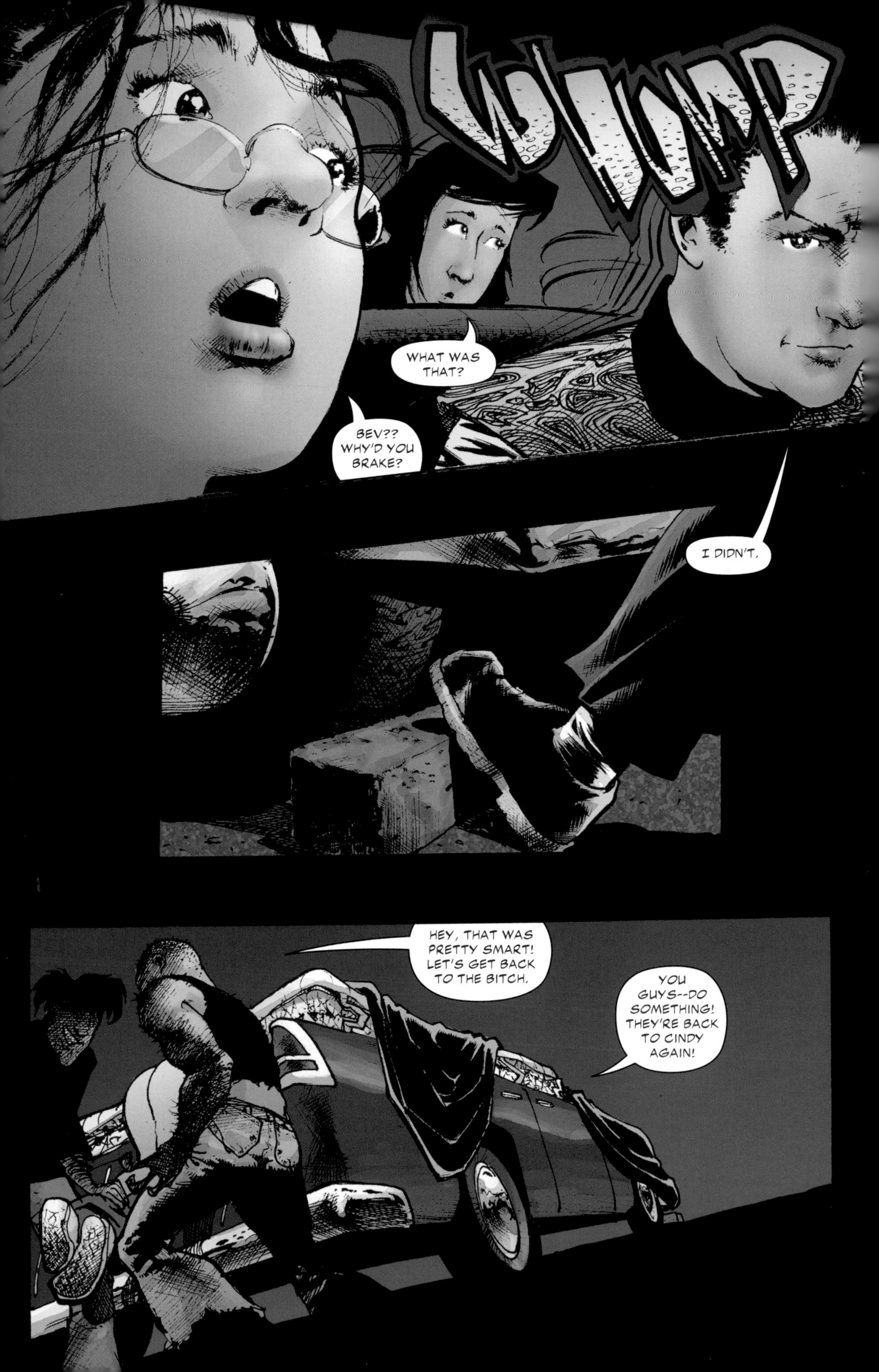
WHUMP
WHAT WAS THAT?
BEV?? WHY'D YOU BRAKE?
I DIDN'T.
HEY, THAT WAS PRETTY SMART! LET'S GET BACK TO THE BITCH.
YOU GUYS--DO SOMETHING! THEY'RE BACK TO CINDY AGAIN!

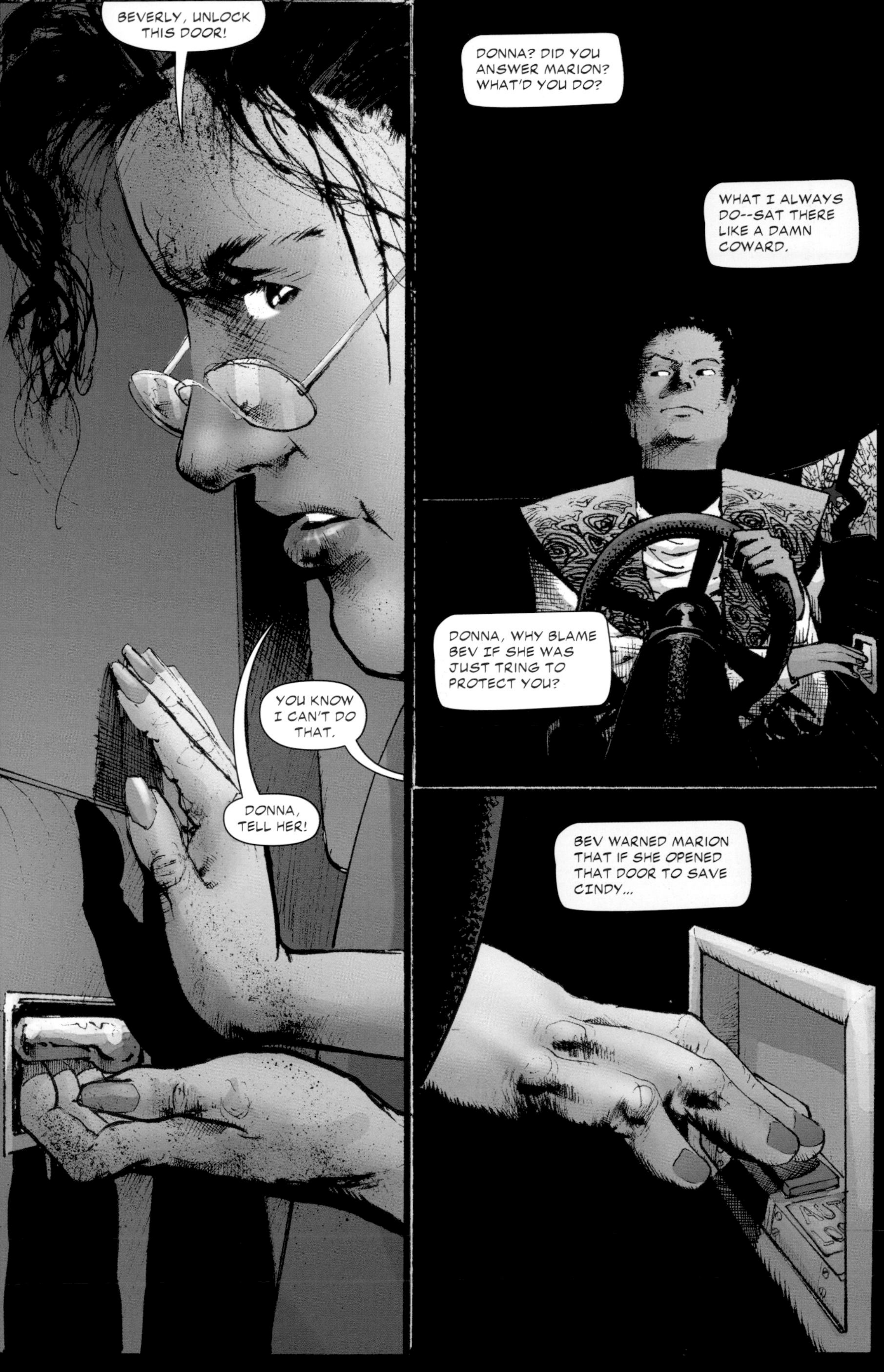

BEVERLY, UNLOCK THIS DOOR!
DONNA? DID YOU ANSWER MARION? WHAT'D YOU DO?
WHAT I ALWAYS DO--SAT THERE LIKE A DAMN COWARD.
DONNA, WHY BLAME BEV IF SHE WAS JUST TRING TO PROTECT YOU?
YOU KNOW I CAN'T DO THAT.
DONNA, TELL HER!
BEV WARNED MARION THAT IF SHE OPENED THAT DOOR TO SAVE CINDY...

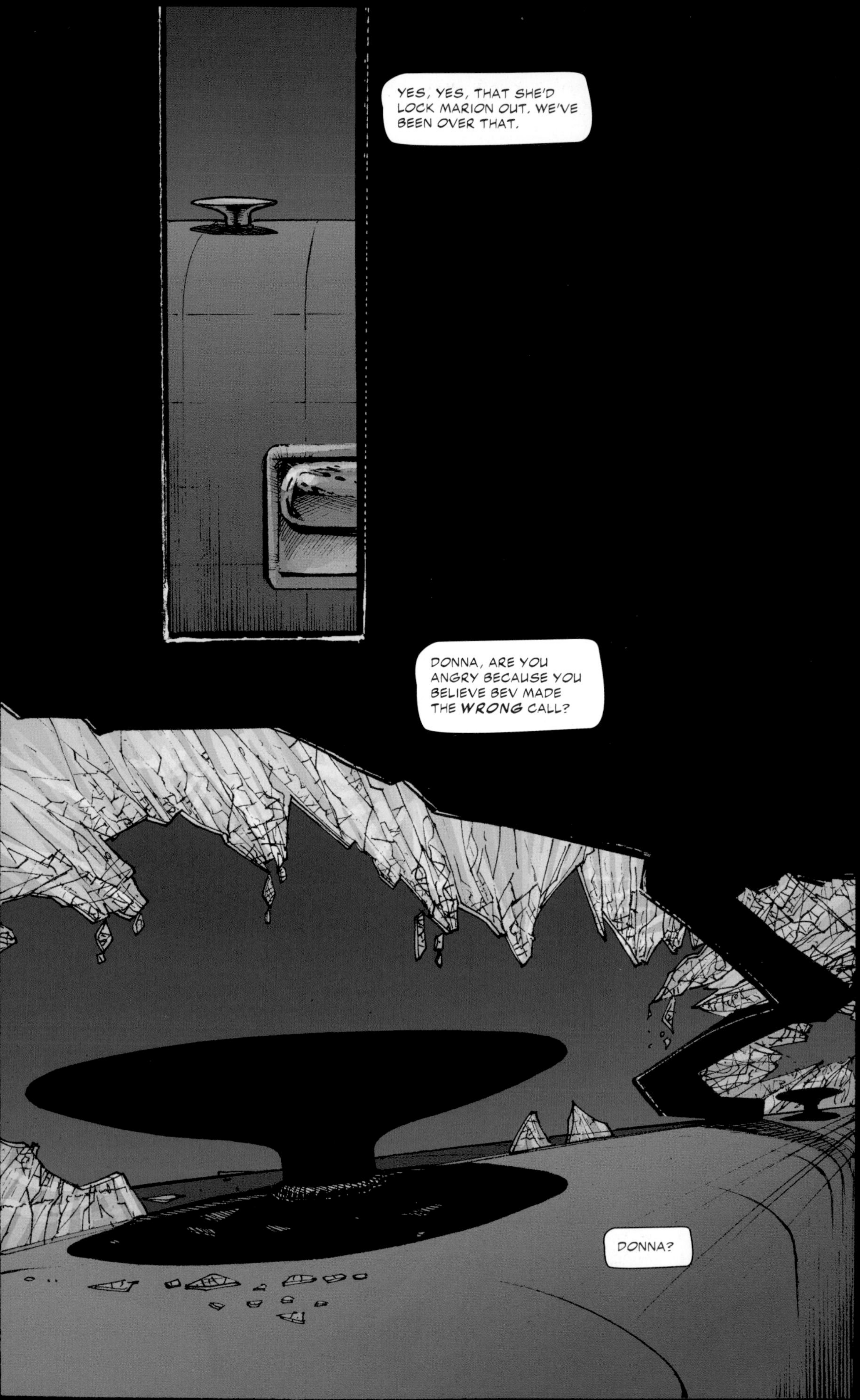
YES, YES, THAT SHE'D LOCK MARION OUT. WE'VE BEEN OVER THAT.
DONNA, ARE YOU ANGRY BECAUSE YOU BELIEVE BEV MADE THE WRONG CALL?
DONNA?

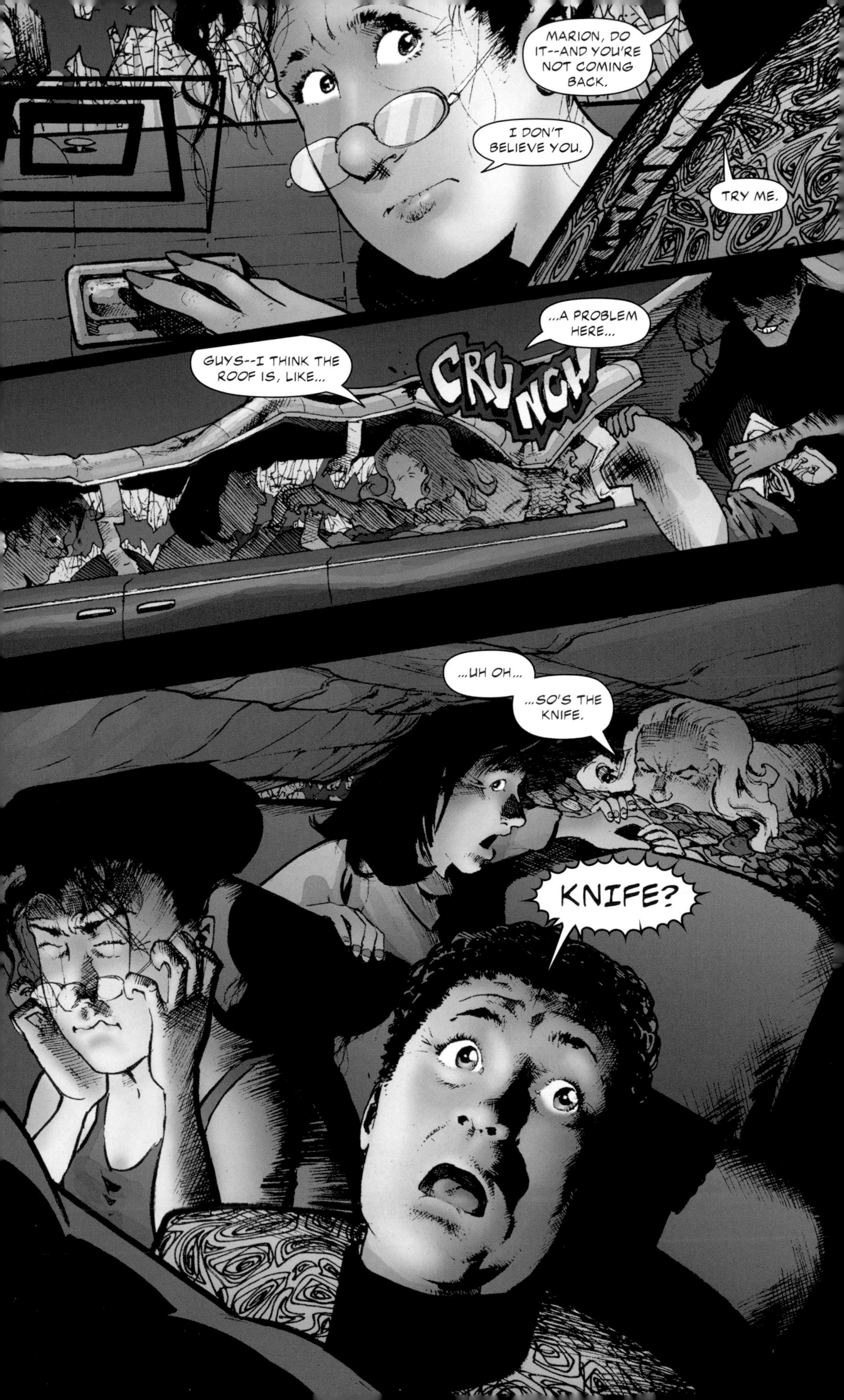
MARION, DO IT--AND YOU'RE NOT COMING BACK.
I DON'T BELIEVE YOU.
TRY ME.
GUYS--I THINK THE ROOF IS, LIKE...
CRUNCH
...A PROBLEM HERE...
...UH OH...
...SO'S THE KNIFE.
KNIFE?

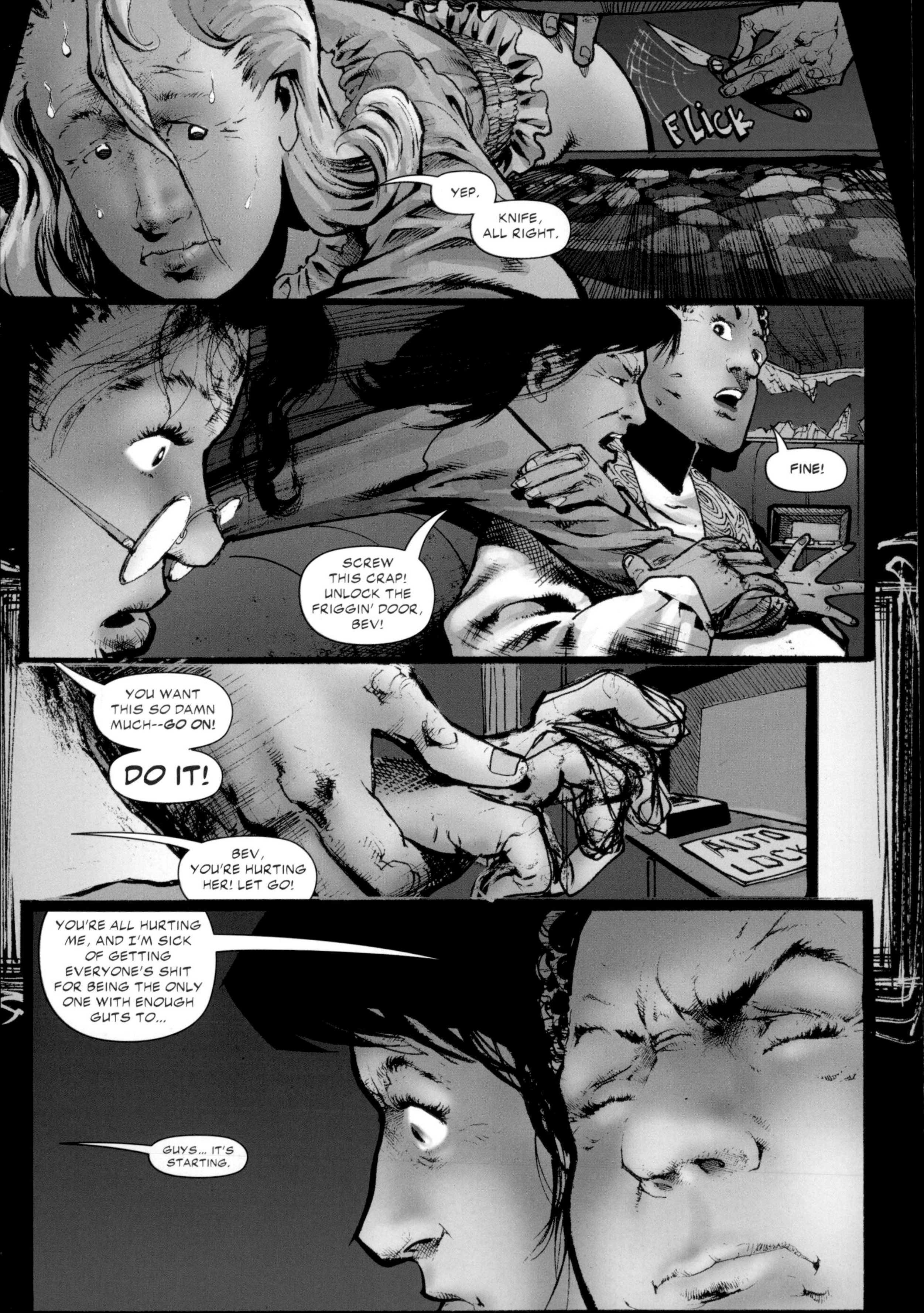
FLICK
YEP.
KNIFE, ALL RIGHT.
FINE!
SCREW THIS CRAP! UNLOCK THE FRIGGIN' DOOR, BEV!
YOU WANT THIS SO DAMN MUCH--GO ON!
DO IT!
AUTO LOCK
BEV, YOU'RE HURTING HER! LET GO!
YOU'RE ALL HURTING ME, AND I'M SICK OF GETTING EVERYONE'S SHIT FOR BEING THE ONLY ONE WITH ENOUGH GUTS TO...
GUYS... IT'S STARTING.

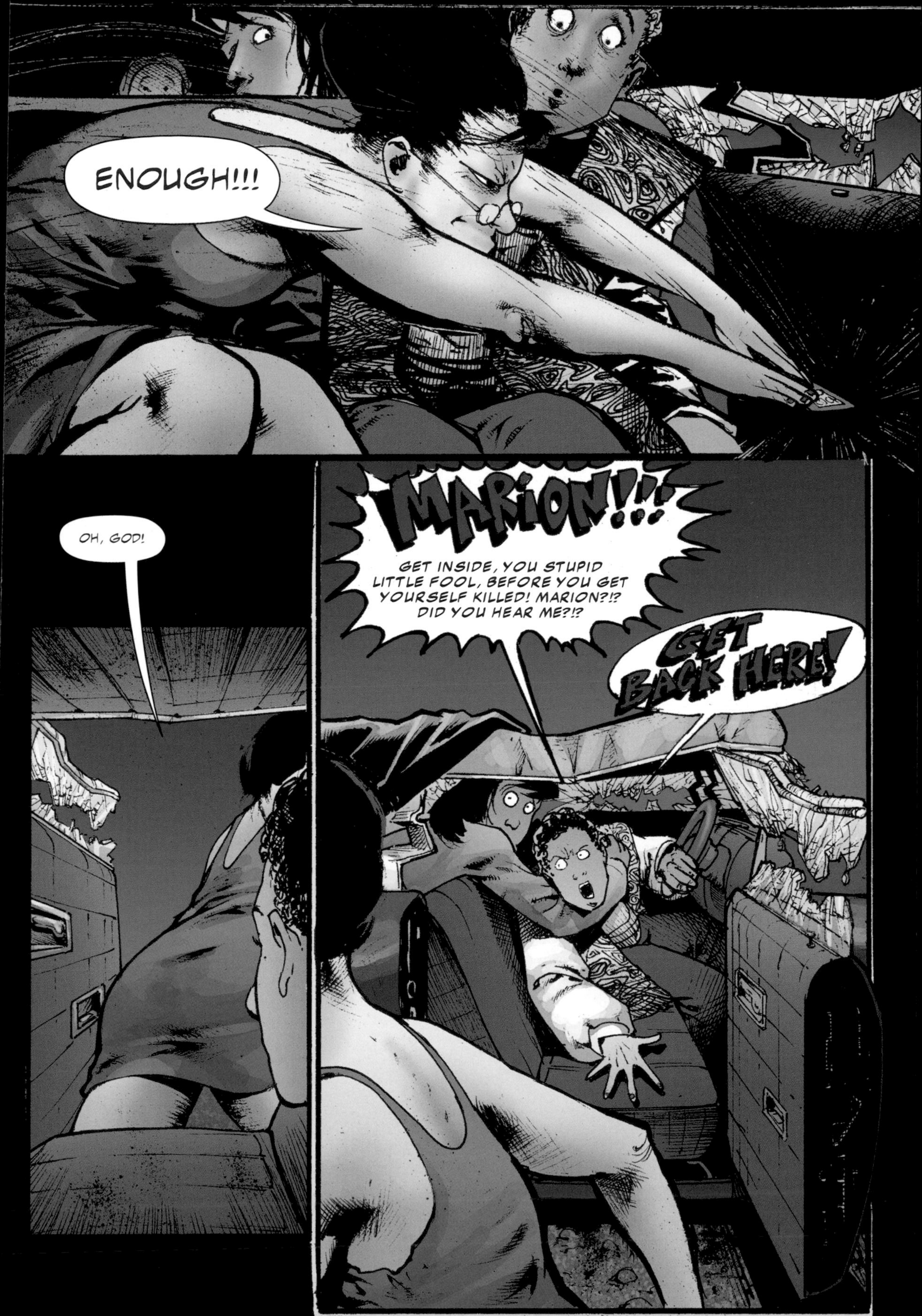
ENOUGH!!!
OH, GOD!
MARION!!!
GET INSIDE, YOU STUPID LITTLE FOOL, BEFORE YOU GET YOURSELF KILLED! MARION?!? DID YOU HEAR ME?!?
GET BACK HERE!

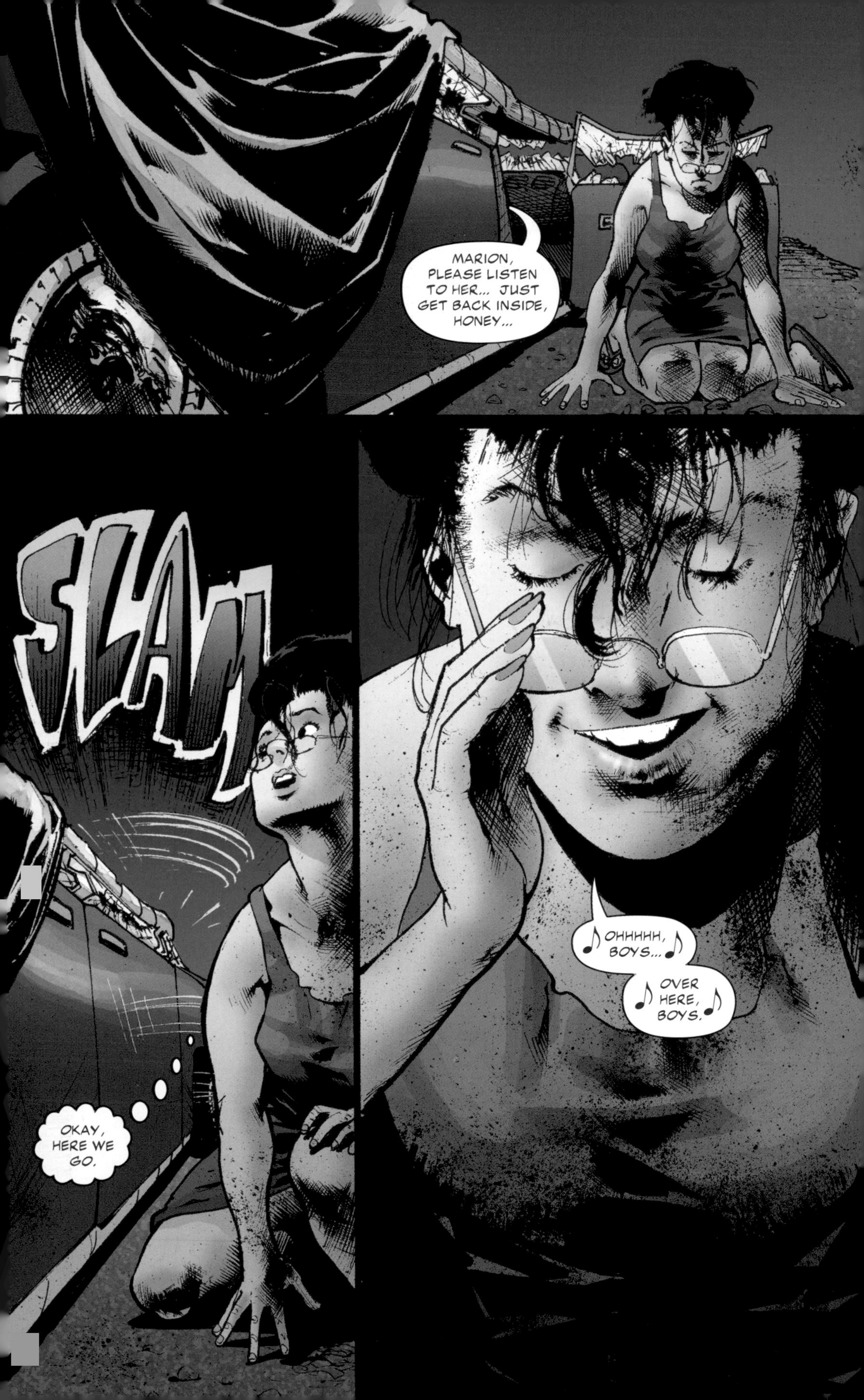

MARION, PLEASE LISTEN TO HER... JUST GET BACK INSIDE, HONEY...
SLAM
OKAY, HERE WE GO.
♪ OHHHHH, BOYS... ♪
♪ OVER HERE, BOYS. ♪

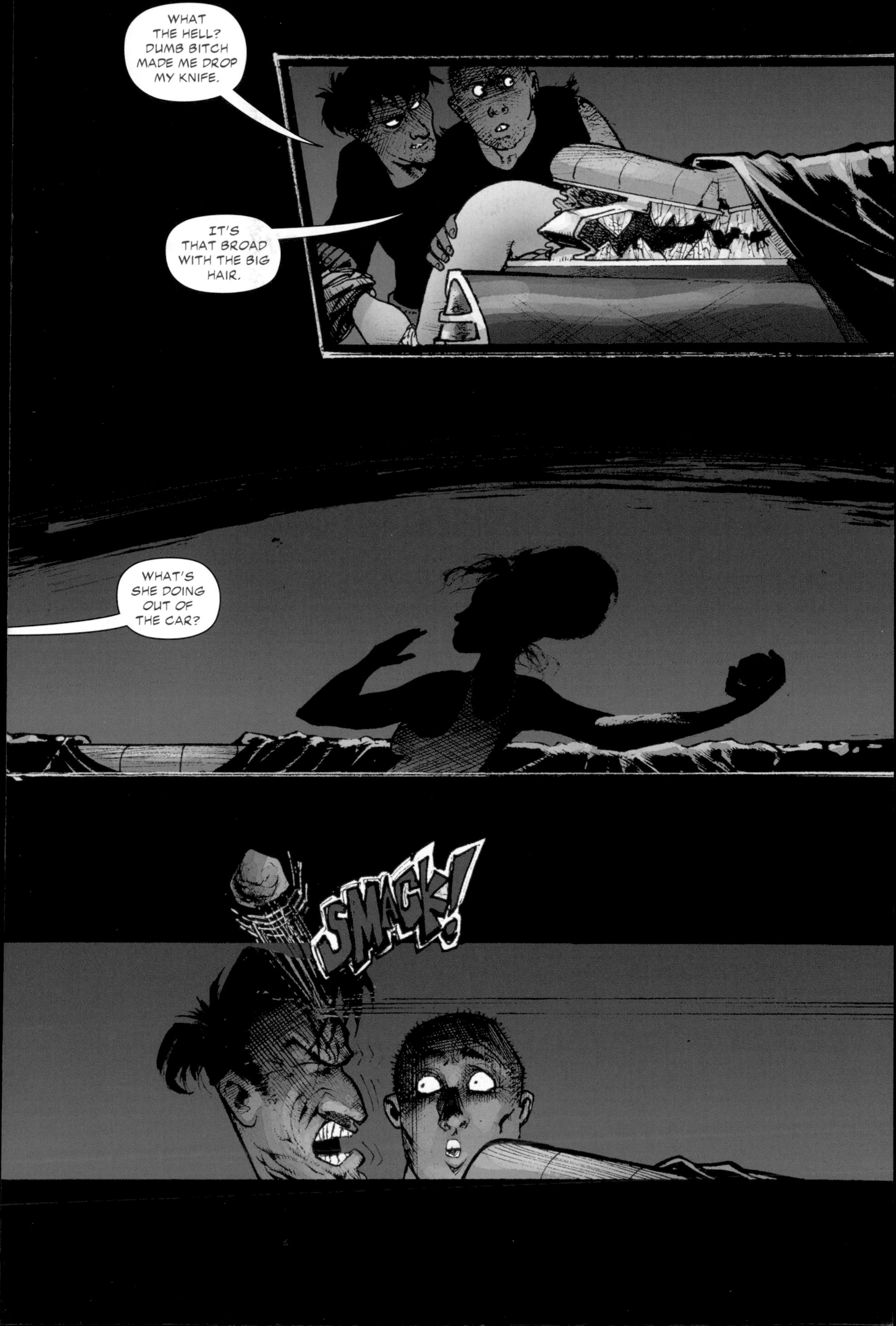
WHAT THE HELL? DUMB BITCH MADE ME DROP MY KNIFE.
IT'S THAT BROAD WITH THE BIG HAIR.
WHAT'S SHE DOING OUT OF THE CAR?
SMACK!

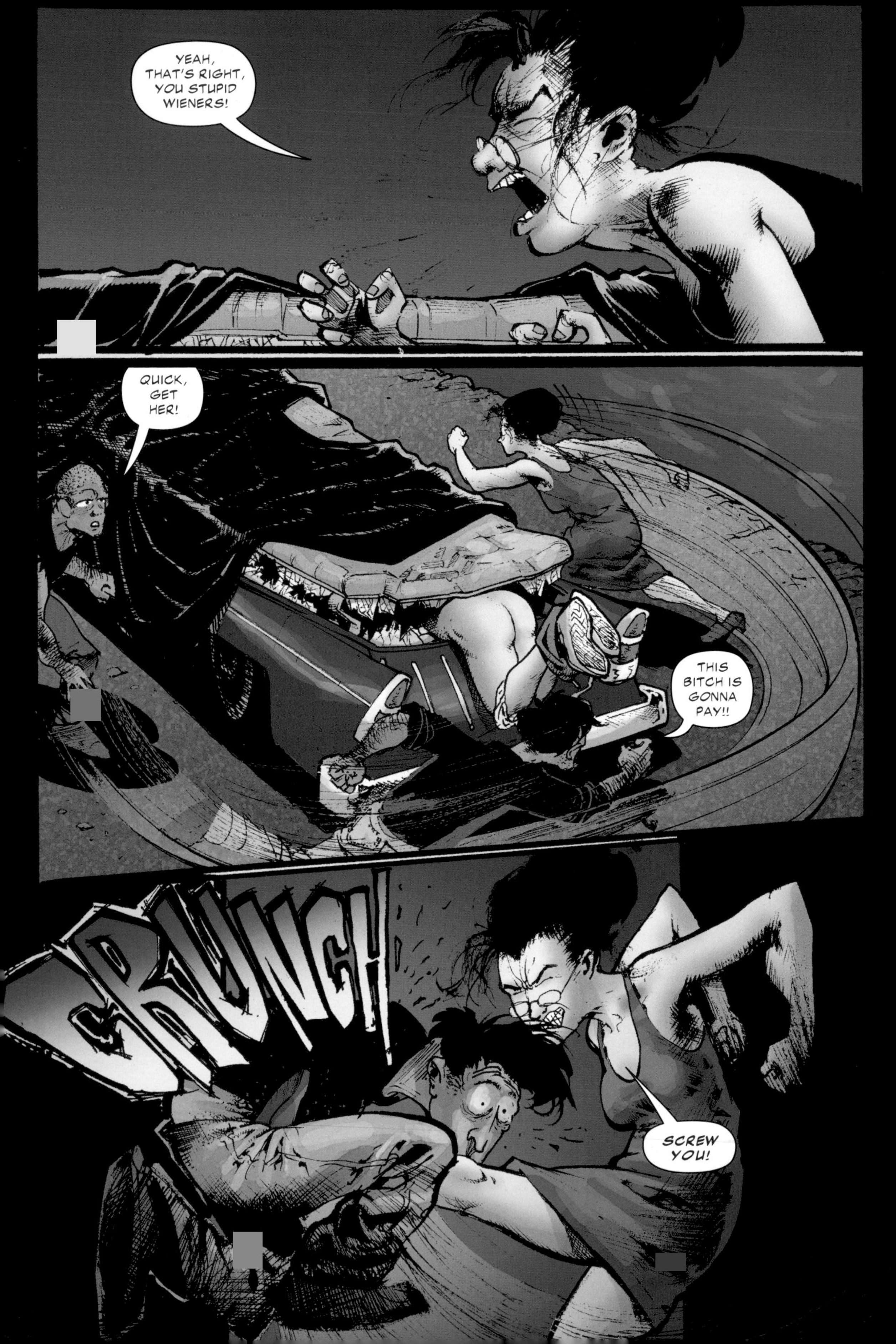
YEAH, THAT'S RIGHT, YOU STUPID WIENERS!
QUICK, GET HER!
THIS BITCH IS GONNA PAY!!
CRUNCH
SCREW YOU!

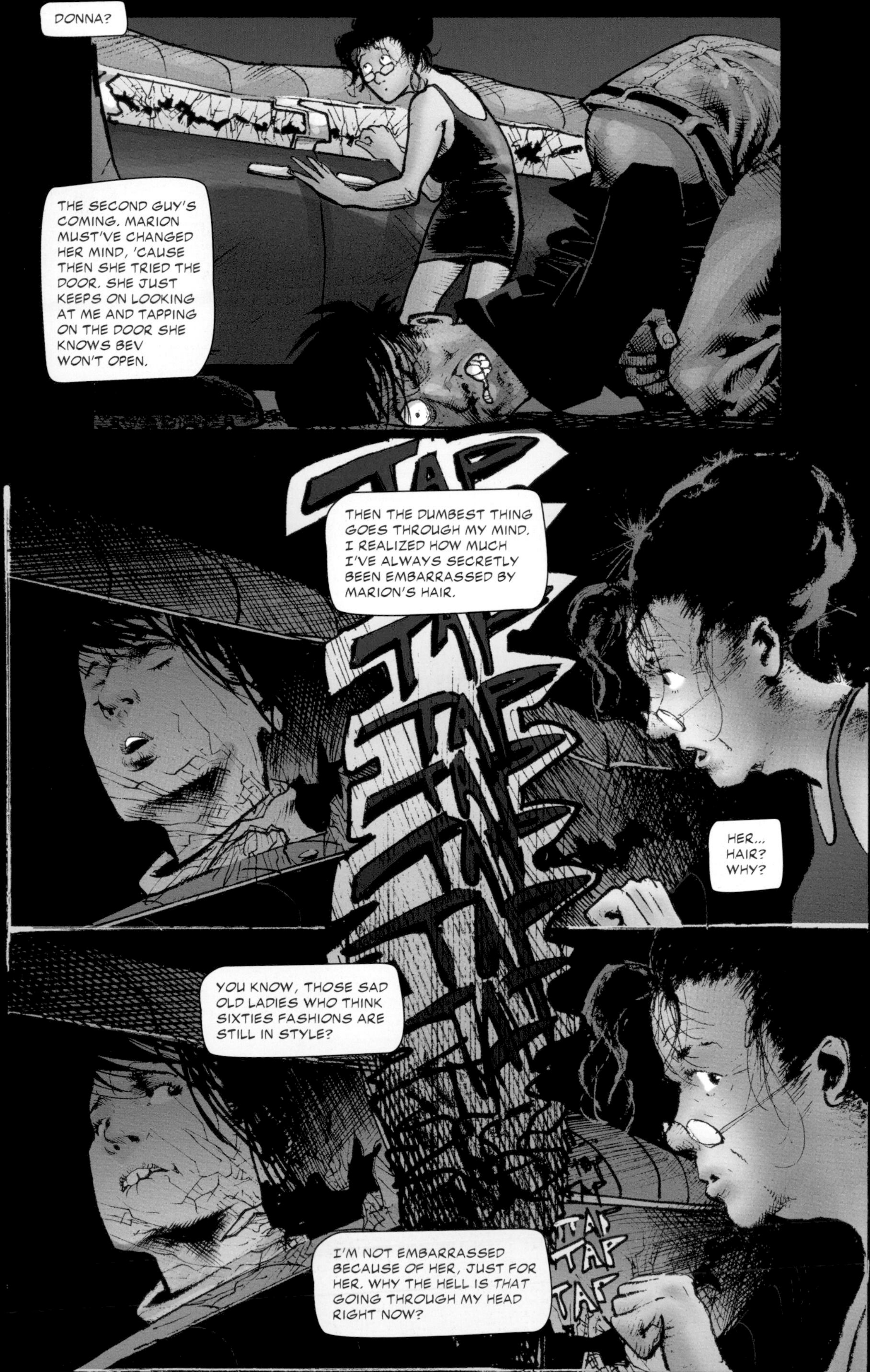
DONNA?
THE SECOND GUY'S COMING. MARION MUST'VE CHANGED HER MIND, 'CAUSE THEN SHE TRIED THE DOOR. SHE JUST KEEPS ON LOOKING AT ME AND TAPPING ON THE DOOR SHE KNOWS BEV WON'T OPEN.
TAP
THEN THE DUMBEST THING GOES THROUGH MY MIND. I REALIZED HOW MUCH I'VE ALWAYS SECRETLY BEEN EMBARRASSED BY MARION'S HAIR.
HER... HAIR? WHY?
YOU KNOW, THOSE SAD OLD LADIES WHO THINK SIXTIES FASHIONS ARE STILL IN STYLE?
I'M NOT EMBARRASSED BECAUSE OF HER, JUST FOR HER. WHY THE HELL IS THAT GOING THROUGH MY HEAD RIGHT NOW?
TAP
TAP
TAP

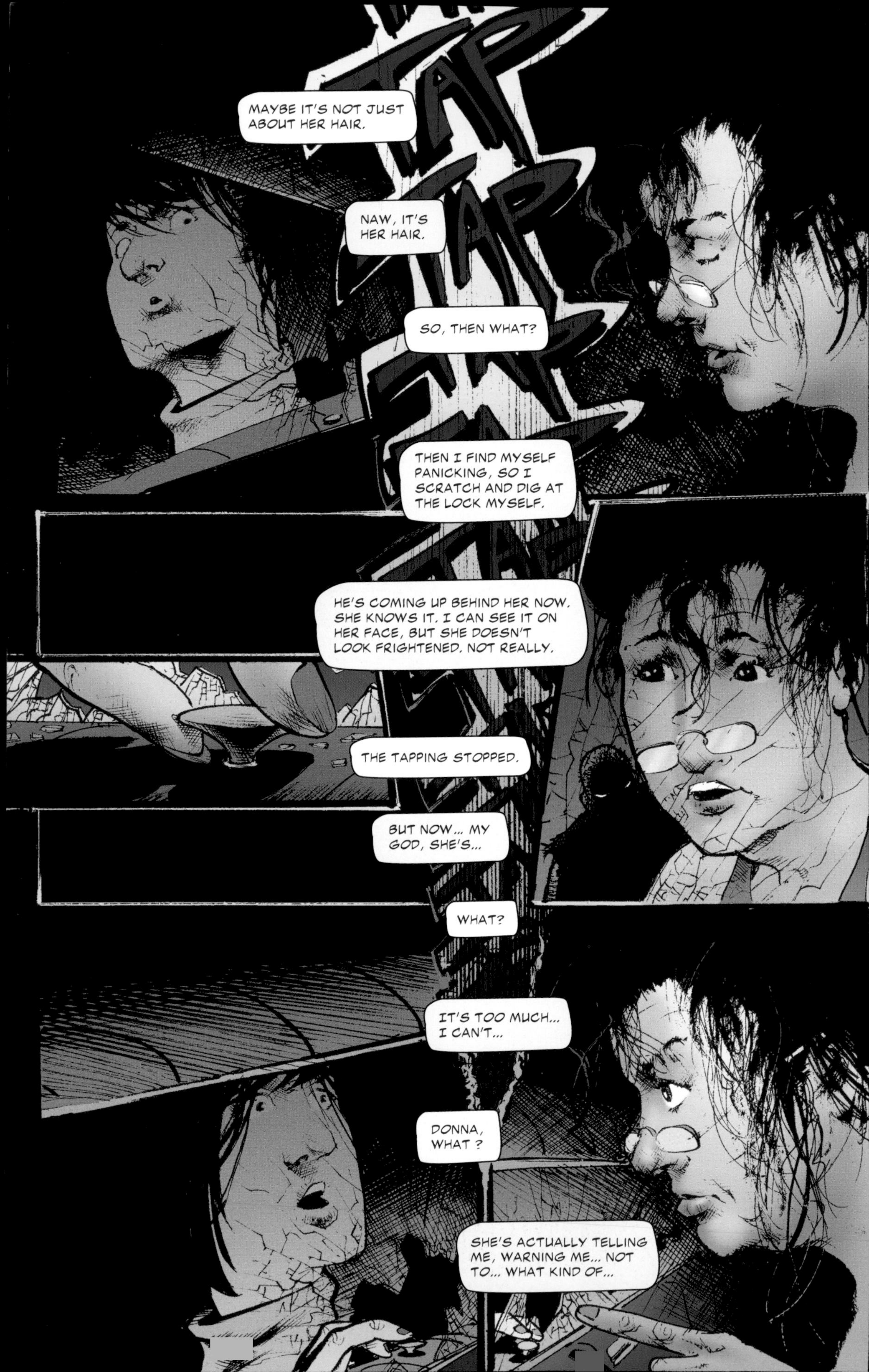

TAP TAP TAP
MAYBE IT'S NOT JUST ABOUT HER HAIR.
NAW, IT'S HER HAIR.
SO, THEN WHAT?
THEN I FIND MYSELF PANICKING, SO I SCRATCH AND DIG AT THE LOCK MYSELF.
HE'S COMING UP BEHIND HER NOW. SHE KNOWS IT. I CAN SEE IT ON HER FACE, BUT SHE DOESN'T LOOK FRIGHTENED. NOT REALLY.
THE TAPPING STOPPED.
BUT NOW... MY GOD, SHE'S...
WHAT?
IT'S TOO MUCH... I CAN'T...
DONNA, WHAT ?
SHE'S ACTUALLY TELLING ME, WARNING ME... NOT TO... WHAT KIND OF...

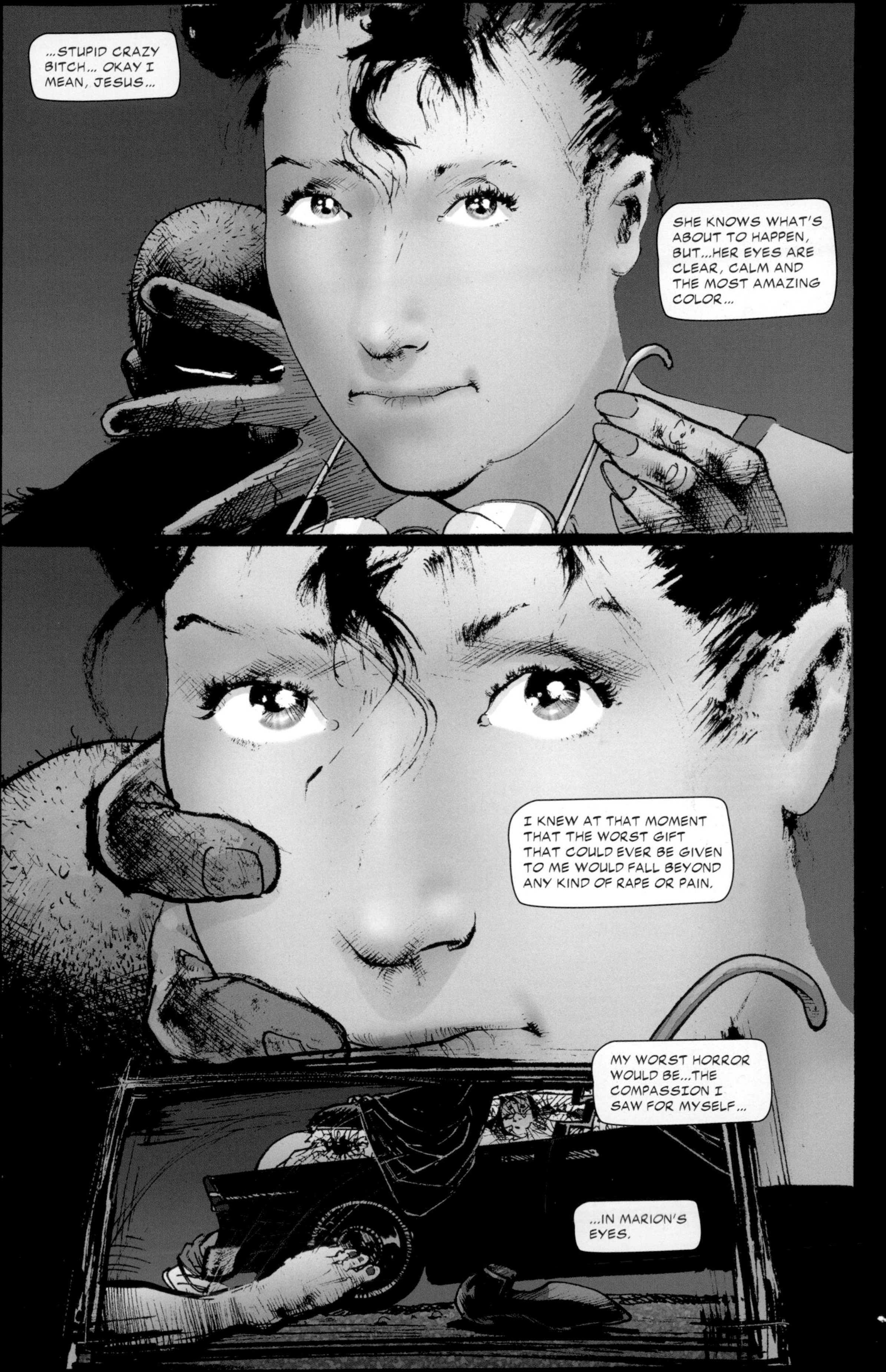
...STUPID CRAZY BITCH... OKAY I MEAN, JESUS...
SHE KNOWS WHAT'S ABOUT TO HAPPEN, BUT...HER EYES ARE CLEAR, CALM AND THE MOST AMAZING COLOR...
I KNEW AT THAT MOMENT THAT THE WORST GIFT THAT COULD EVER BE GIVEN TO ME WOULD FALL BEYOND ANY KIND OF RAPE OR PAIN.
MY WORST HORROR WOULD BE...THE COMPASSION I SAW FOR MYSELF...
...IN MARION'S EYES.

PANT

PANT

OKAY, DONNA...SO NOW MARION IS...?

YUP, MY BILE'S RISING INSIDE BECAUSE BEV IS APPARENTLY STILL TOO GUTLESS TO DO ANYTHING BUT SIT THERE AND WATCH--

PANT

PANT

I STILL DON'T BUY YOUR ANGER AT BEV. IT DOESN'T ADD UP.

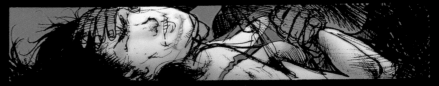

SHE'S TOO EASY A WAY OUT, AND YOU KNOW IT. I FEEL LIKE THERE'S SOMETHING ELSE YOU'RE HOLDING BACK.

PANT

PANT

PANT

PANT

PANT

SO NOW YOU THINK I'M LYING?

PANT

I DIDN'T SAY THAT. I KNOW YOU AND BEVERLY WERE THERE WATCHING MARION'S RAPE, WITH CINDY WEDGED IN THE BACK.

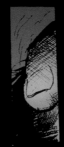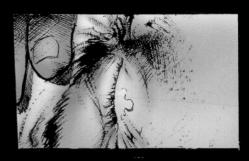

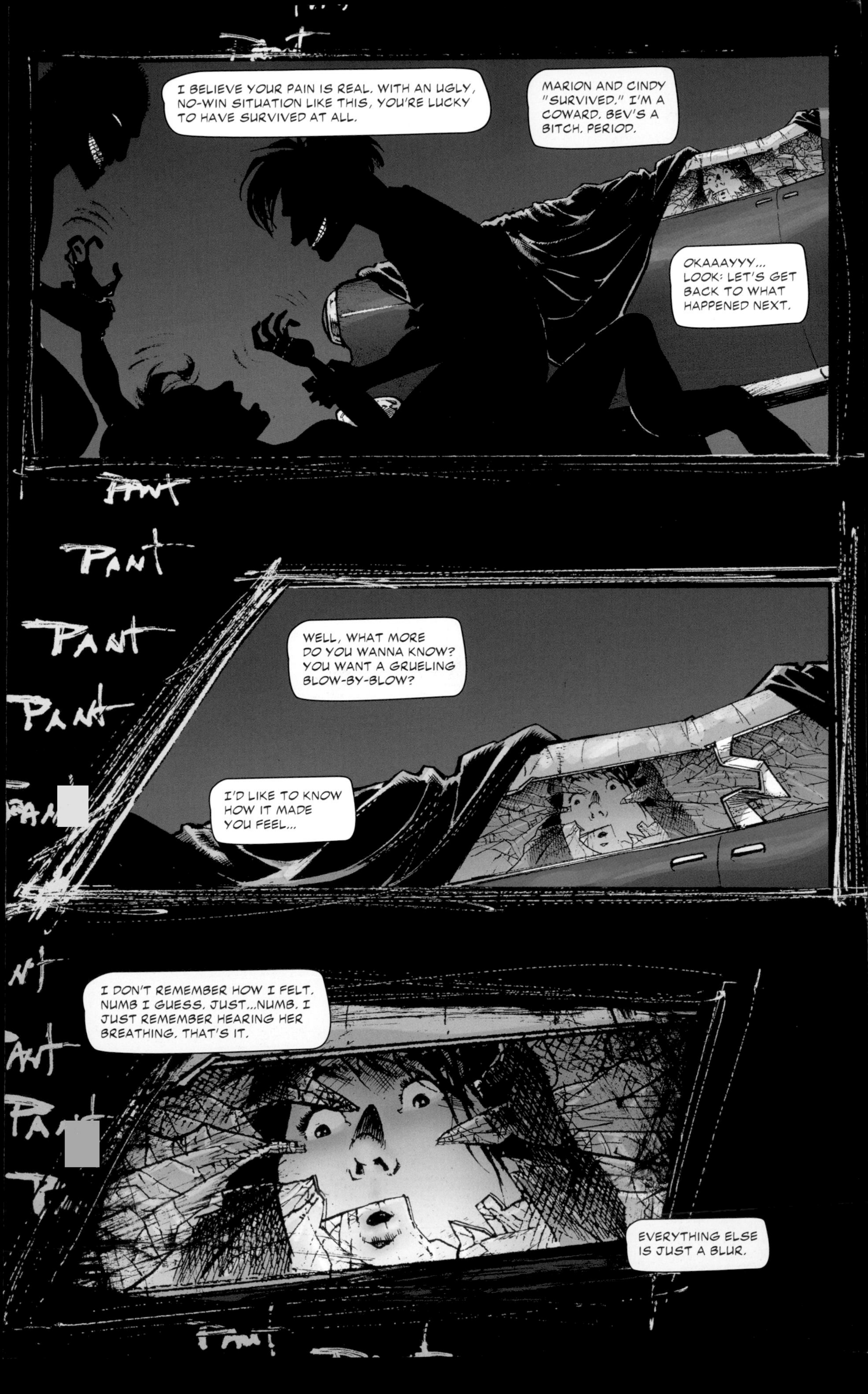
I BELIEVE YOUR PAIN IS REAL. WITH AN UGLY, NO-WIN SITUATION LIKE THIS, YOU'RE LUCKY TO HAVE SURVIVED AT ALL.
MARION AND CINDY "SURVIVED." I'M A COWARD. BEV'S A BITCH. PERIOD.
OKAAAYYY... LOOK: LET'S GET BACK TO WHAT HAPPENED NEXT.
PANT
PANT
PANT
PANT
WELL, WHAT MORE DO YOU WANNA KNOW? YOU WANT A GRUELING BLOW-BY-BLOW?
I'D LIKE TO KNOW HOW IT MADE YOU FEEL...
I DON'T REMEMBER HOW I FELT. NUMB I GUESS. JUST...NUMB. I JUST REMEMBER HEARING HER BREATHING. THAT'S IT.
EVERYTHING ELSE IS JUST A BLUR.

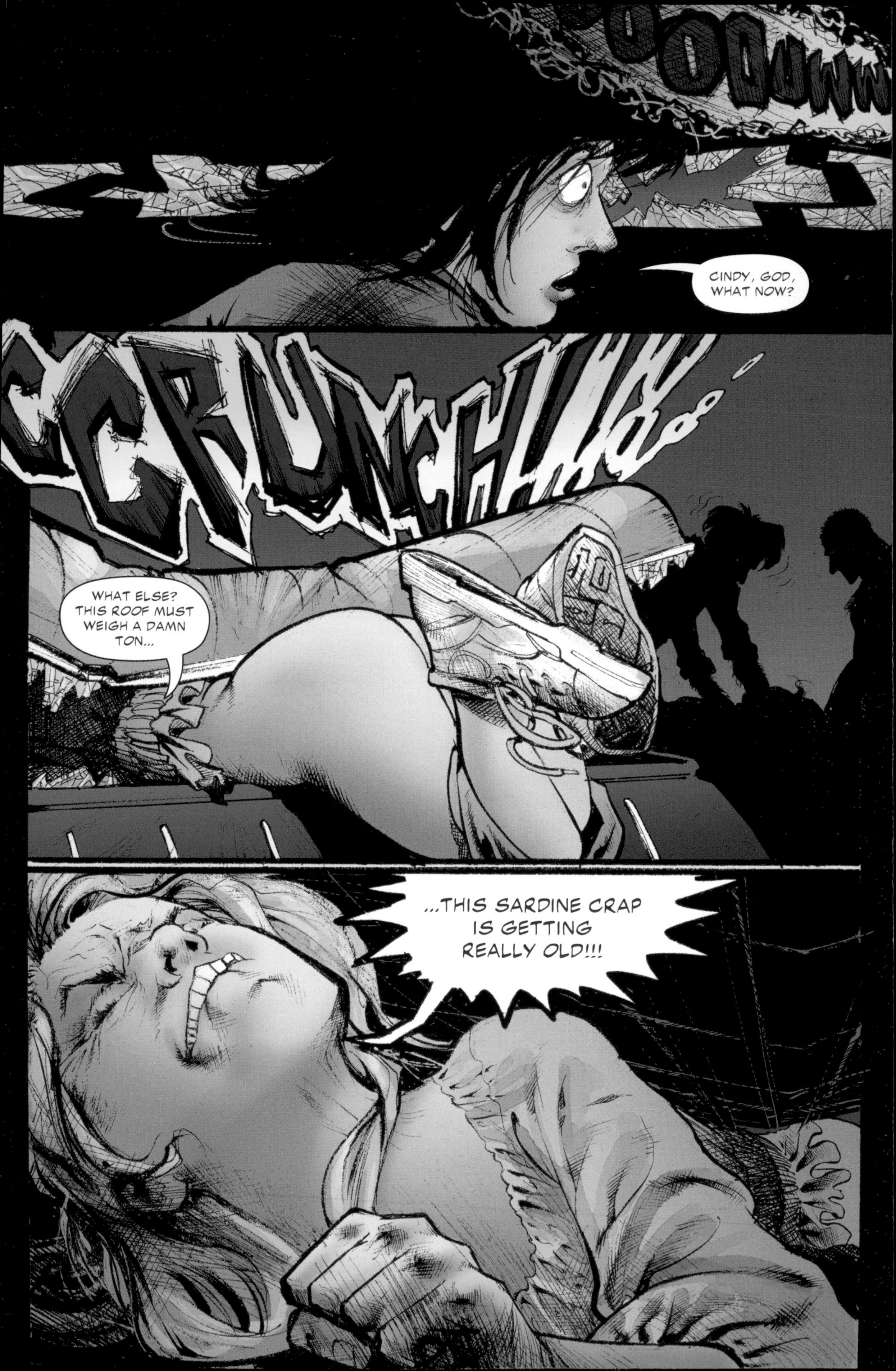
CINDY, GOD, WHAT NOW?
CRUNCH
WHAT ELSE? THIS ROOF MUST WEIGH A DAMN TON...
...THIS SARDINE CRAP IS GETTING REALLY OLD!!!

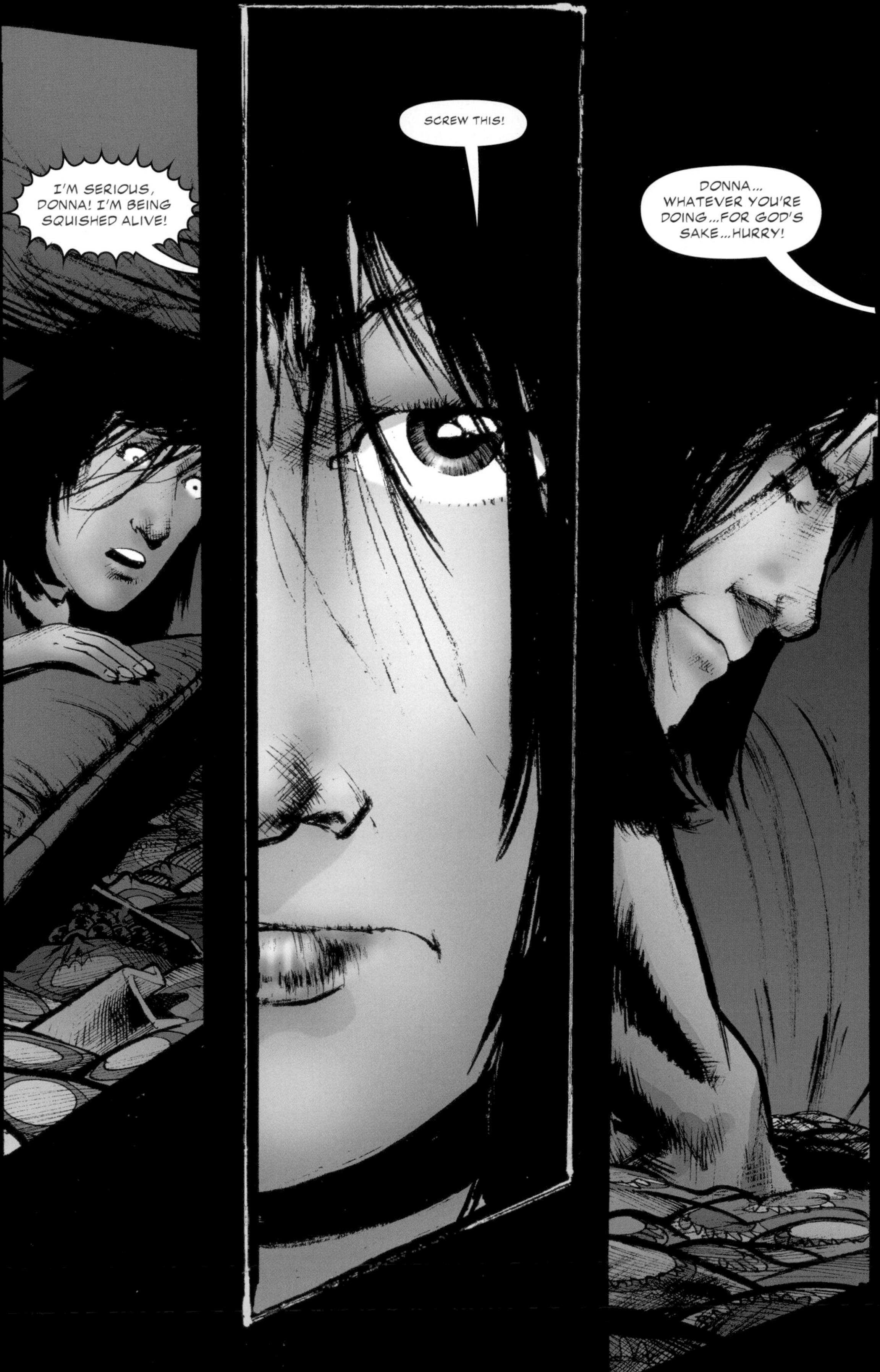
I'M SERIOUS, DONNA! I'M BEING SQUISHED ALIVE!
SCREW THIS!
DONNA... WHATEVER YOU'RE DOING...FOR GOD'S SAKE...HURRY!

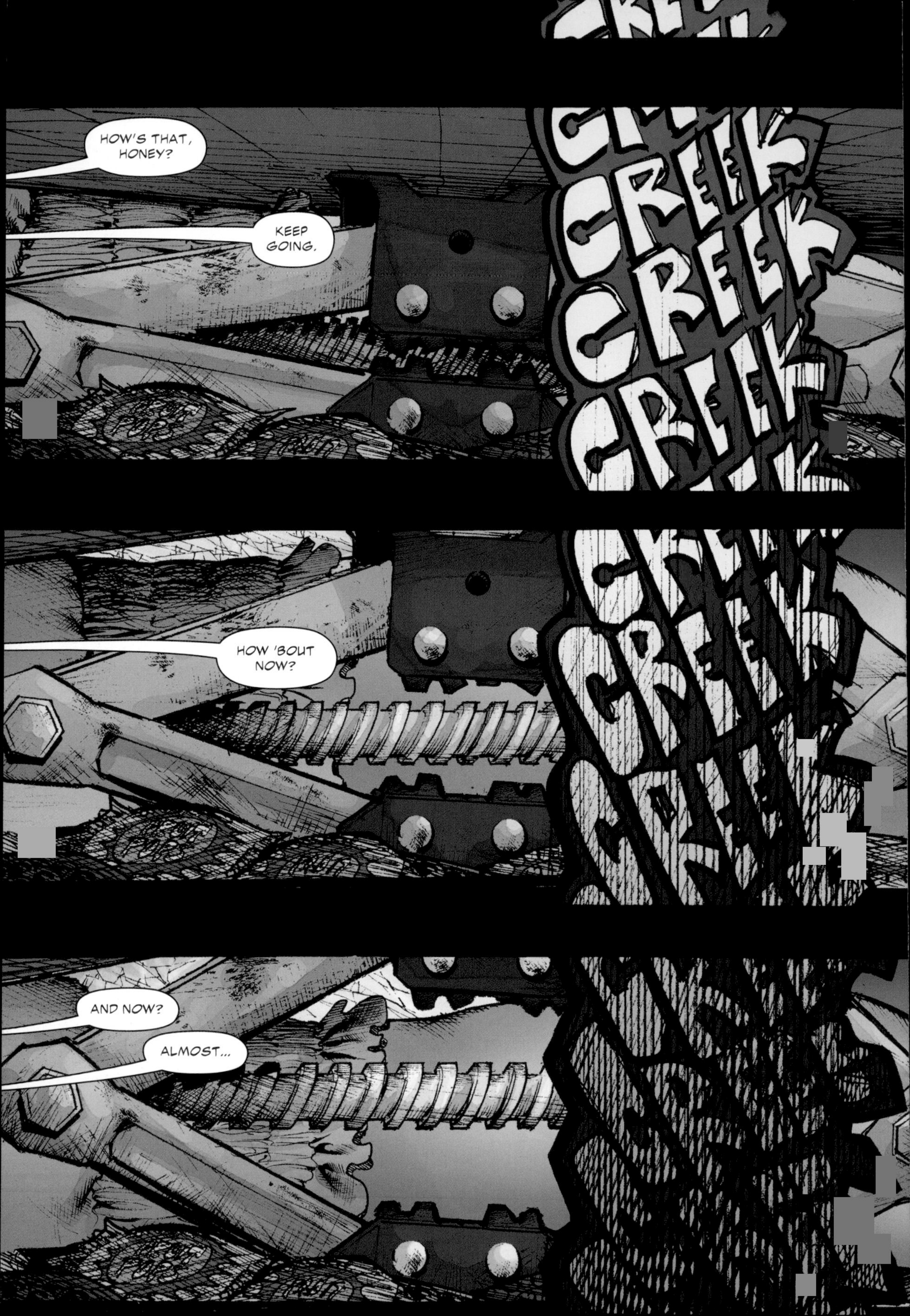
HOW'S THAT, HONEY?
CREEK
CREEK
CREEK
KEEP GOING.
CREEK
HOW 'BOUT NOW?
CREEK
AND NOW?
ALMOST...

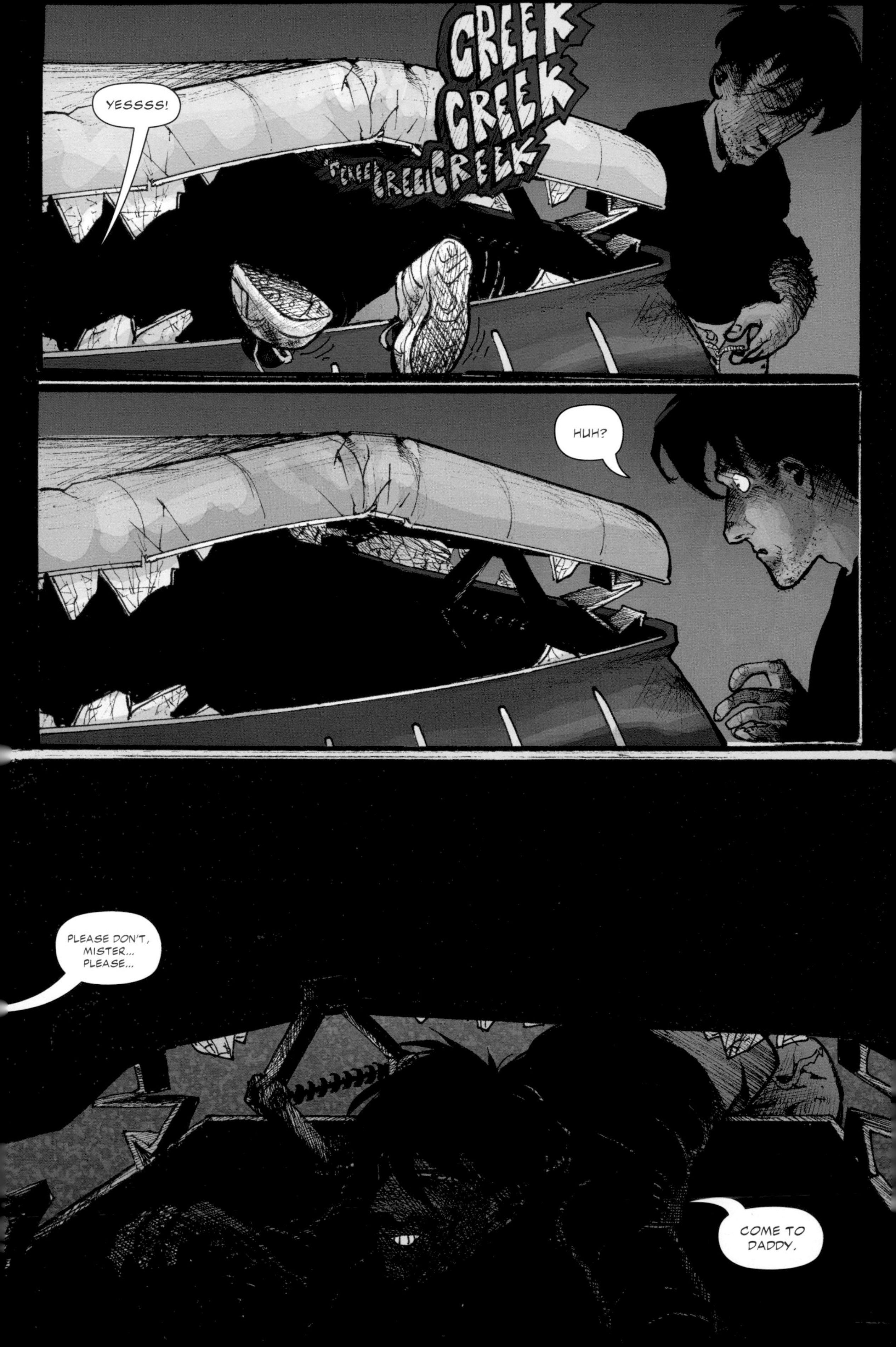
CREEK
CREEK
YESSSS!
CREEK
HUH?
PLEASE DON'T, MISTER... PLEASE...
COME TO DADDY.

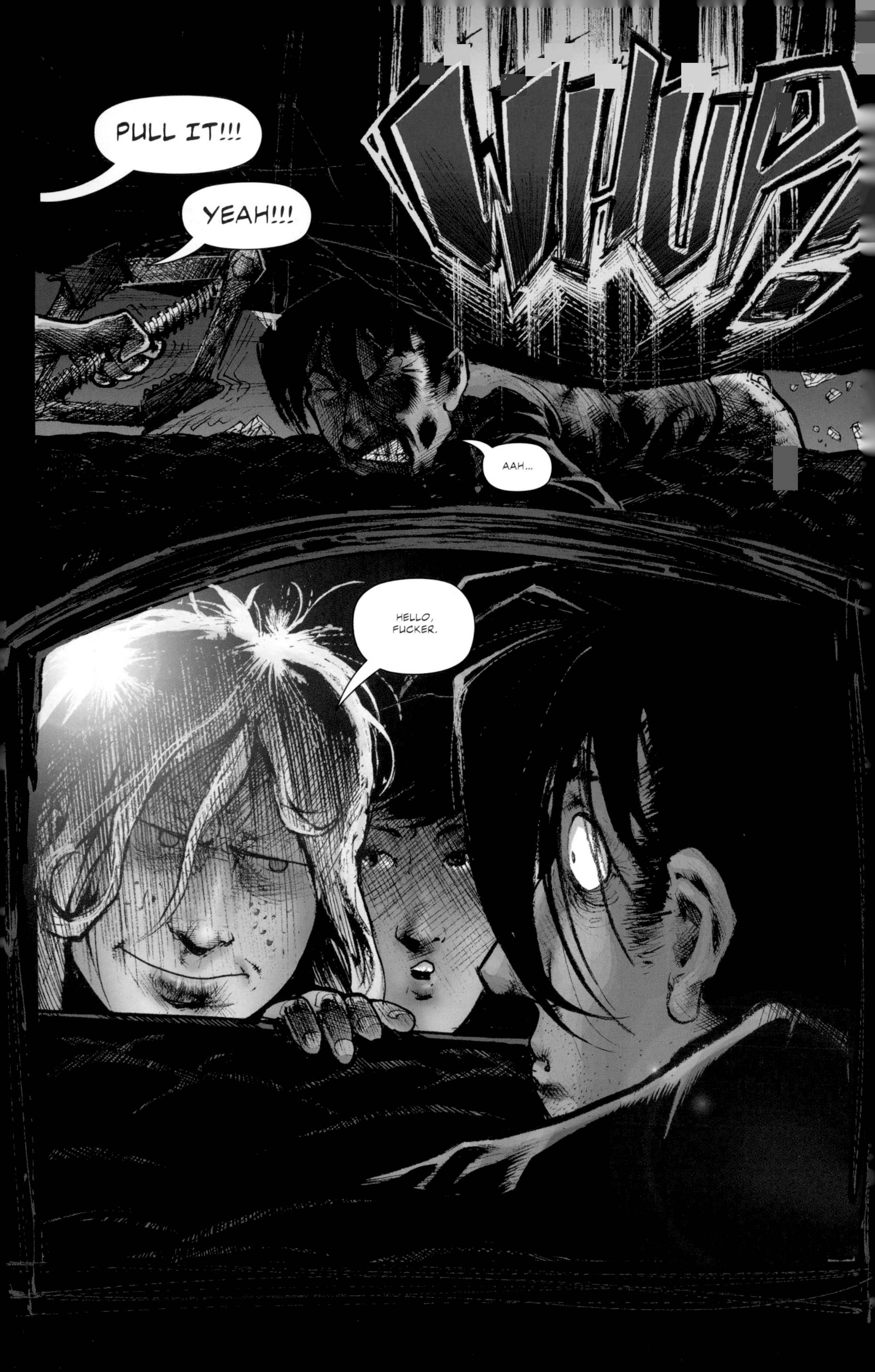
PULL IT!!!
YEAH!!!
WHUP
AAH...
HELLO, FUCKER.

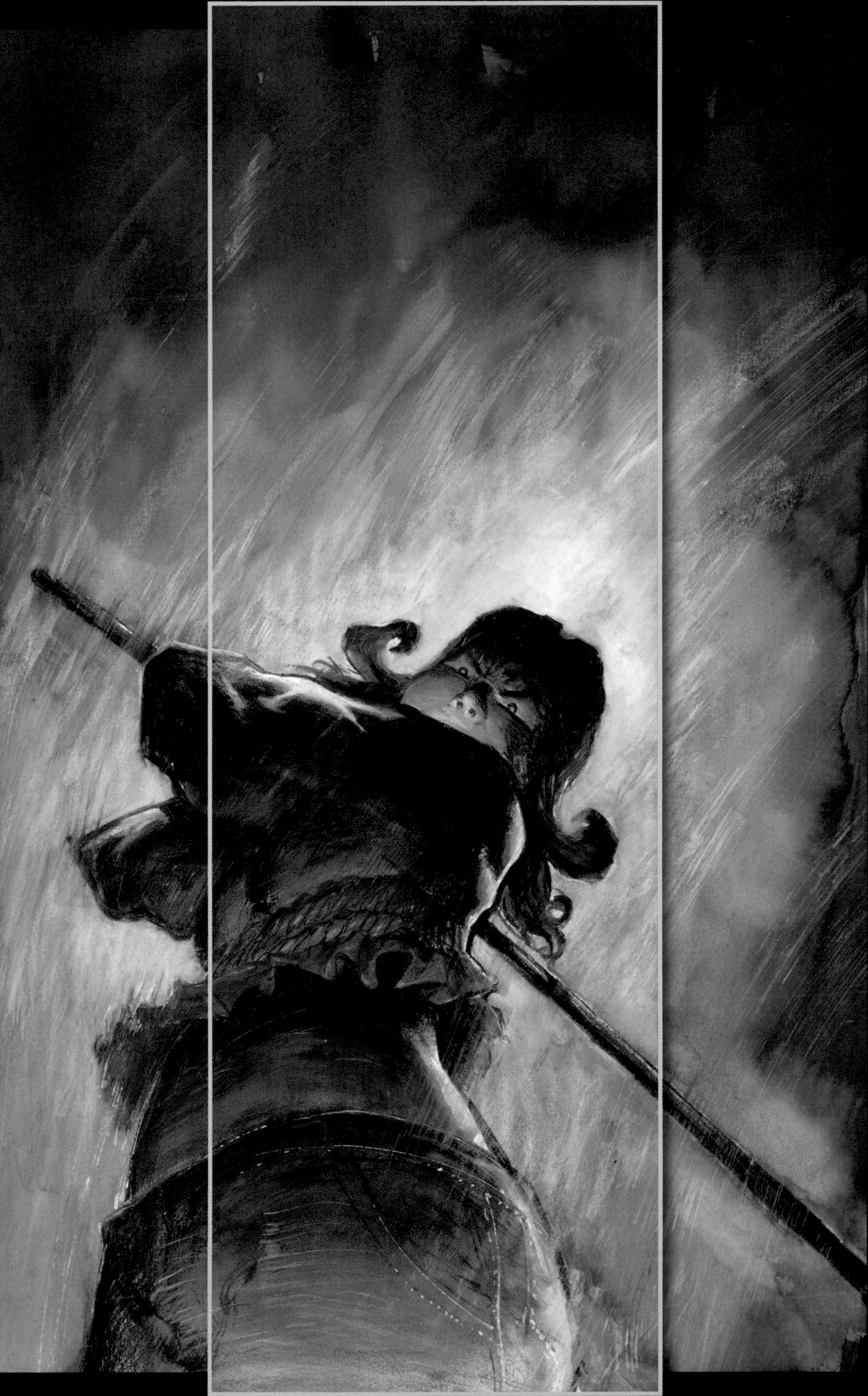

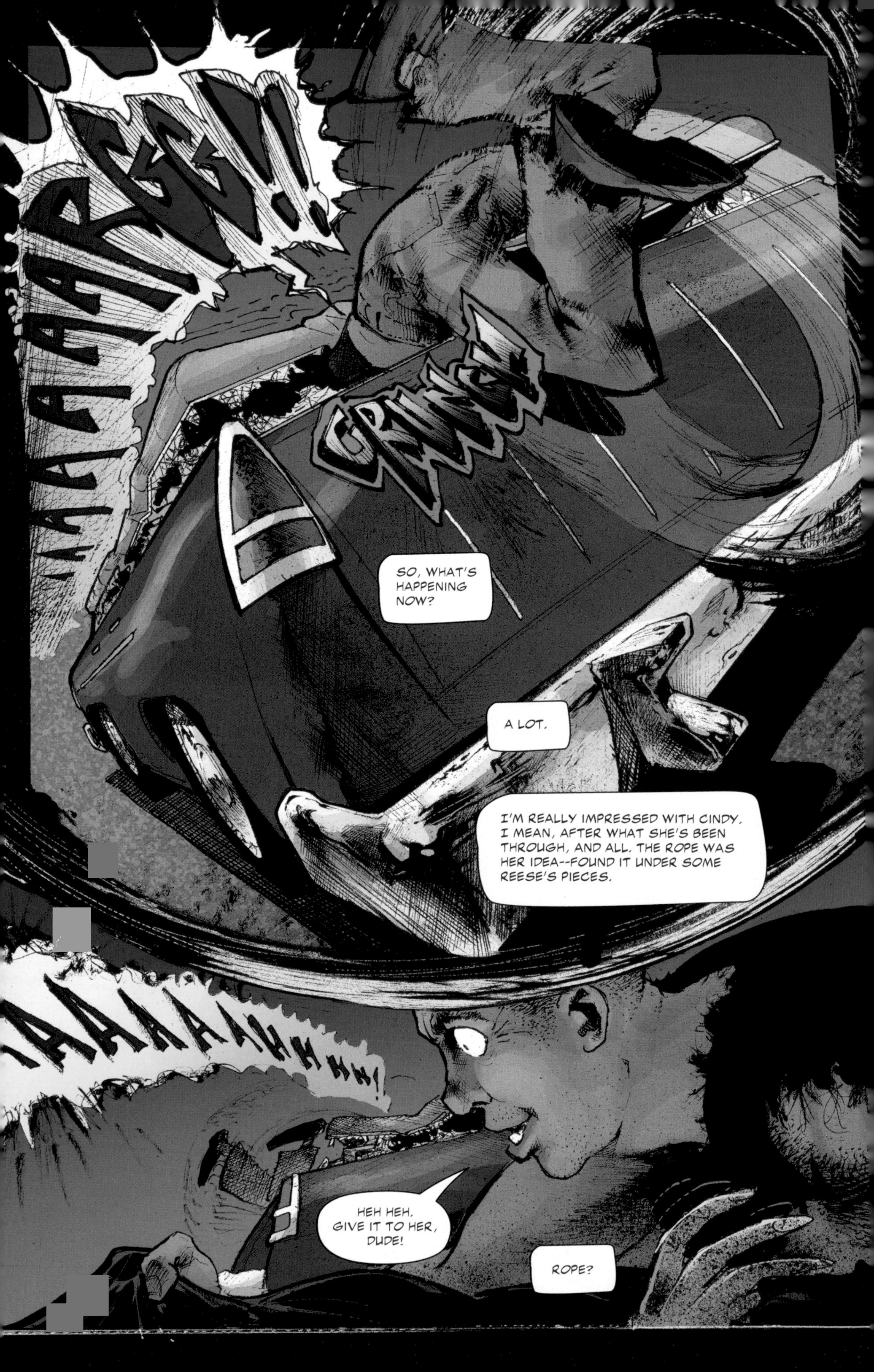
AAAAARGG!!
GRINCH
SO, WHAT'S HAPPENING NOW?
A LOT.
I'M REALLY IMPRESSED WITH CINDY. I MEAN, AFTER WHAT SHE'S BEEN THROUGH, AND ALL. THE ROPE WAS HER IDEA--FOUND IT UNDER SOME REESE'S PIECES.
AAAAAAHHHH!
HEH HEH. GIVE IT TO HER, DUDE!
ROPE?

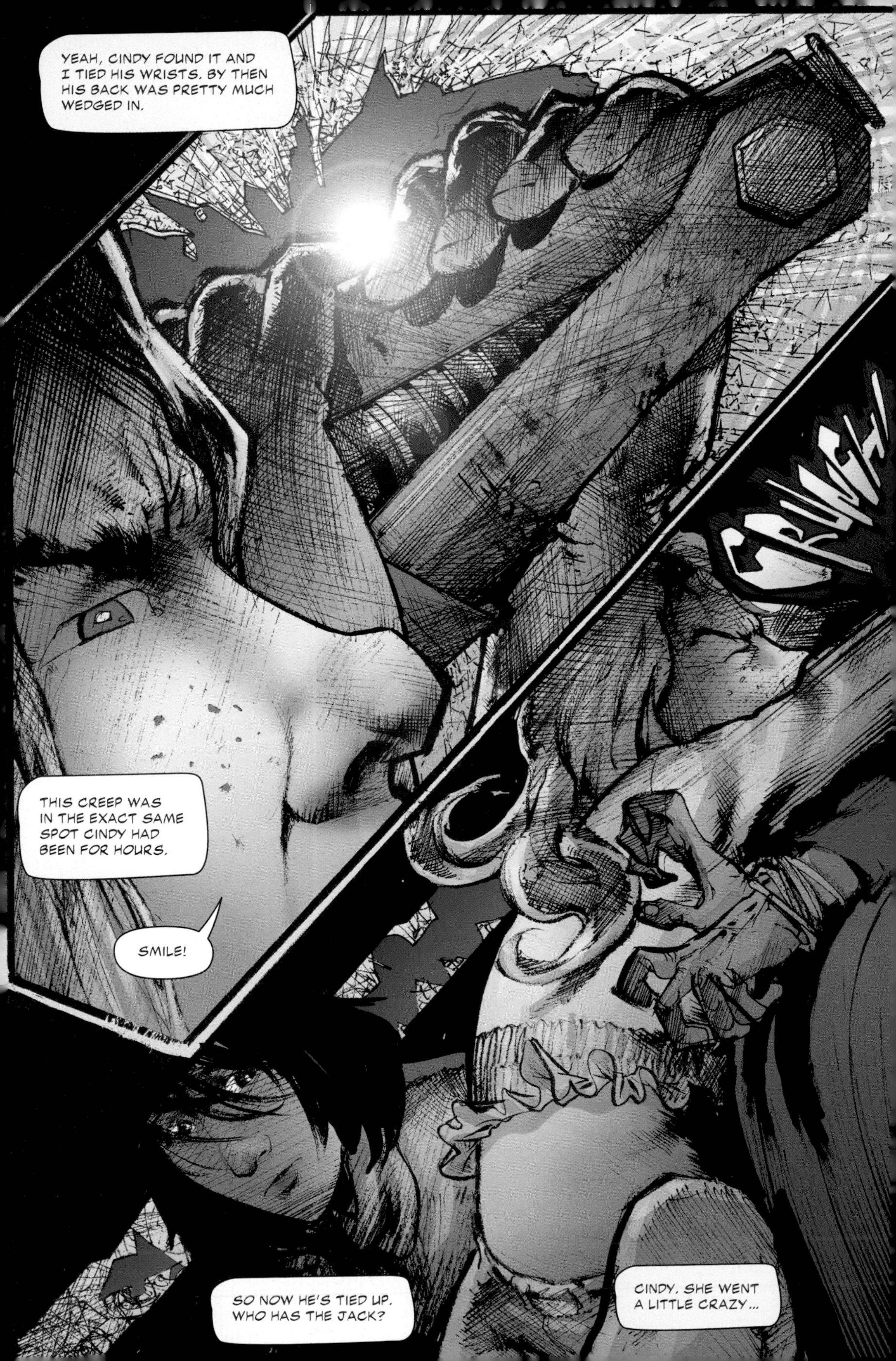
YEAH, CINDY FOUND IT AND I TIED HIS WRISTS. BY THEN HIS BACK WAS PRETTY MUCH WEDGED IN.
CRUNCH!
THIS CREEP WAS IN THE EXACT SAME SPOT CINDY HAD BEEN FOR HOURS.
SMILE!
SO NOW HE'S TIED UP. WHO HAS THE JACK?
CINDY. SHE WENT A LITTLE CRAZY...

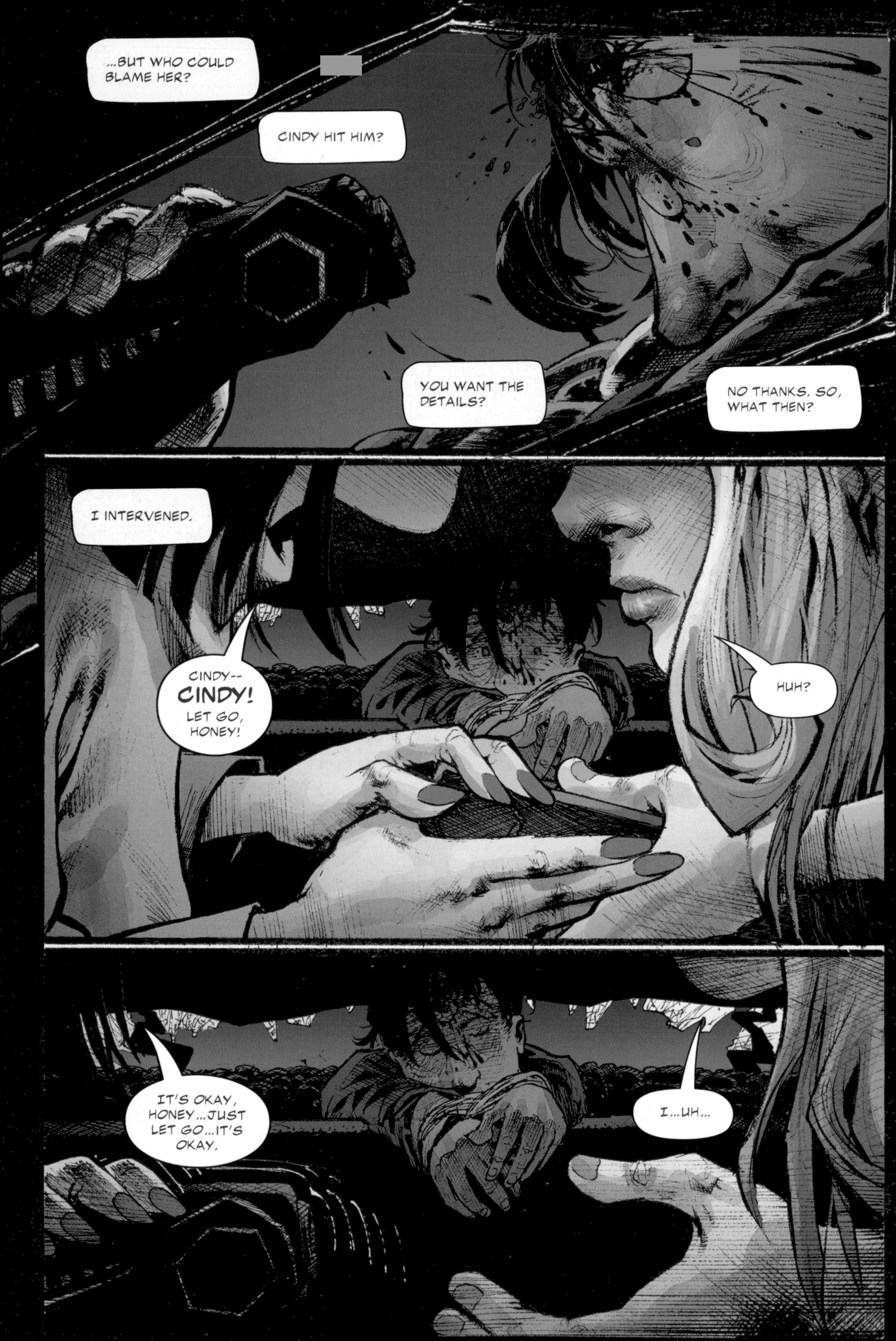
...BUT WHO COULD BLAME HER?
CINDY HIT HIM?
YOU WANT THE DETAILS?
NO THANKS. SO, WHAT THEN?
I INTERVENED.
CINDY-- CINDY! LET GO, HONEY!
HUH?
IT'S OKAY, HONEY...JUST LET GO...IT'S OKAY.
I...UH...

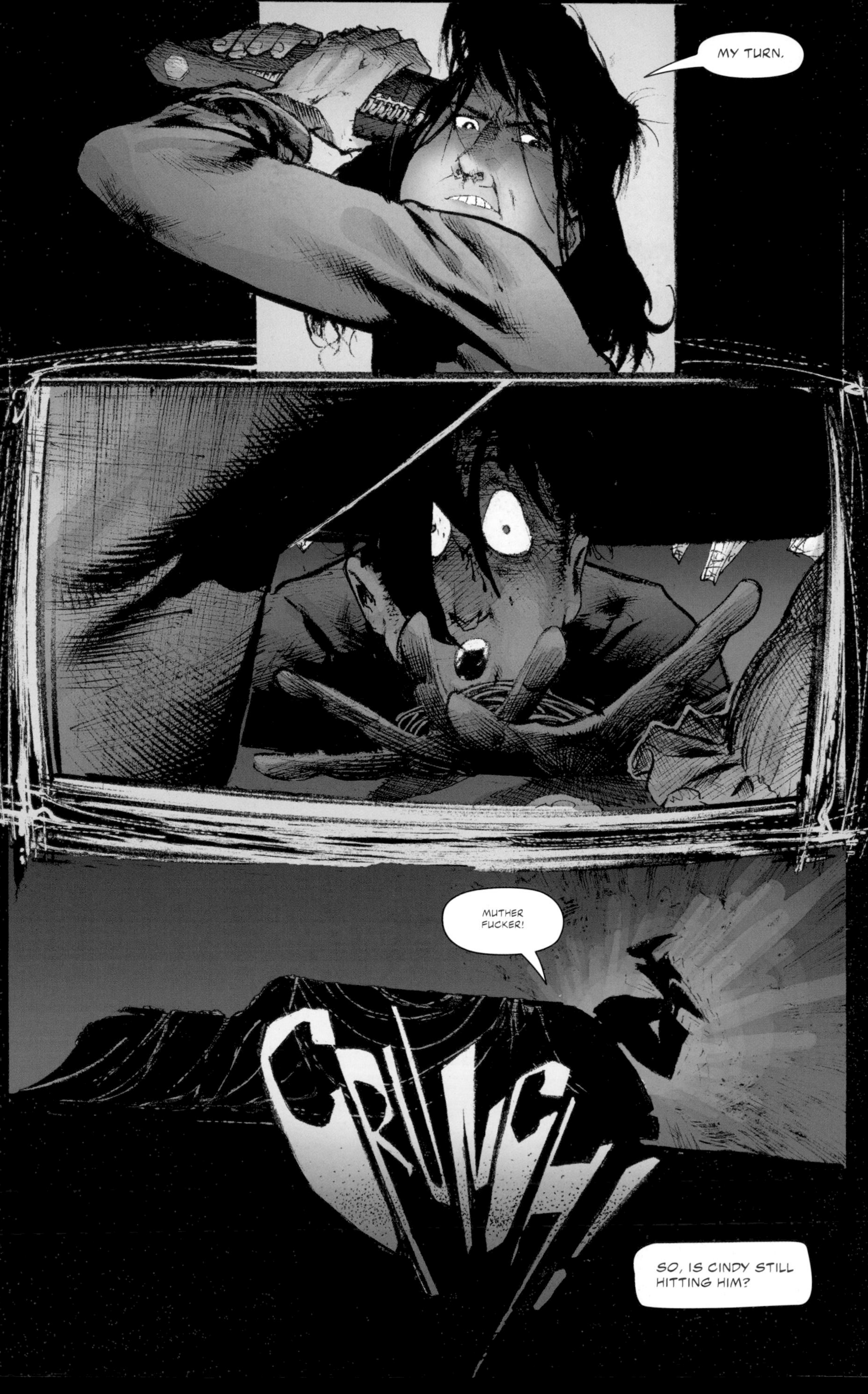
MY TURN.
MUTHER FUCKER!
SO, IS CINDY STILL HITTING HIM?

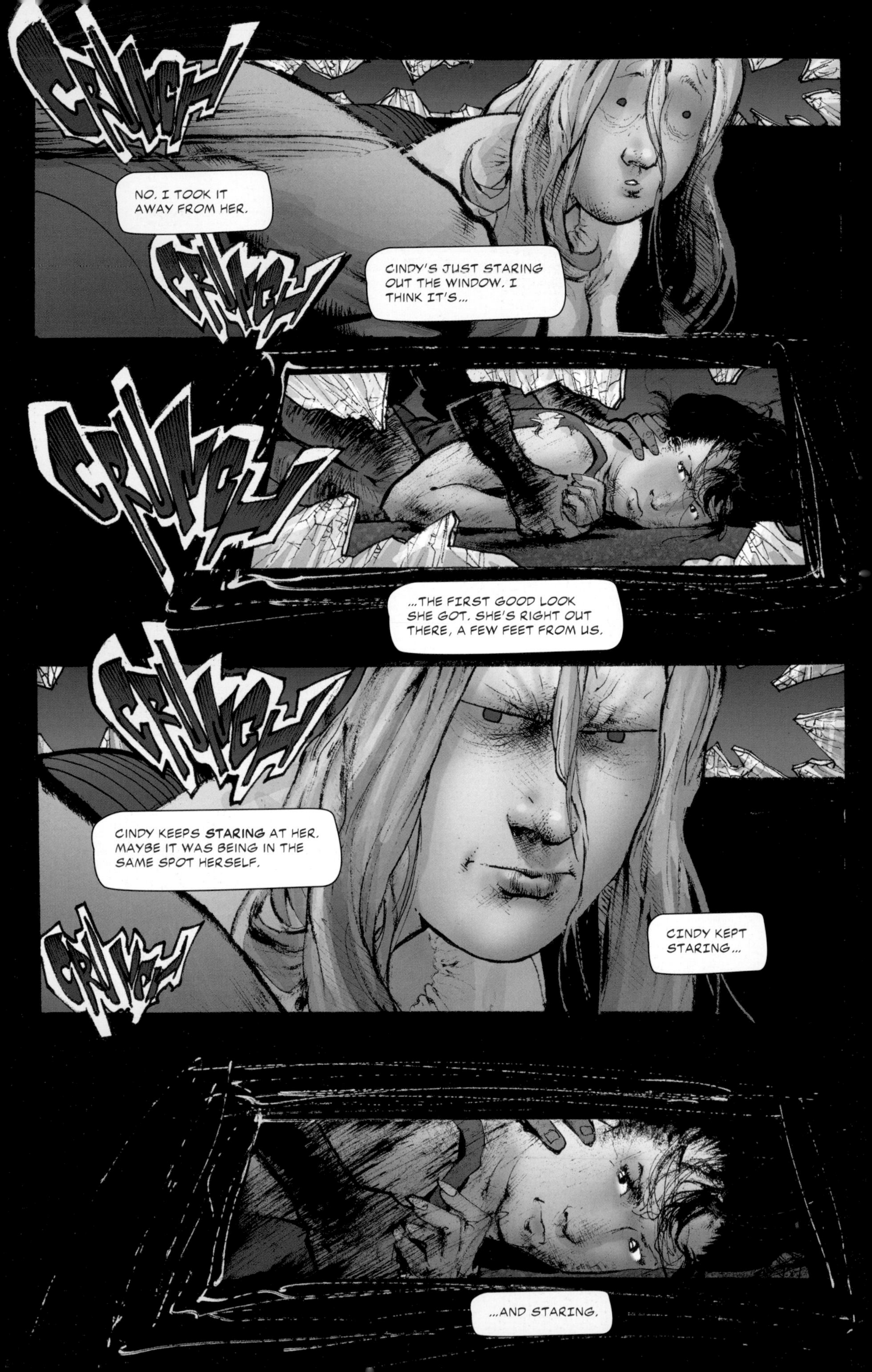
CRUNCH
NO. I TOOK IT AWAY FROM HER.
CRUNCH
CINDY'S JUST STARING OUT THE WINDOW. I THINK IT'S...
CRUNCH
...THE FIRST GOOD LOOK SHE GOT. SHE'S RIGHT OUT THERE, A FEW FEET FROM US.
CRUNCH
CINDY KEEPS STARING AT HER. MAYBE IT WAS BEING IN THE SAME SPOT HERSELF.
CRUNCH
CINDY KEPT STARING...
...AND STARING.

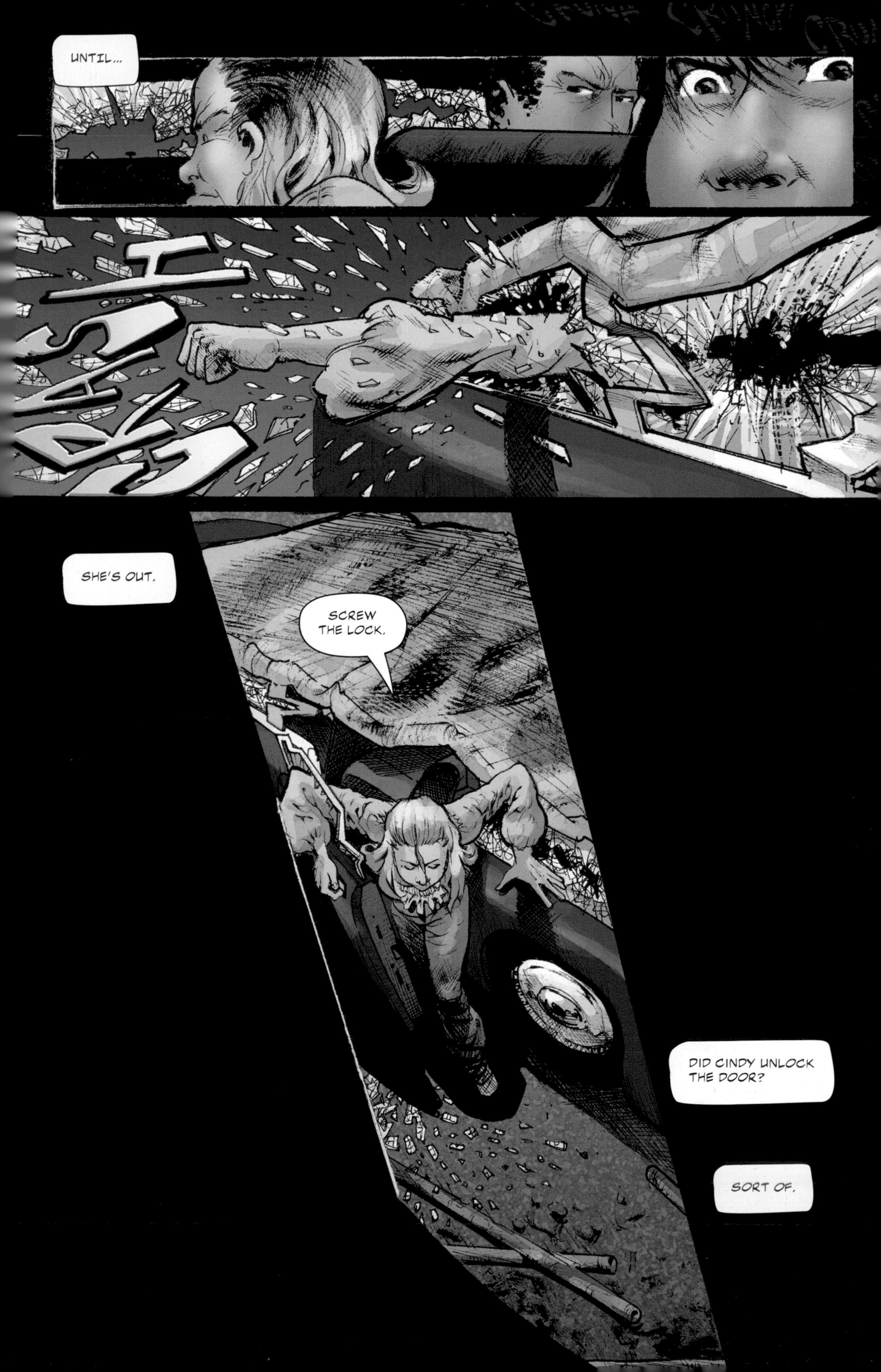
UNTIL...
CRASH
SHE'S OUT.
SCREW THE LOCK.
DID CINDY UNLOCK THE DOOR?
SORT OF.

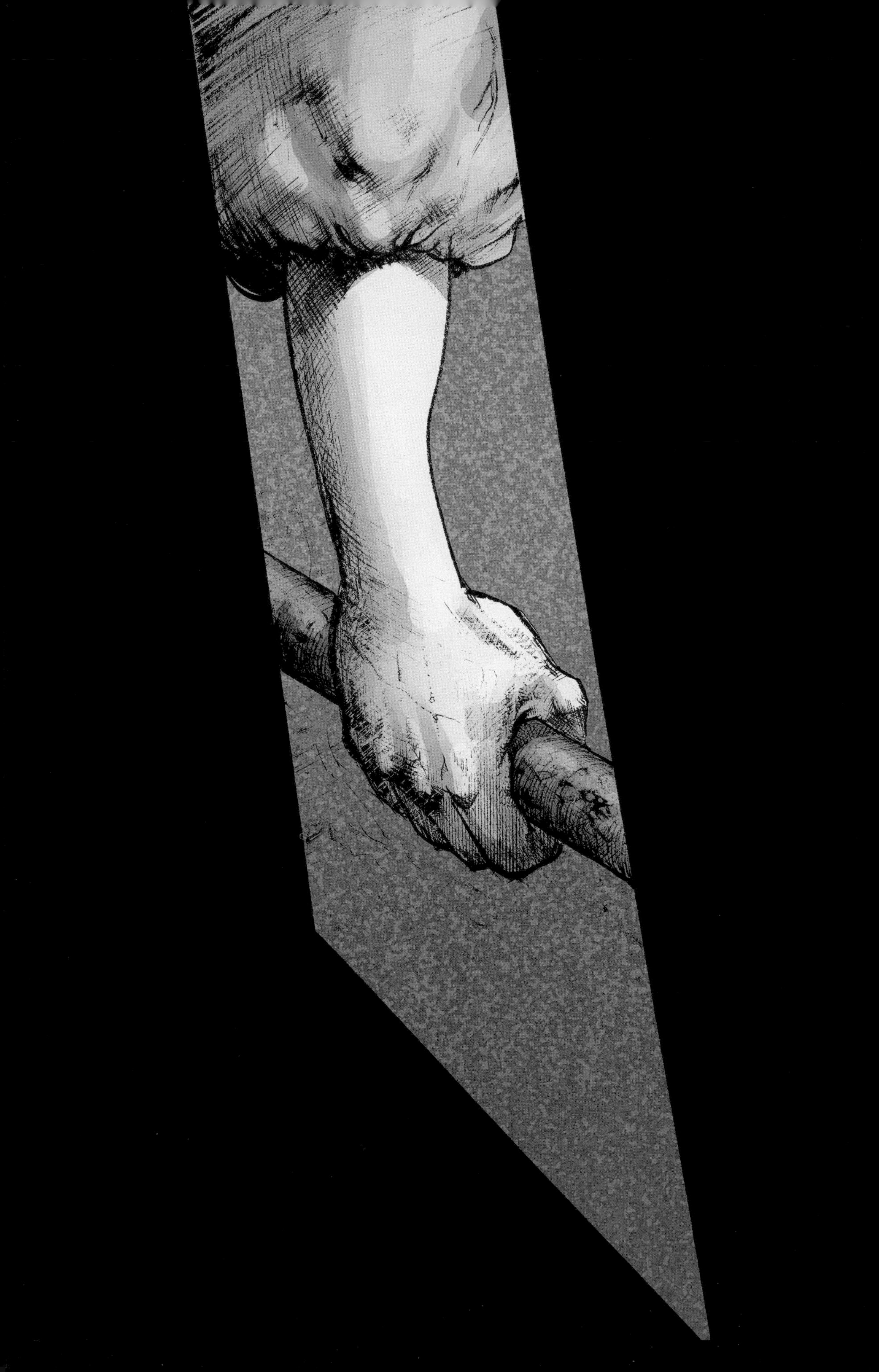

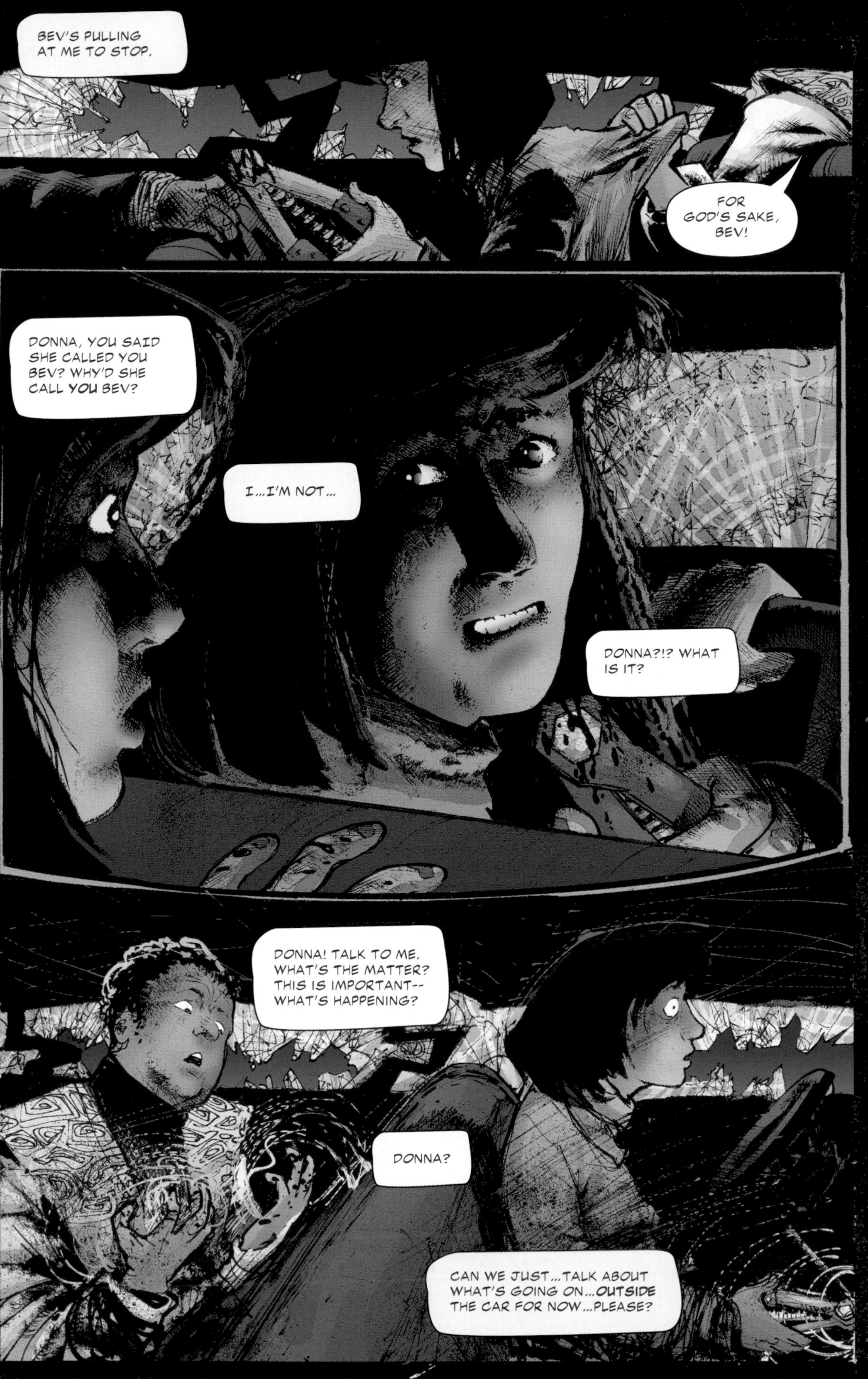
BEV'S PULLING AT ME TO STOP.
FOR GOD'S SAKE, BEV!
DONNA, YOU SAID SHE CALLED YOU BEV? WHY'D SHE CALL YOU BEV?
I...I'M NOT...
DONNA?!? WHAT IS IT?
DONNA! TALK TO ME. WHAT'S THE MATTER? THIS IS IMPORTANT-- WHAT'S HAPPENING?
DONNA?
CAN WE JUST...TALK ABOUT WHAT'S GOING ON...OUTSIDE THE CAR FOR NOW...PLEASE?

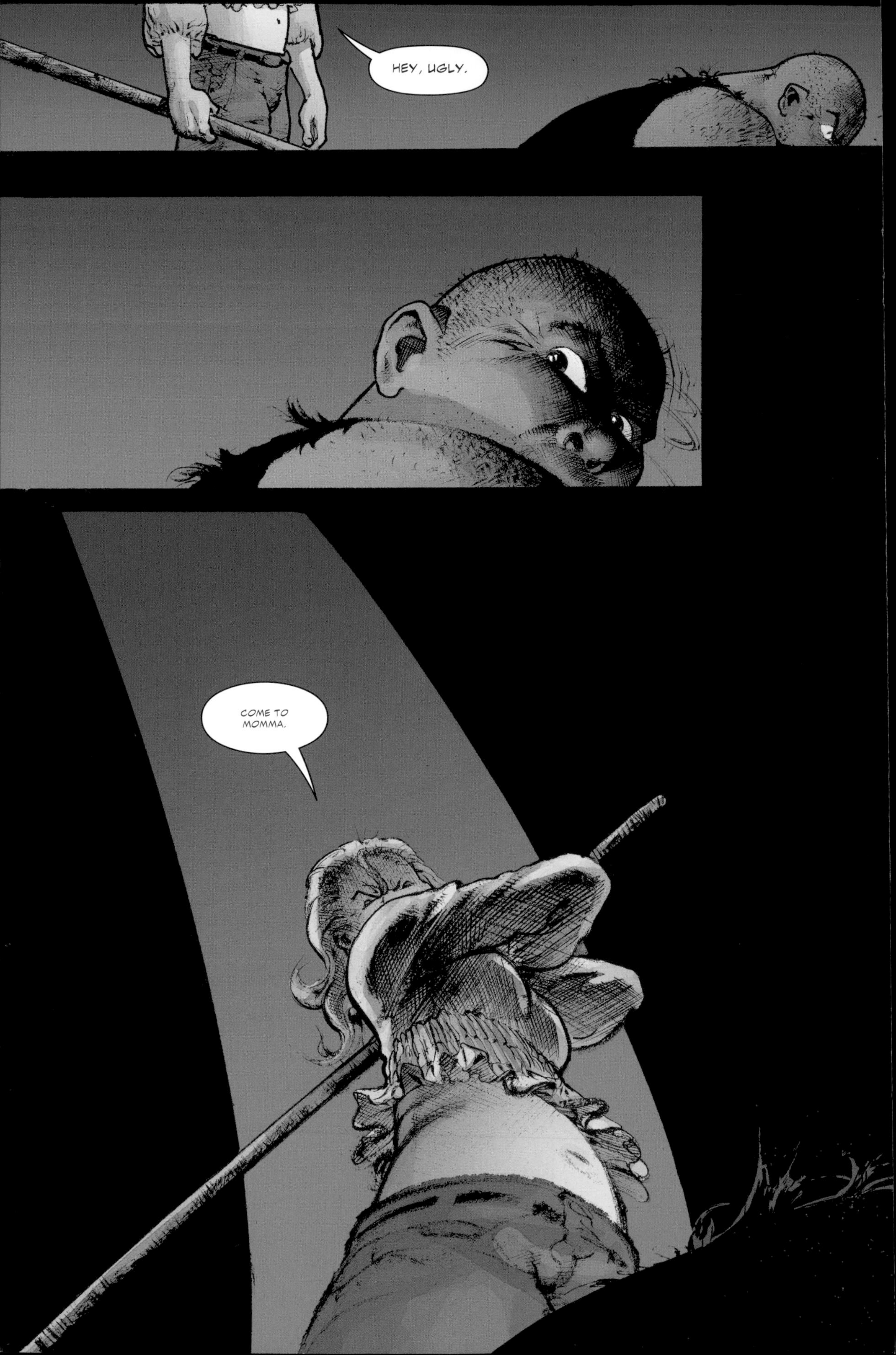
HEY, UGLY.
COME TO MOMMA.

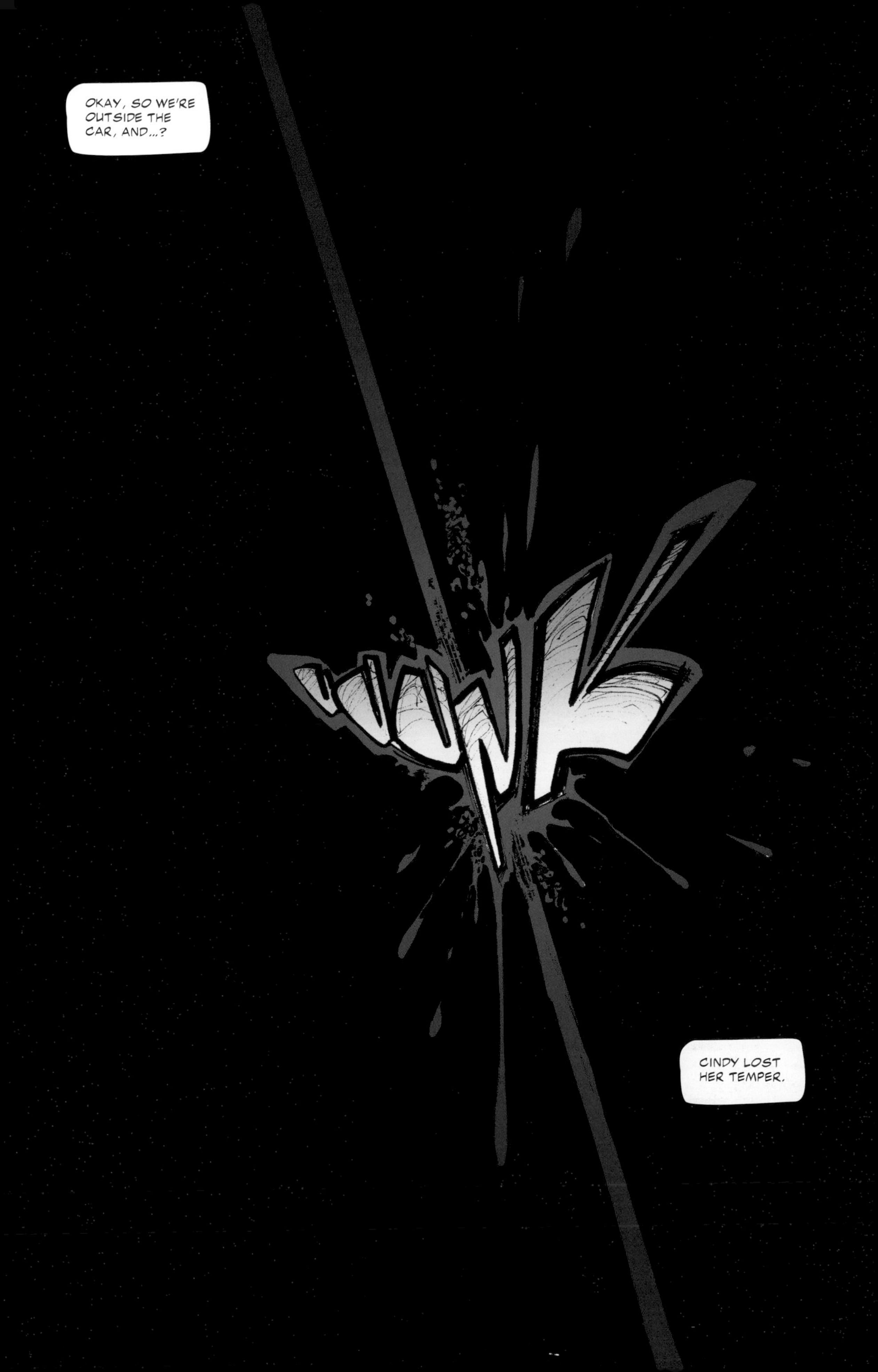
OKAY, SO WE'RE OUTSIDE THE CAR, AND...?
CINDY LOST HER TEMPER.

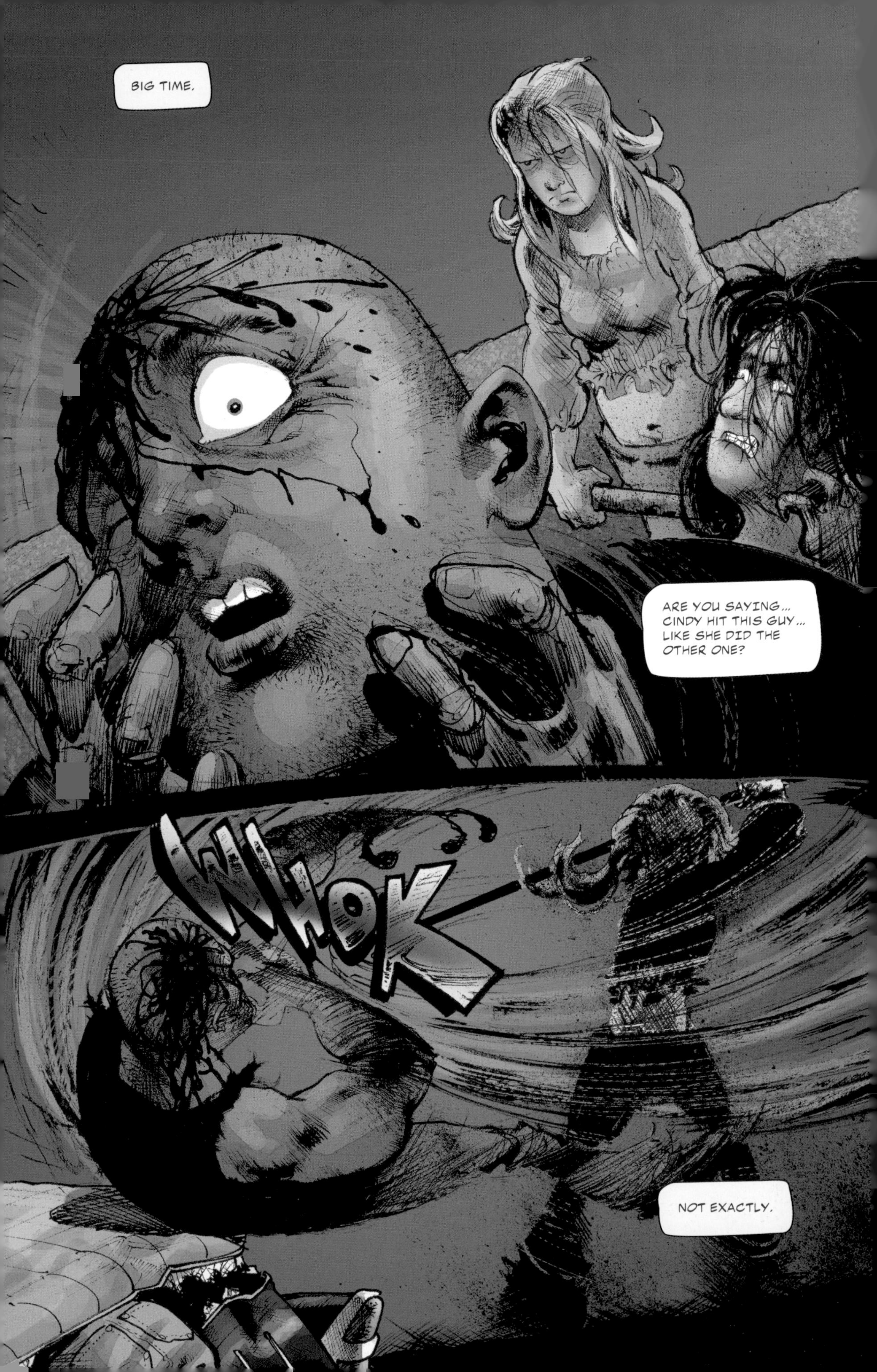
BIG TIME.
ARE YOU SAYING... CINDY HIT THIS GUY... LIKE SHE DID THE OTHER ONE?
WHOK
NOT EXACTLY.

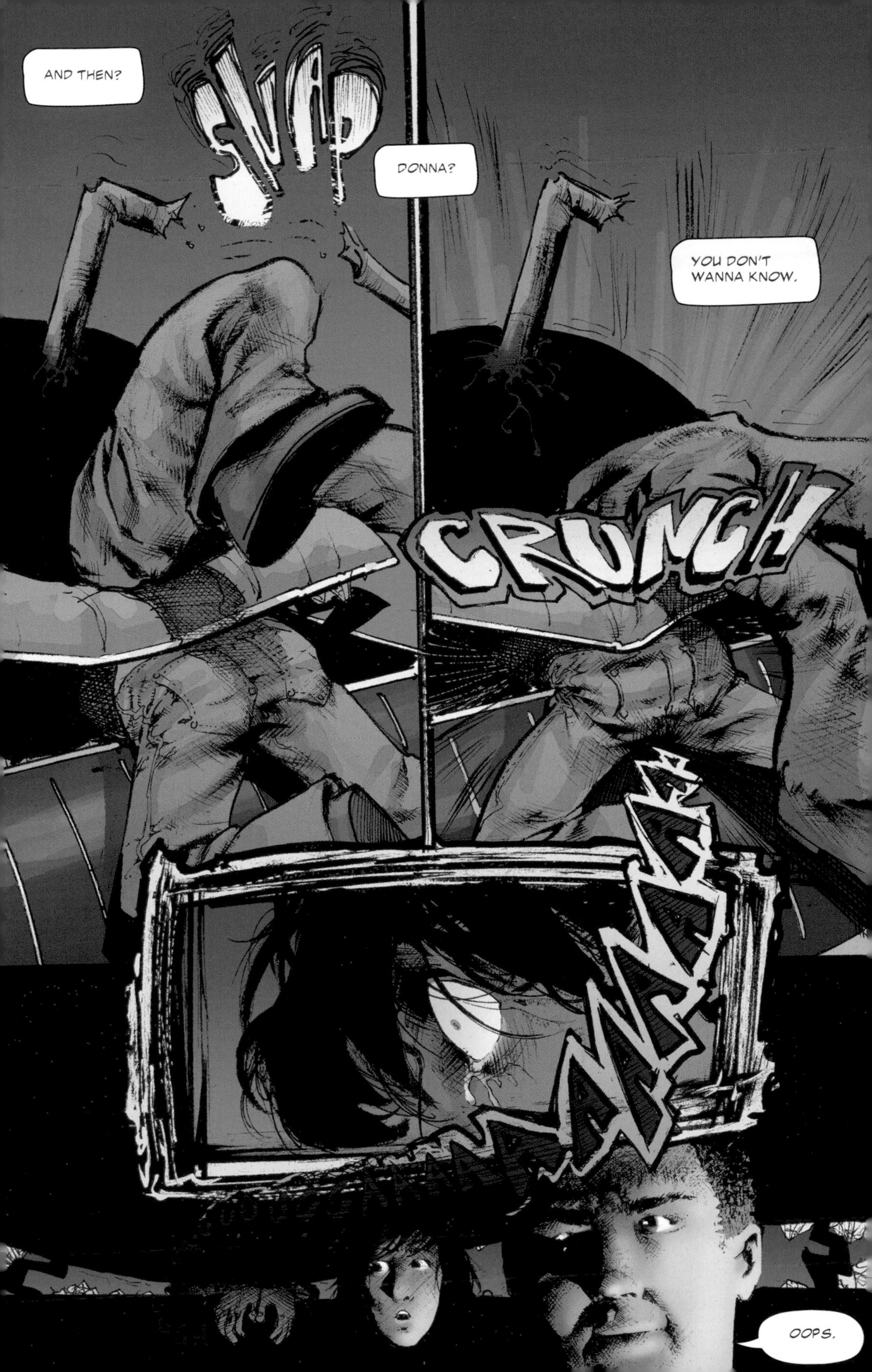
AND THEN?
SNAP
DONNA?
YOU DON'T WANNA KNOW.
CRUNCH
OOPS.

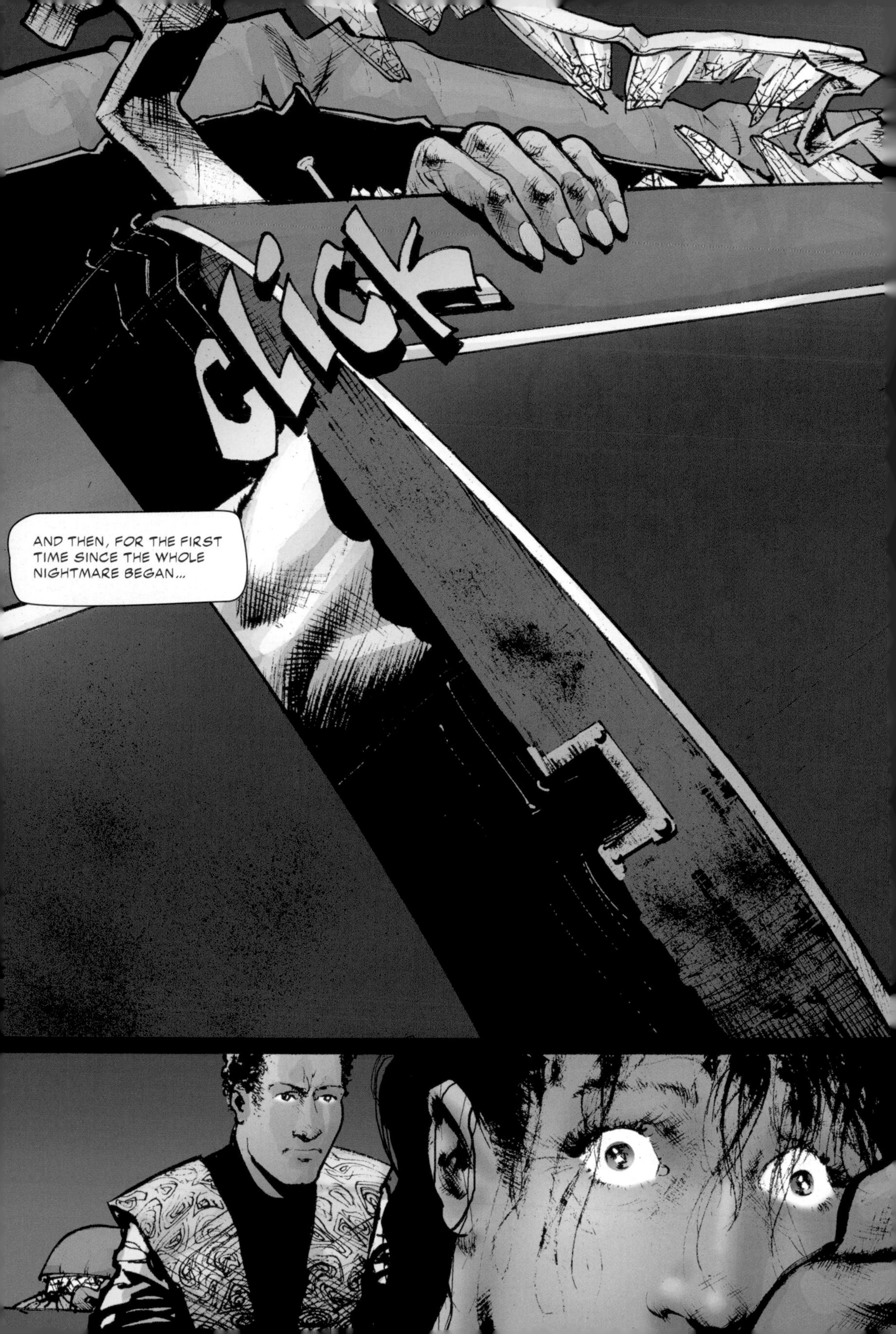
CLICK
AND THEN, FOR THE FIRST TIME SINCE THE WHOLE NIGHTMARE BEGAN...

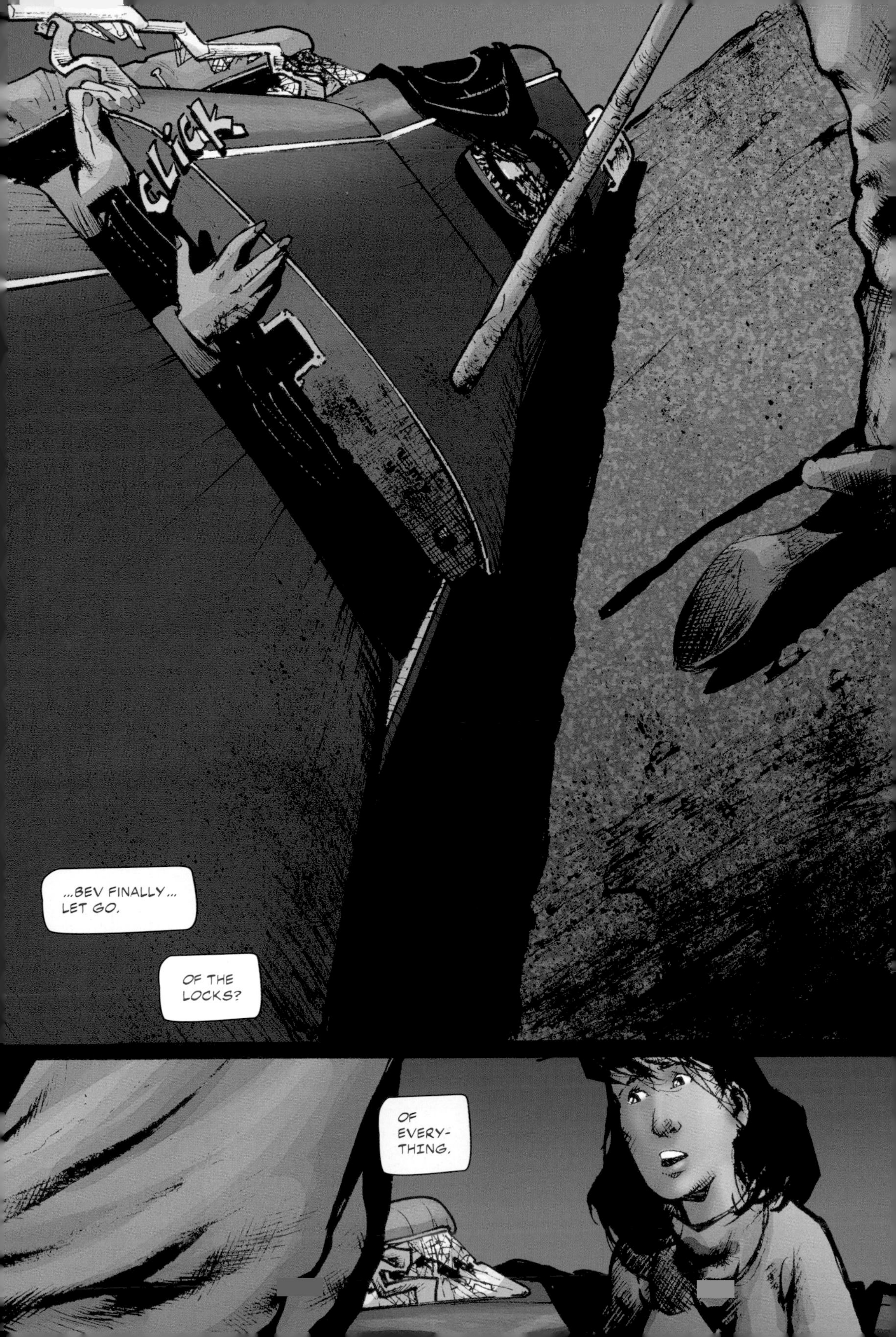
CLICK
...BEV FINALLY... LET GO.
OF THE LOCKS?
OF EVERY-THING.

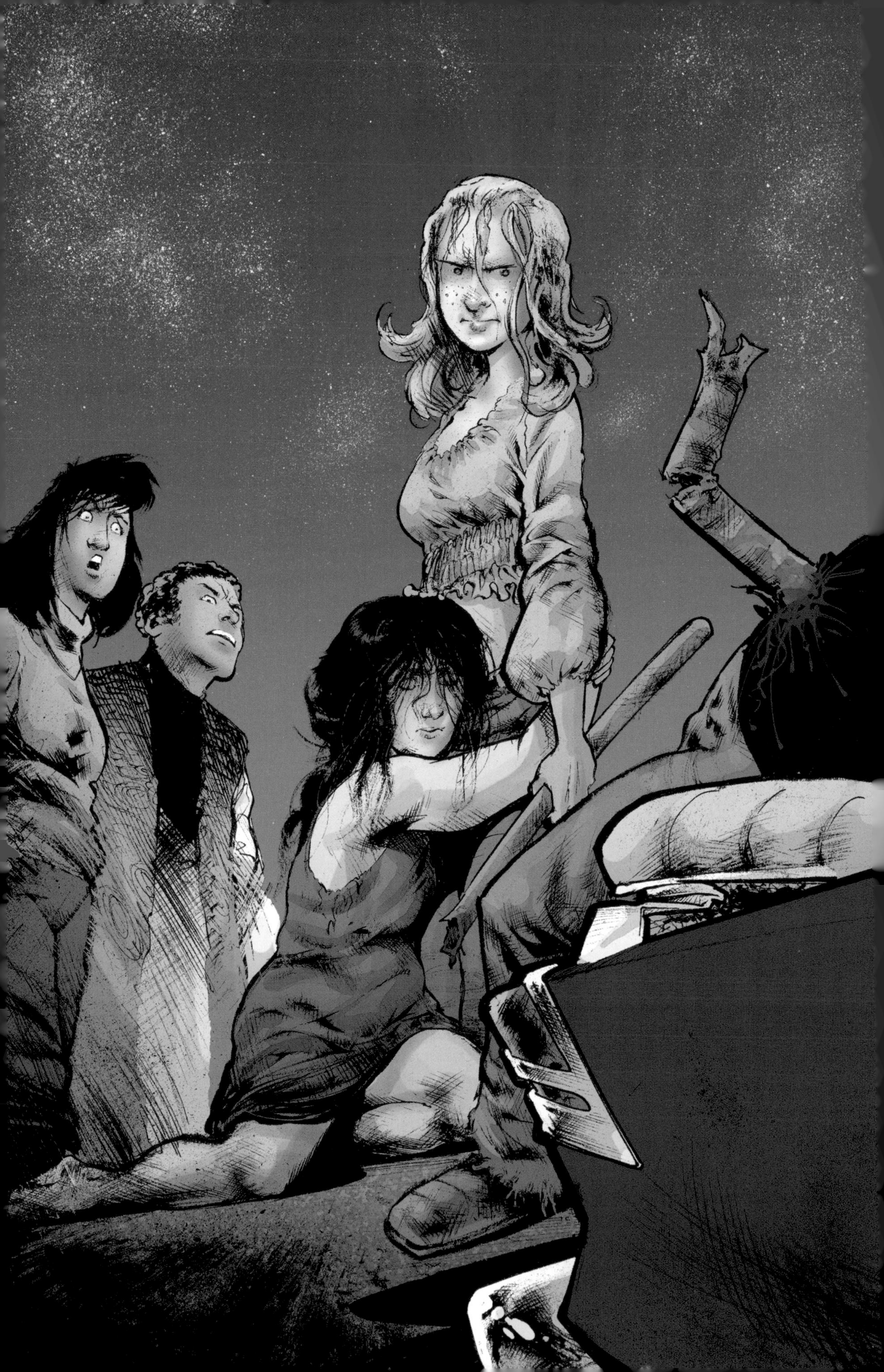

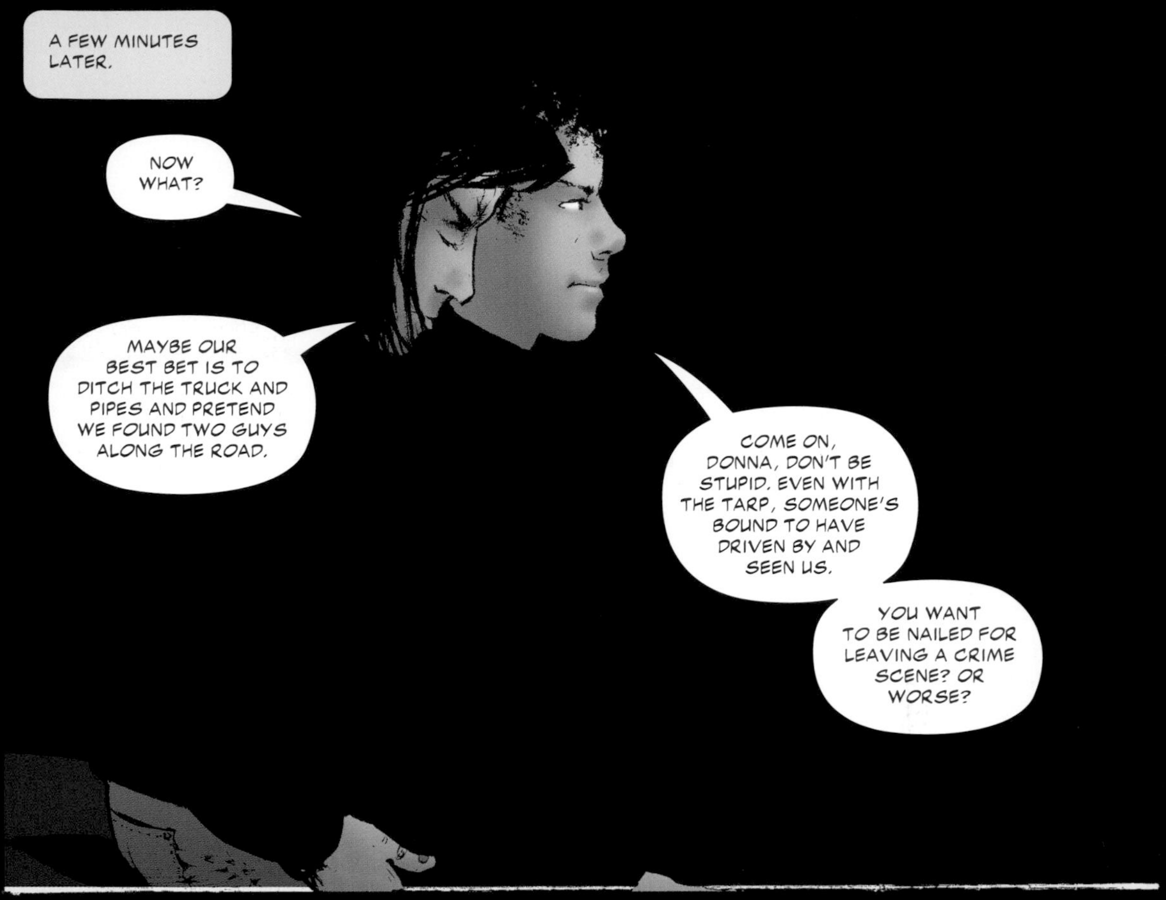
A FEW MINUTES LATER.
NOW WHAT?
MAYBE OUR BEST BET IS TO DITCH THE TRUCK AND PIPES AND PRETEND WE FOUND TWO GUYS ALONG THE ROAD.
COME ON, DONNA, DON'T BE STUPID. EVEN WITH THE TARP, SOMEONE'S BOUND TO HAVE DRIVEN BY AND SEEN US.
YOU WANT TO BE NAILED FOR LEAVING A CRIME SCENE? OR WORSE?

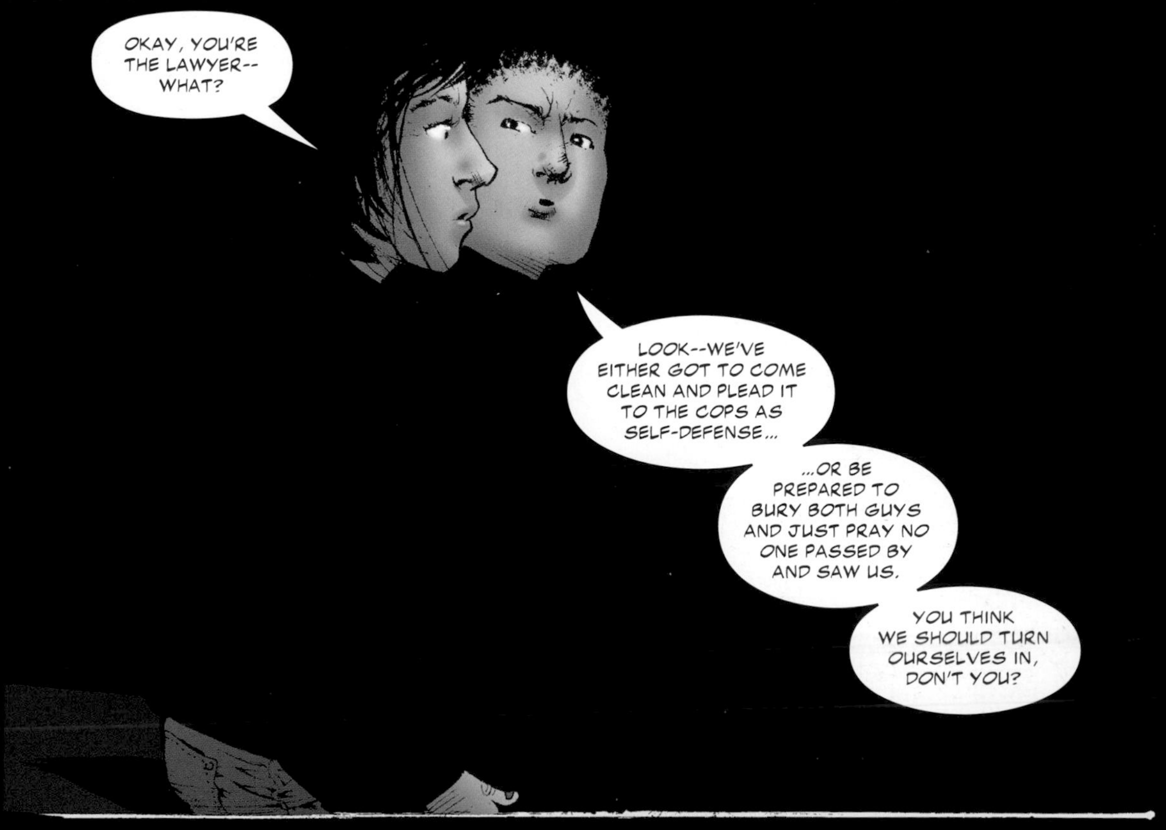
OKAY, YOU'RE THE LAWYER-- WHAT?
LOOK--WE'VE EITHER GOT TO COME CLEAN AND PLEAD IT TO THE COPS AS SELF-DEFENSE...
...OR BE PREPARED TO BURY BOTH GUYS AND JUST PRAY NO ONE PASSED BY AND SAW US.
YOU THINK WE SHOULD TURN OURSELVES IN, DON'T YOU?

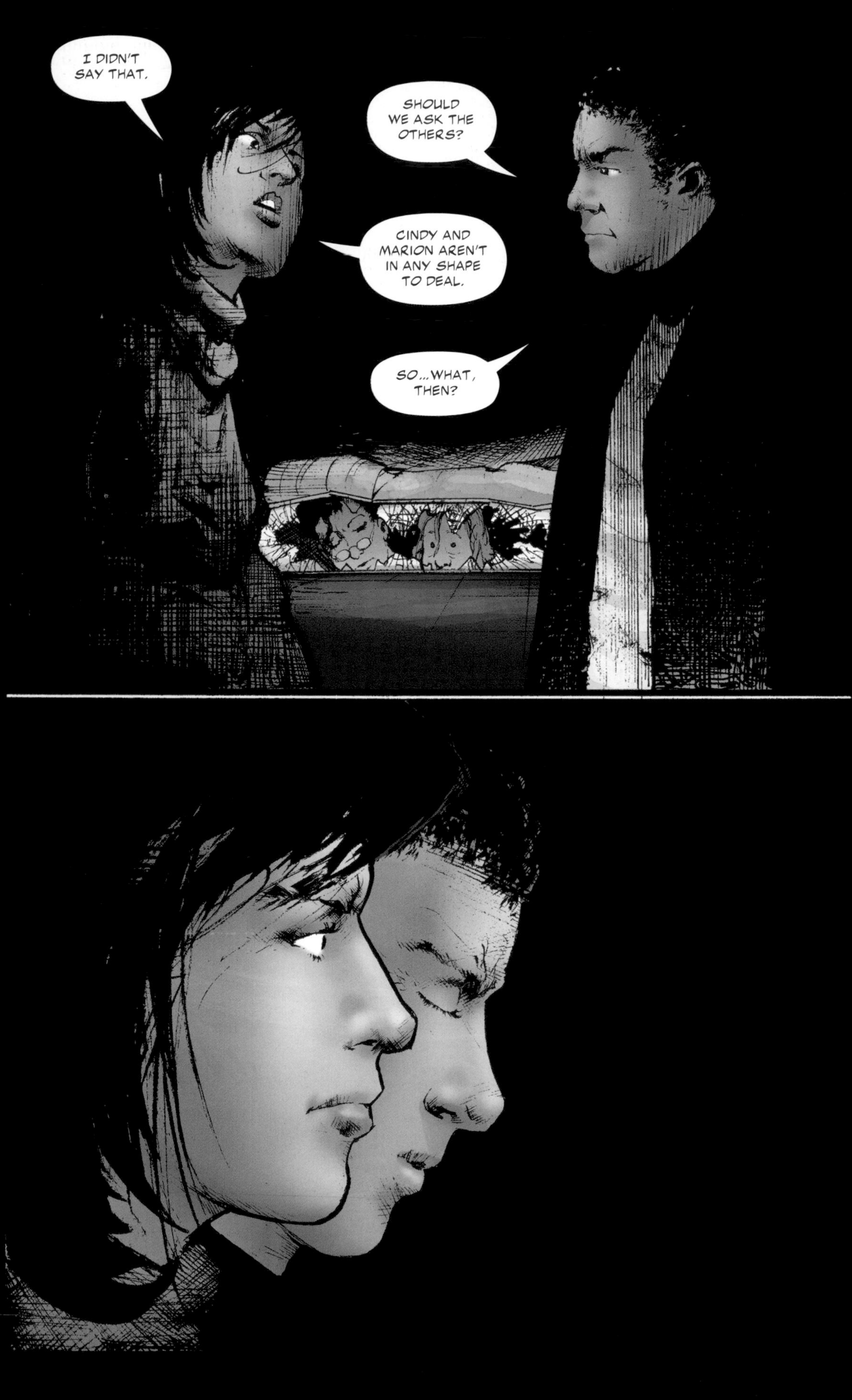
I DIDN'T SAY THAT.
SHOULD WE ASK THE OTHERS?
CINDY AND MARION AREN'T IN ANY SHAPE TO DEAL.
SO...WHAT, THEN?

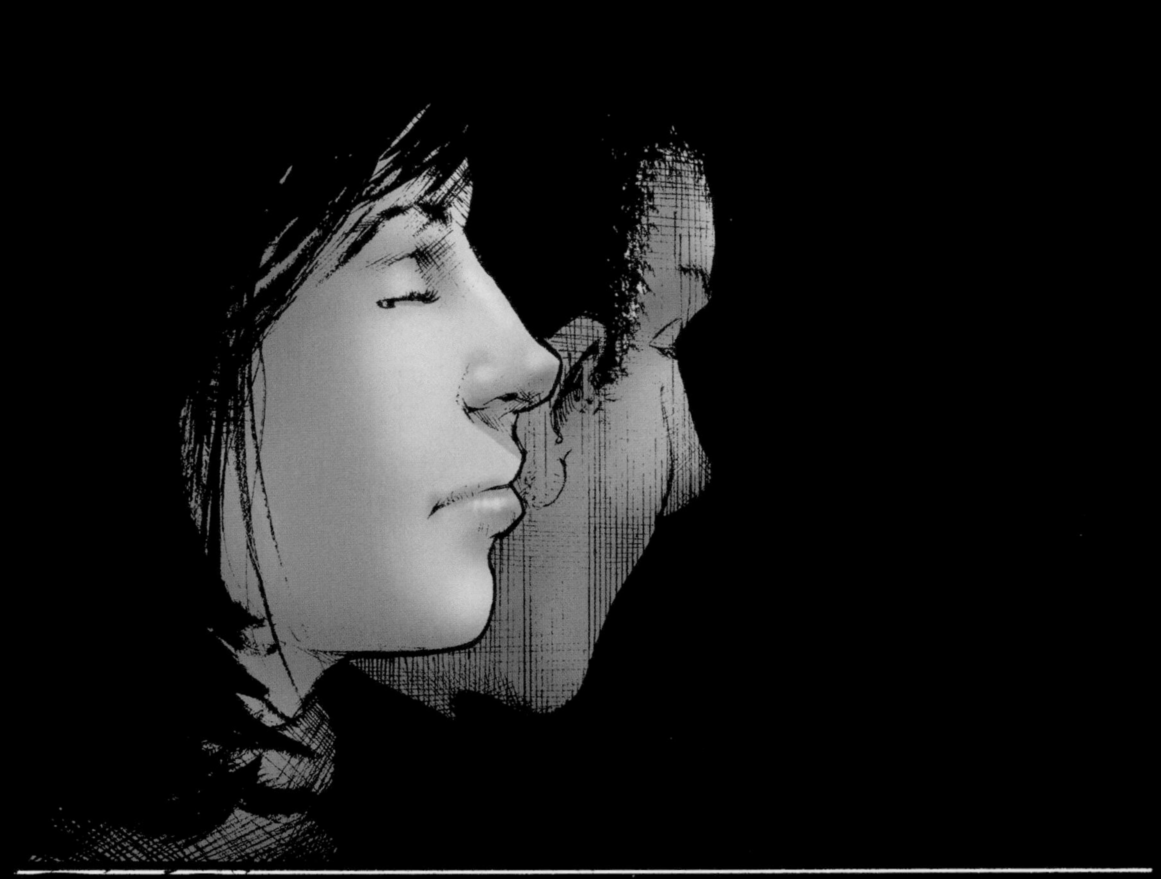
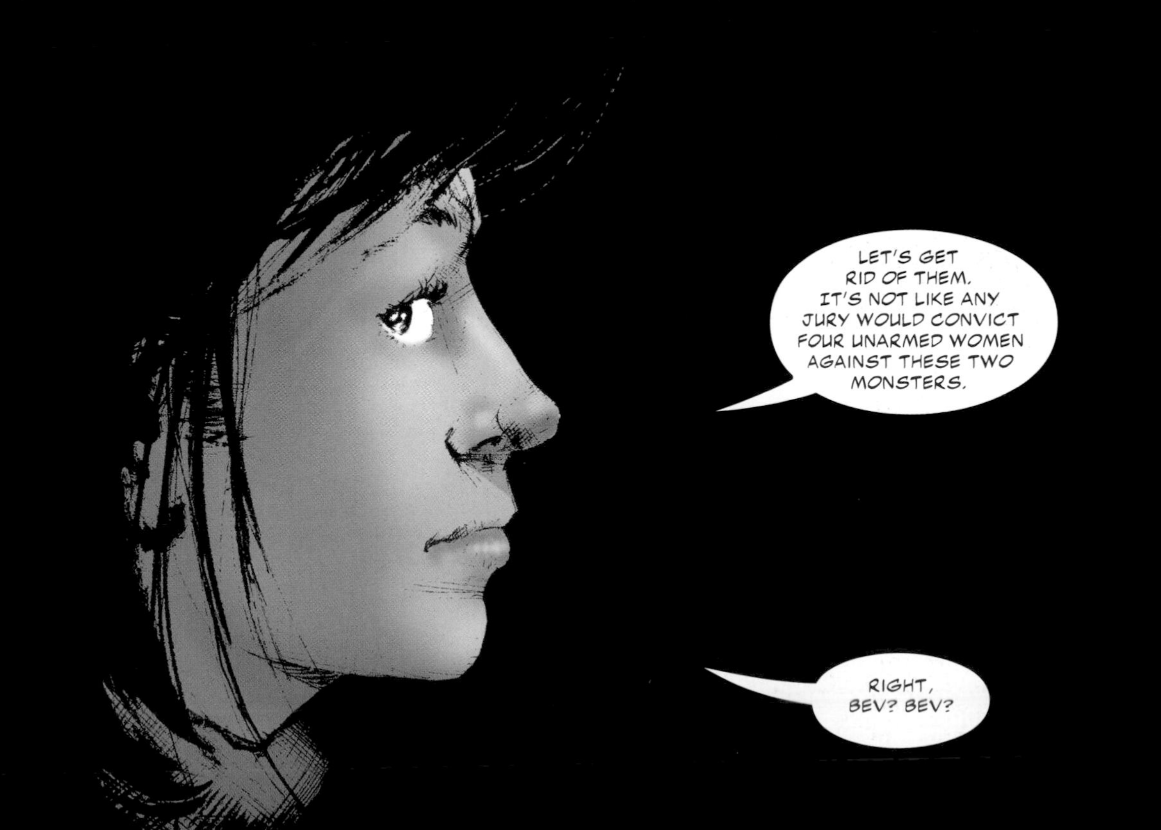
LET'S GET RID OF THEM. IT'S NOT LIKE ANY JURY WOULD CONVICT FOUR UNARMED WOMEN AGAINST THESE TWO MONSTERS.
RIGHT, BEV? BEV?

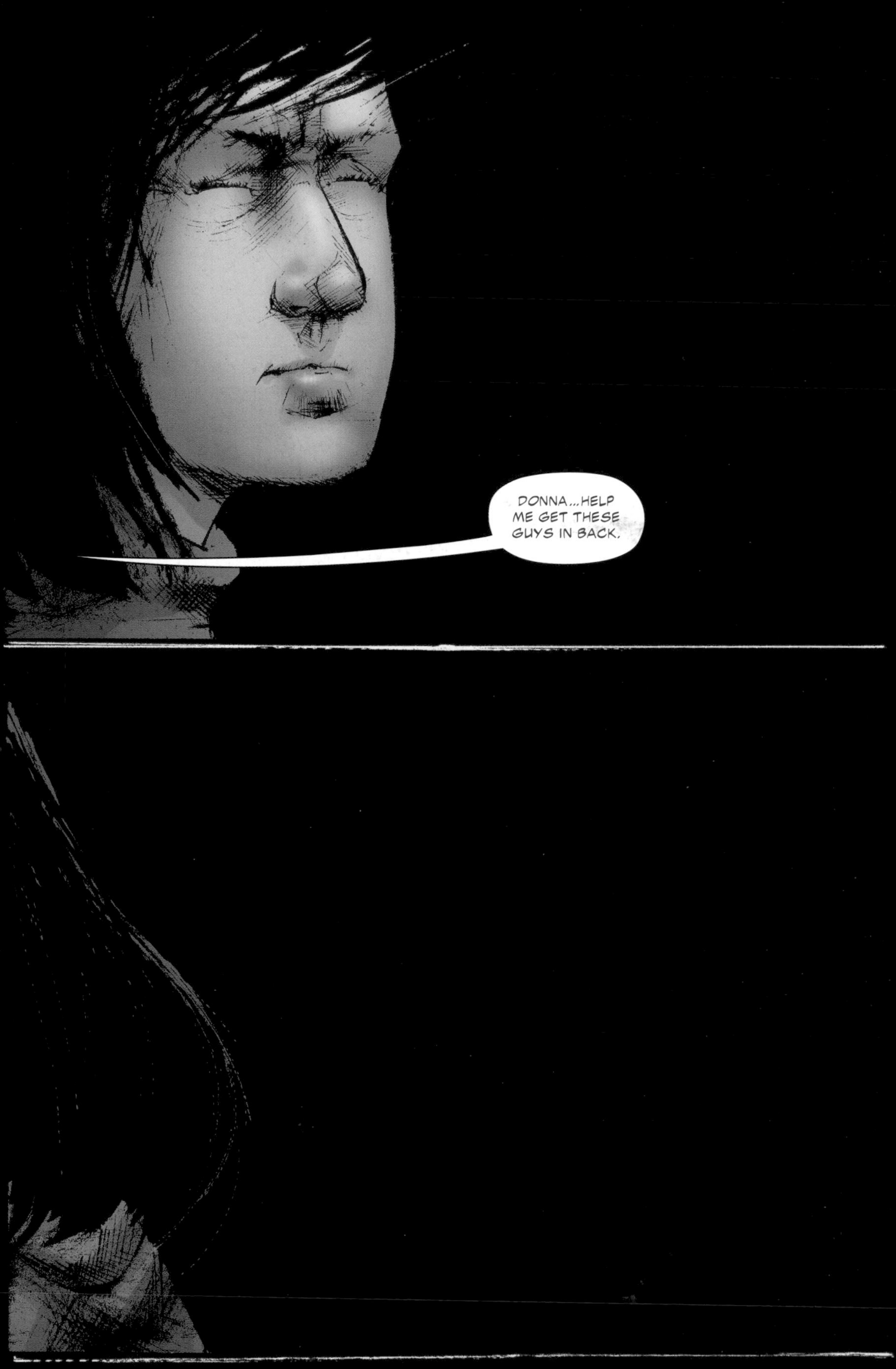
DONNA...HELP ME GET THESE GUYS IN BACK.

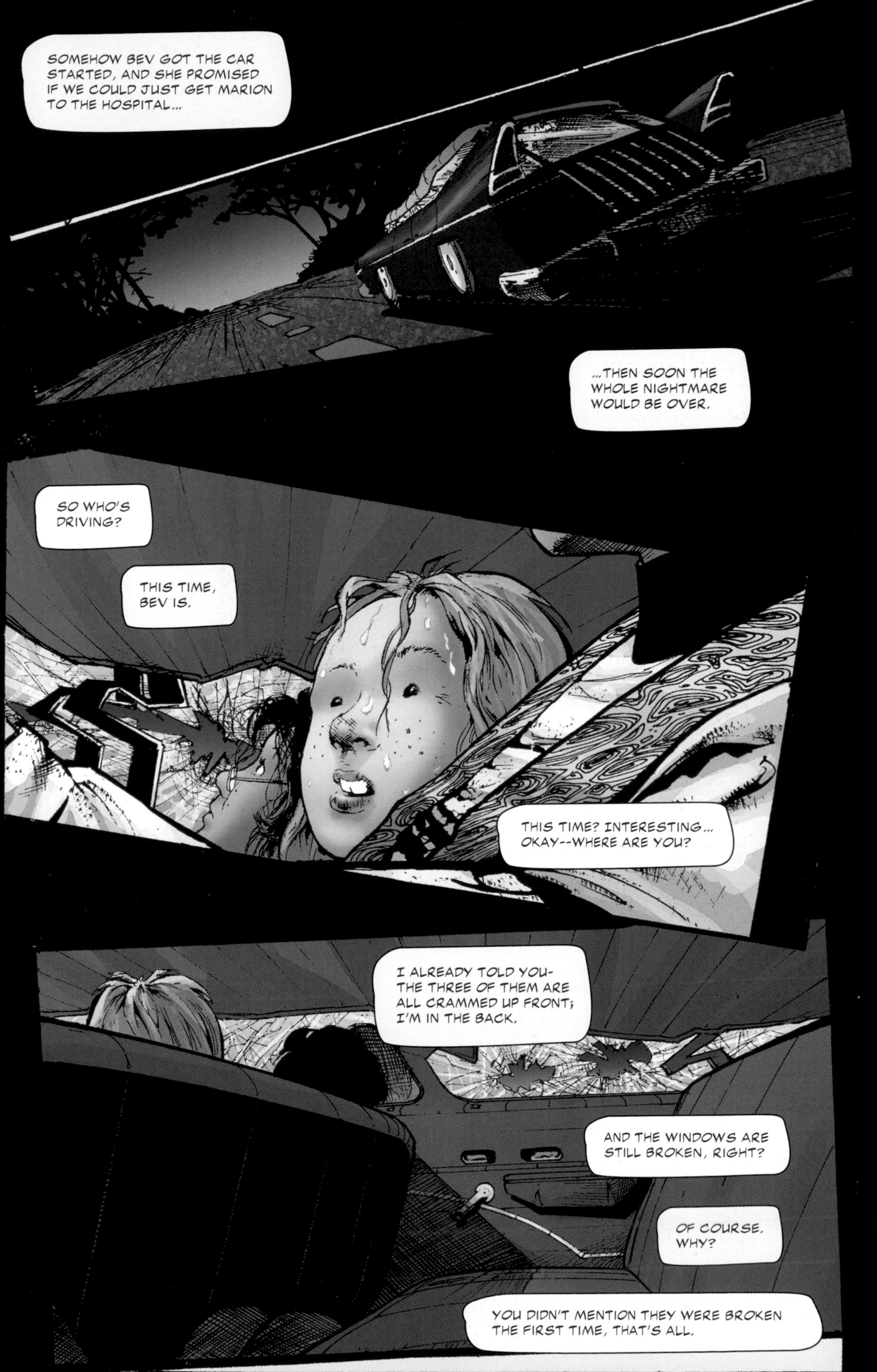
SOMEHOW BEV GOT THE CAR STARTED, AND SHE PROMISED IF WE COULD JUST GET MARION TO THE HOSPITAL...
...THEN SOON THE WHOLE NIGHTMARE WOULD BE OVER.
SO WHO'S DRIVING?
THIS TIME, BEV IS.
THIS TIME? INTERESTING... OKAY--WHERE ARE YOU?
I ALREADY TOLD YOU- THE THREE OF THEM ARE ALL CRAMMED UP FRONT; I'M IN THE BACK.
AND THE WINDOWS ARE STILL BROKEN, RIGHT?
OF COURSE. WHY?
YOU DIDN'T MENTION THEY WERE BROKEN THE FIRST TIME, THAT'S ALL.

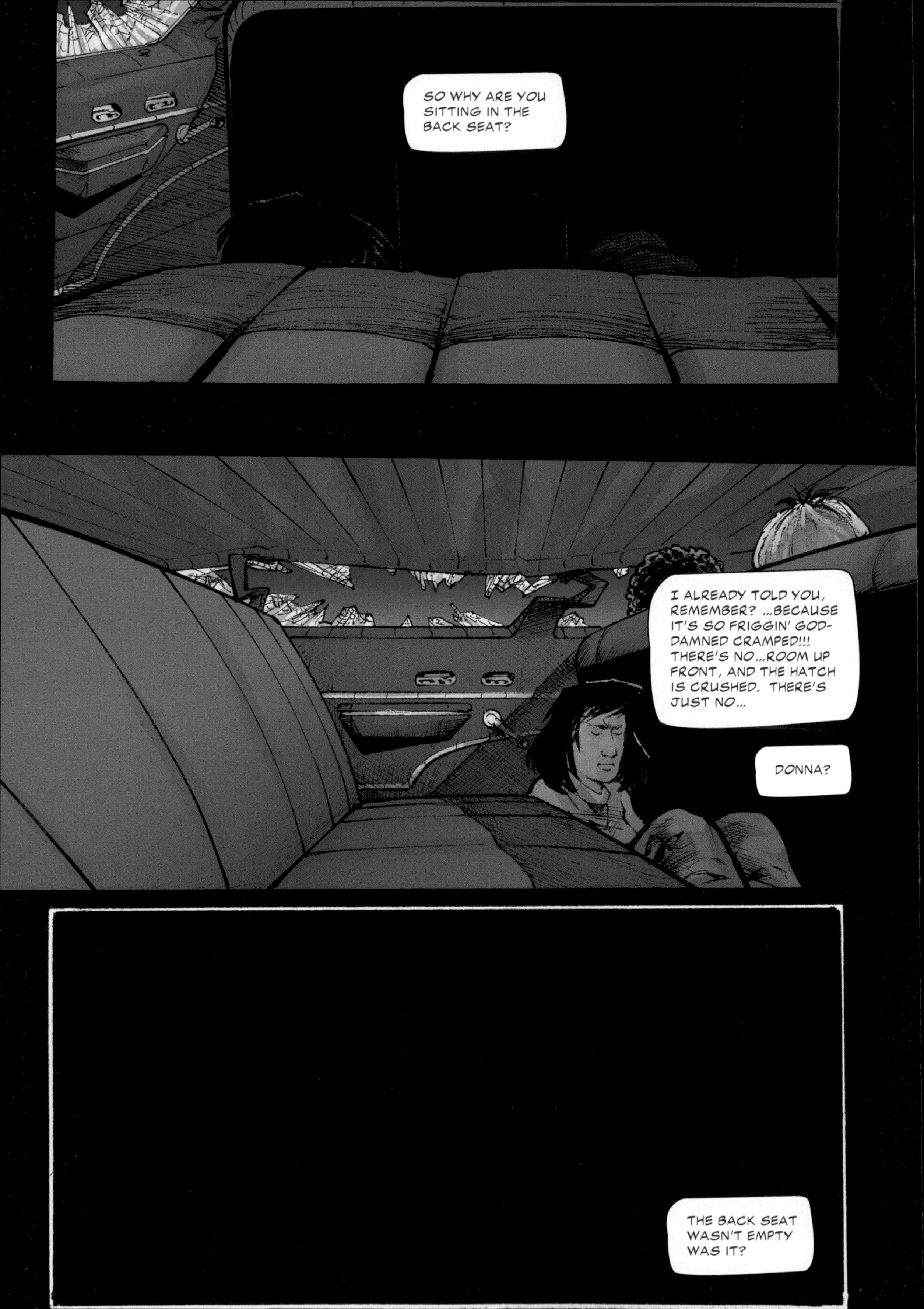
SO WHY ARE YOU SITTING IN THE BACK SEAT?
I ALREADY TOLD YOU, REMEMBER? ...BECAUSE IT'S SO FRIGGIN' GOD-DAMNED CRAMPED!!! THERE'S NO...ROOM UP FRONT, AND THE HATCH IS CRUSHED. THERE'S JUST NO...
DONNA?
THE BACK SEAT WASN'T EMPTY WAS IT?

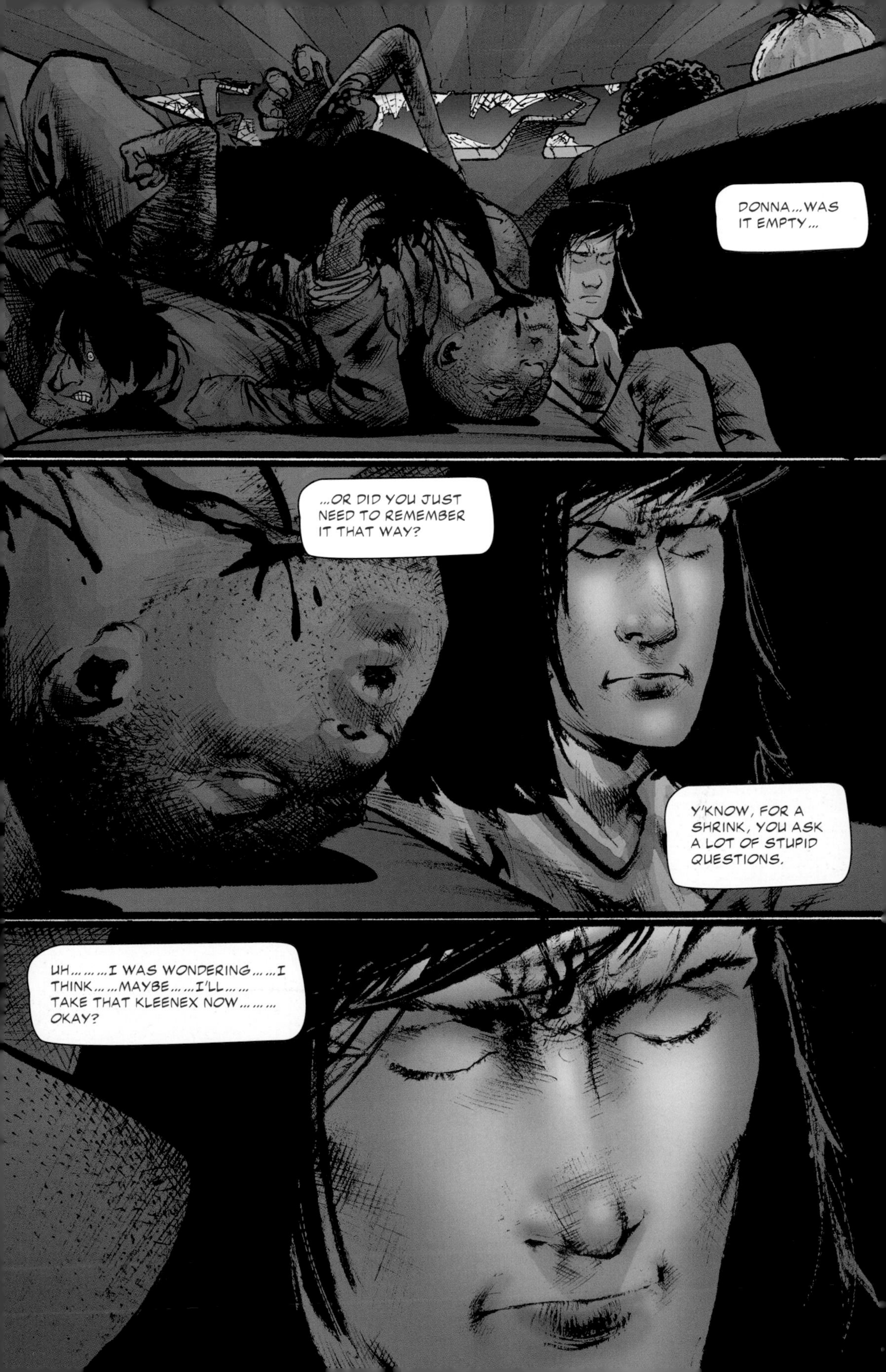
DONNA...WAS IT EMPTY...
...OR DID YOU JUST NEED TO REMEMBER IT THAT WAY?
Y'KNOW, FOR A SHRINK, YOU ASK A LOT OF STUPID QUESTIONS.
UH.........I WAS WONDERING......I THINK......MAYBE......I'LL......TAKE THAT KLEENEX NOW.........OKAY?

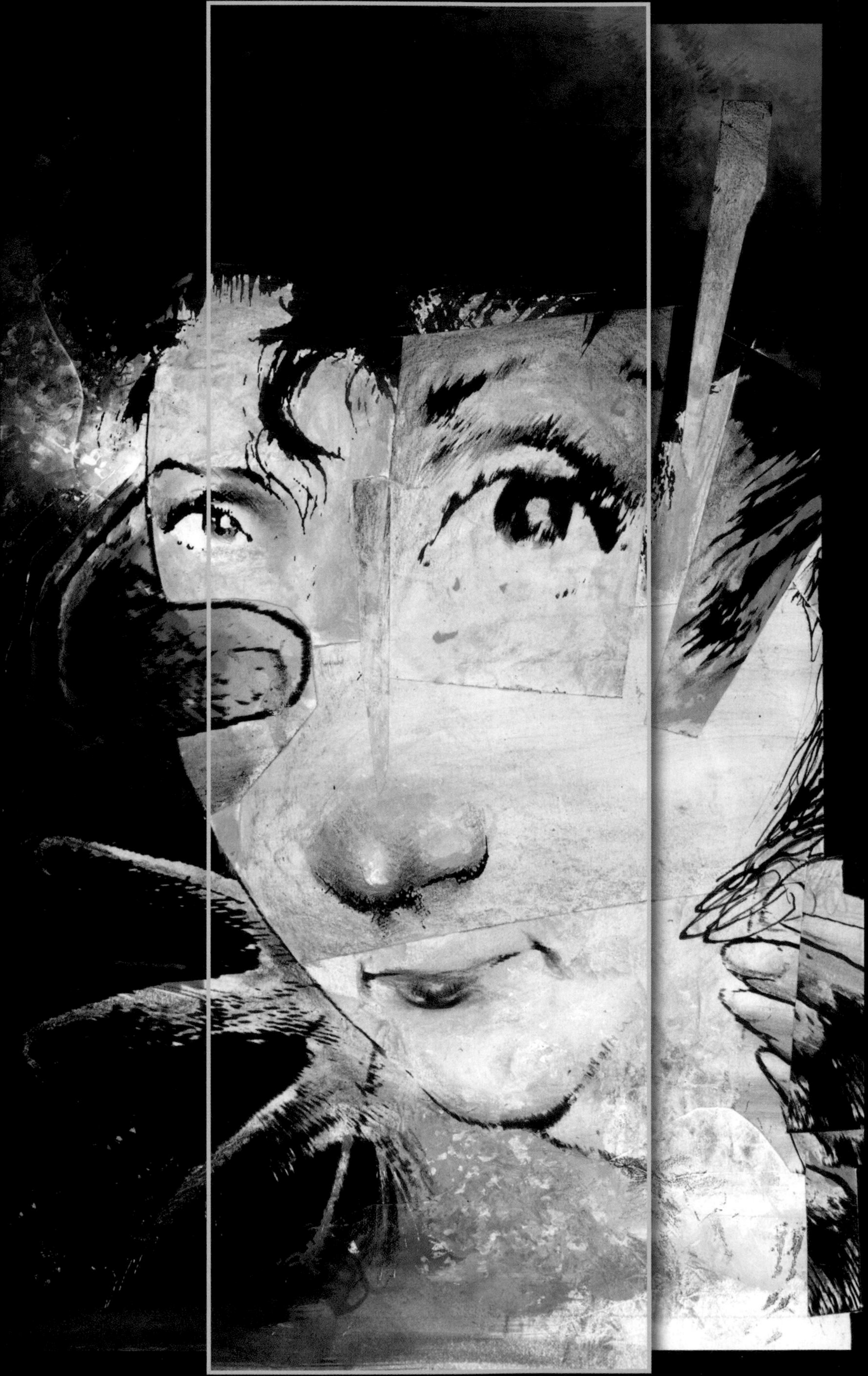

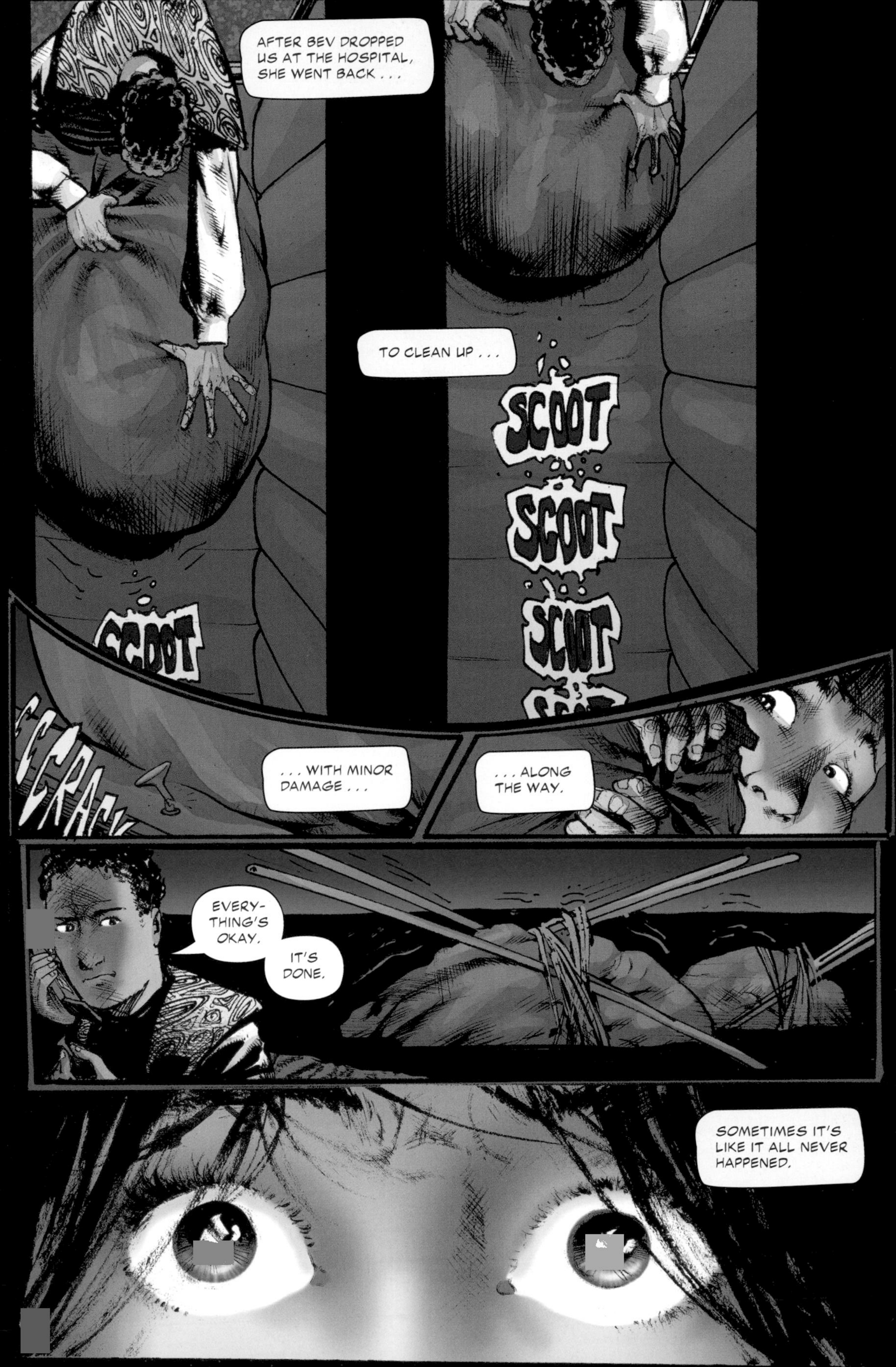
AFTER BEV DROPPED US AT THE HOSPITAL, SHE WENT BACK . . .
TO CLEAN UP . . .
SCOOT
SCOOT
SCOOT
. . . WITH MINOR DAMAGE . . .
. . . ALONG THE WAY.
EVERY-THING'S OKAY.
IT'S DONE.
SOMETIMES IT'S LIKE IT ALL NEVER HAPPENED.

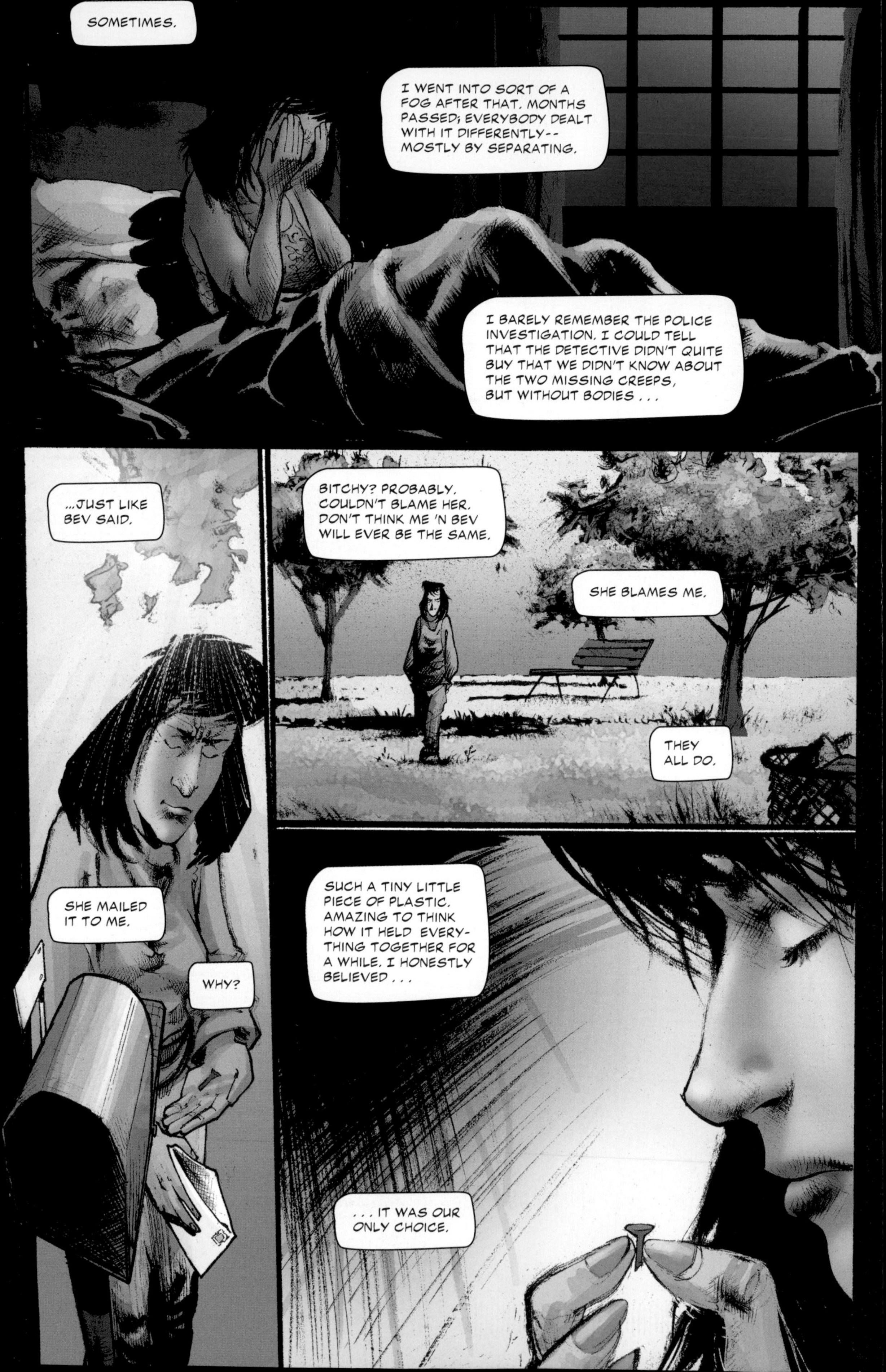
SOMETIMES.
I WENT INTO SORT OF A FOG AFTER THAT. MONTHS PASSED; EVERYBODY DEALT WITH IT DIFFERENTLY-- MOSTLY BY SEPARATING.
I BARELY REMEMBER THE POLICE INVESTIGATION. I COULD TELL THAT THE DETECTIVE DIDN'T QUITE BUY THAT WE DIDN'T KNOW ABOUT THE TWO MISSING CREEPS, BUT WITHOUT BODIES . . .
...JUST LIKE BEV SAID.
BITCHY? PROBABLY. COULDN'T BLAME HER. DON'T THINK ME 'N BEV WILL EVER BE THE SAME.
SHE BLAMES ME.
THEY ALL DO.
SHE MAILED IT TO ME.
WHY?
SUCH A TINY LITTLE PIECE OF PLASTIC. AMAZING TO THINK HOW IT HELD EVERYTHING TOGETHER FOR A WHILE. I HONESTLY BELIEVED . . .
. . . IT WAS OUR ONLY CHOICE.

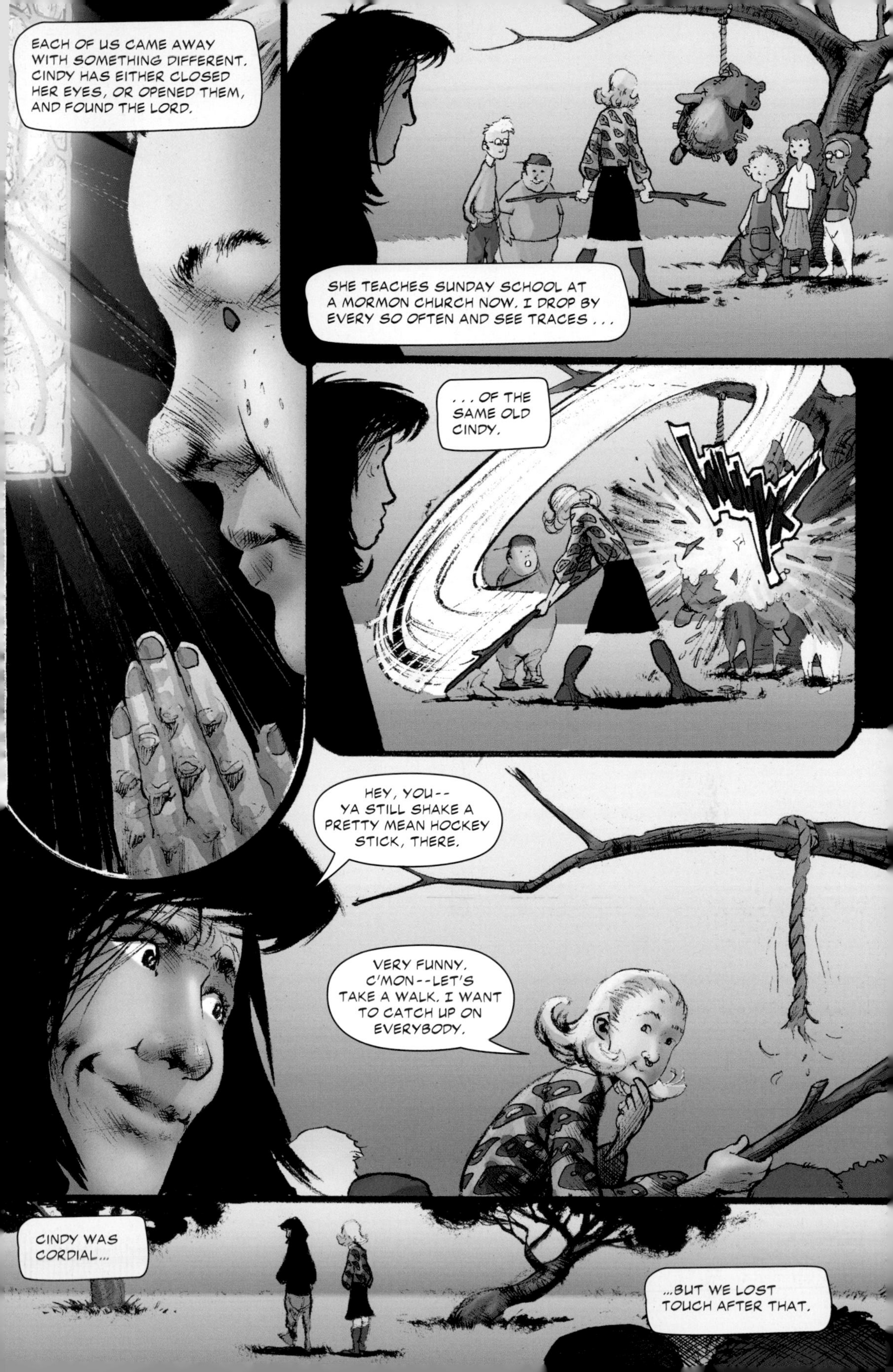
EACH OF US CAME AWAY WITH SOMETHING DIFFERENT. CINDY HAS EITHER CLOSED HER EYES, OR OPENED THEM, AND FOUND THE LORD.
SHE TEACHES SUNDAY SCHOOL AT A MORMON CHURCH NOW. I DROP BY EVERY SO OFTEN AND SEE TRACES . . .
. . . OF THE SAME OLD CINDY.
WHAK
HEY, YOU-- YA STILL SHAKE A PRETTY MEAN HOCKEY STICK, THERE.
VERY FUNNY. C'MON--LET'S TAKE A WALK. I WANT TO CATCH UP ON EVERYBODY.
CINDY WAS CORDIAL...
...BUT WE LOST TOUCH AFTER THAT.

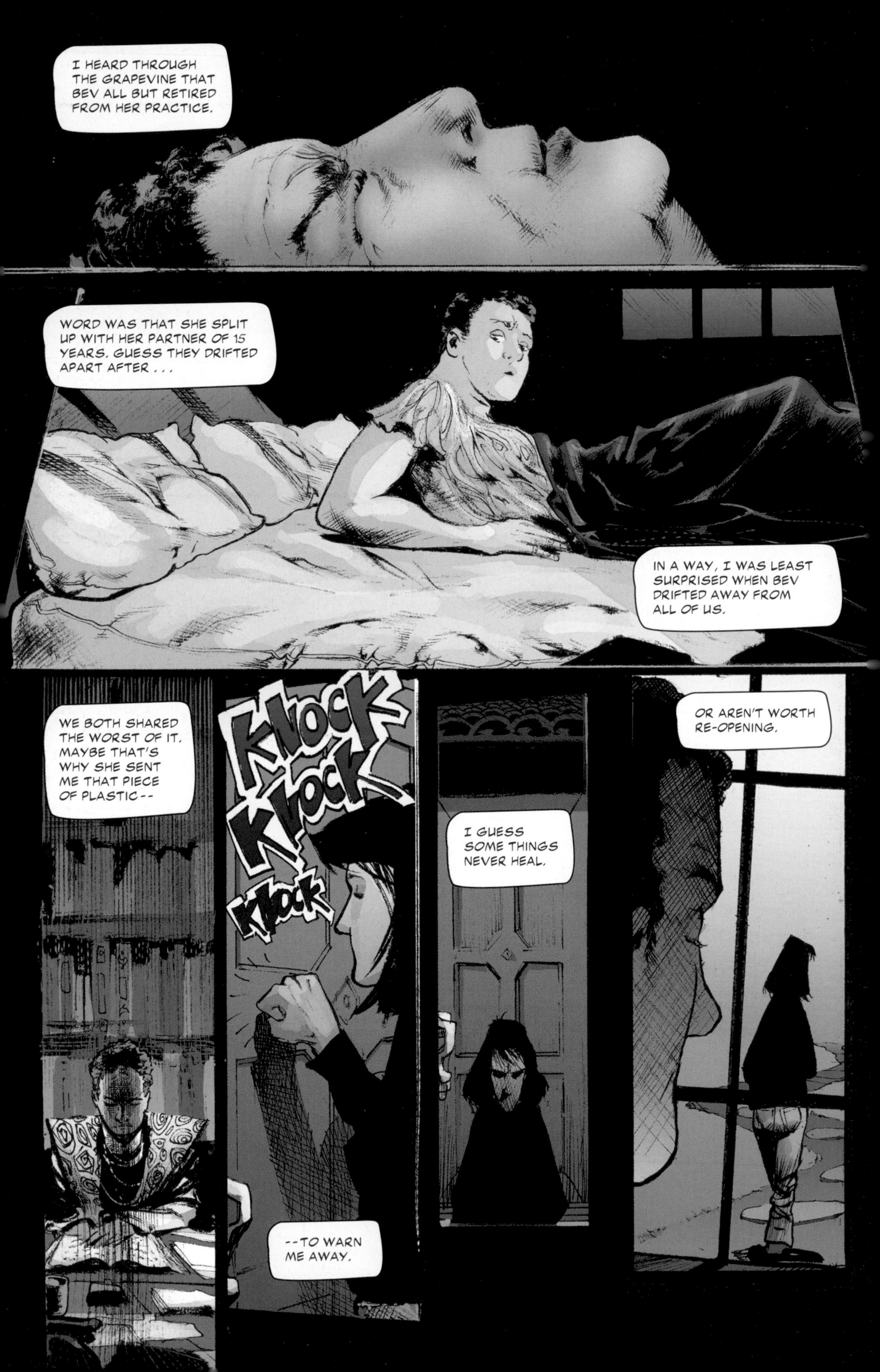
I HEARD THROUGH THE GRAPEVINE THAT BEV ALL BUT RETIRED FROM HER PRACTICE.
WORD WAS THAT SHE SPLIT UP WITH HER PARTNER OF 15 YEARS. GUESS THEY DRIFTED APART AFTER . . .
IN A WAY, I WAS LEAST SURPRISED WHEN BEV DRIFTED AWAY FROM ALL OF US.
WE BOTH SHARED THE WORST OF IT. MAYBE THAT'S WHY SHE SENT ME THAT PIECE OF PLASTIC--
KNOCK KNOCK
KNOCK
--TO WARN ME AWAY.
I GUESS SOME THINGS NEVER HEAL.
OR AREN'T WORTH RE-OPENING.

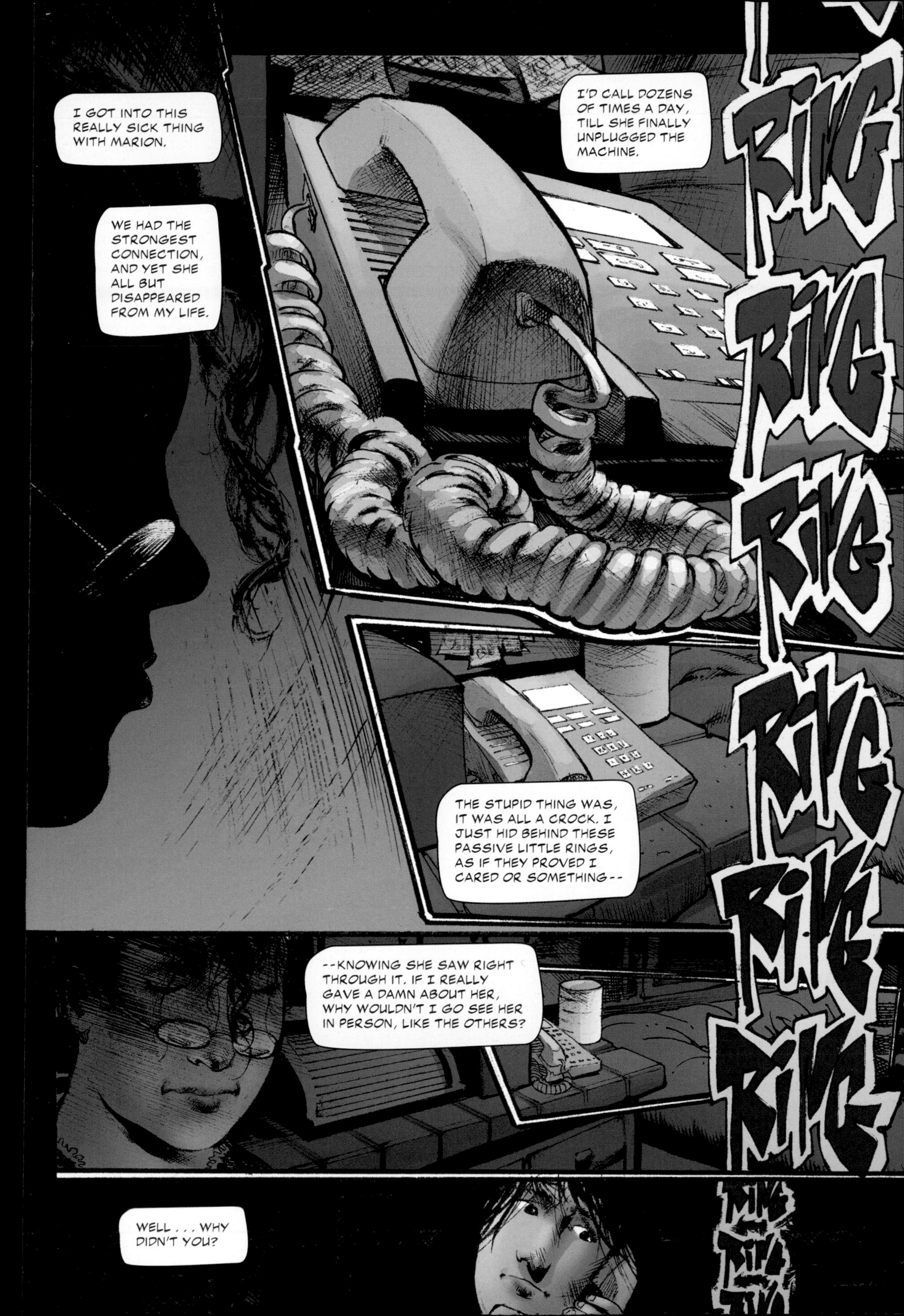
I GOT INTO THIS REALLY SICK THING WITH MARION.
WE HAD THE STRONGEST CONNECTION, AND YET SHE ALL BUT DISAPPEARED FROM MY LIFE.
I'D CALL DOZENS OF TIMES A DAY, TILL SHE FINALLY UNPLUGGED THE MACHINE.
RING
RING
RING
RING
RING
RING
RING
THE STUPID THING WAS, IT WAS ALL A CROCK. I JUST HID BEHIND THESE PASSIVE LITTLE RINGS, AS IF THEY PROVED I CARED OR SOMETHING--
--KNOWING SHE SAW RIGHT THROUGH IT. IF I REALLY GAVE A DAMN ABOUT HER, WHY WOULDN'T I GO SEE HER IN PERSON, LIKE THE OTHERS?
WELL . . . WHY DIDN'T YOU?

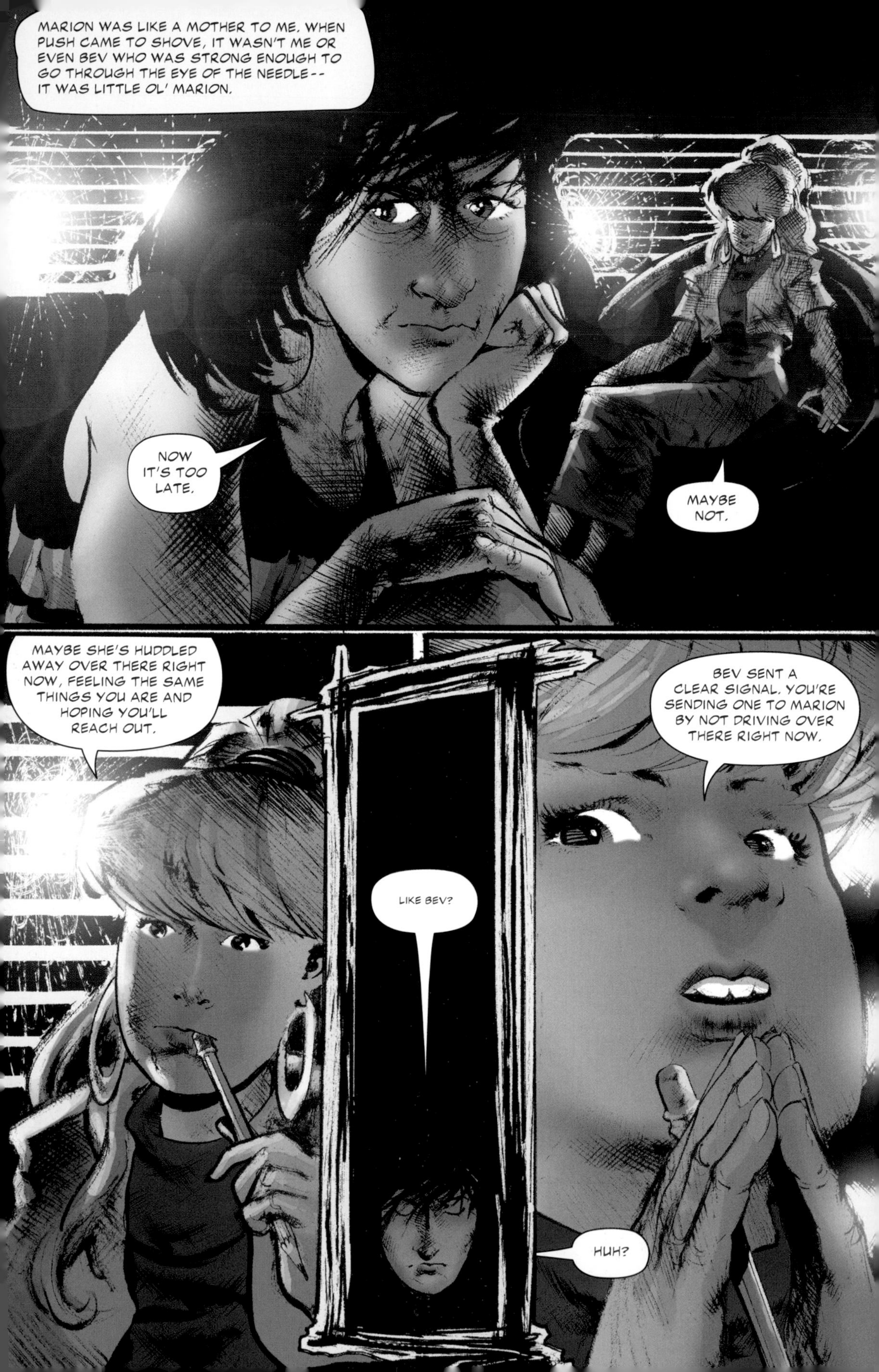
MARION WAS LIKE A MOTHER TO ME. WHEN PUSH CAME TO SHOVE, IT WASN'T ME OR EVEN BEV WHO WAS STRONG ENOUGH TO GO THROUGH THE EYE OF THE NEEDLE-- IT WAS LITTLE OL' MARION.
NOW IT'S TOO LATE.
MAYBE NOT.
MAYBE SHE'S HUDDLED AWAY OVER THERE RIGHT NOW, FEELING THE SAME THINGS YOU ARE AND HOPING YOU'LL REACH OUT.
BEV SENT A CLEAR SIGNAL. YOU'RE SENDING ONE TO MARION BY NOT DRIVING OVER THERE RIGHT NOW.
LIKE BEV?
HUH?

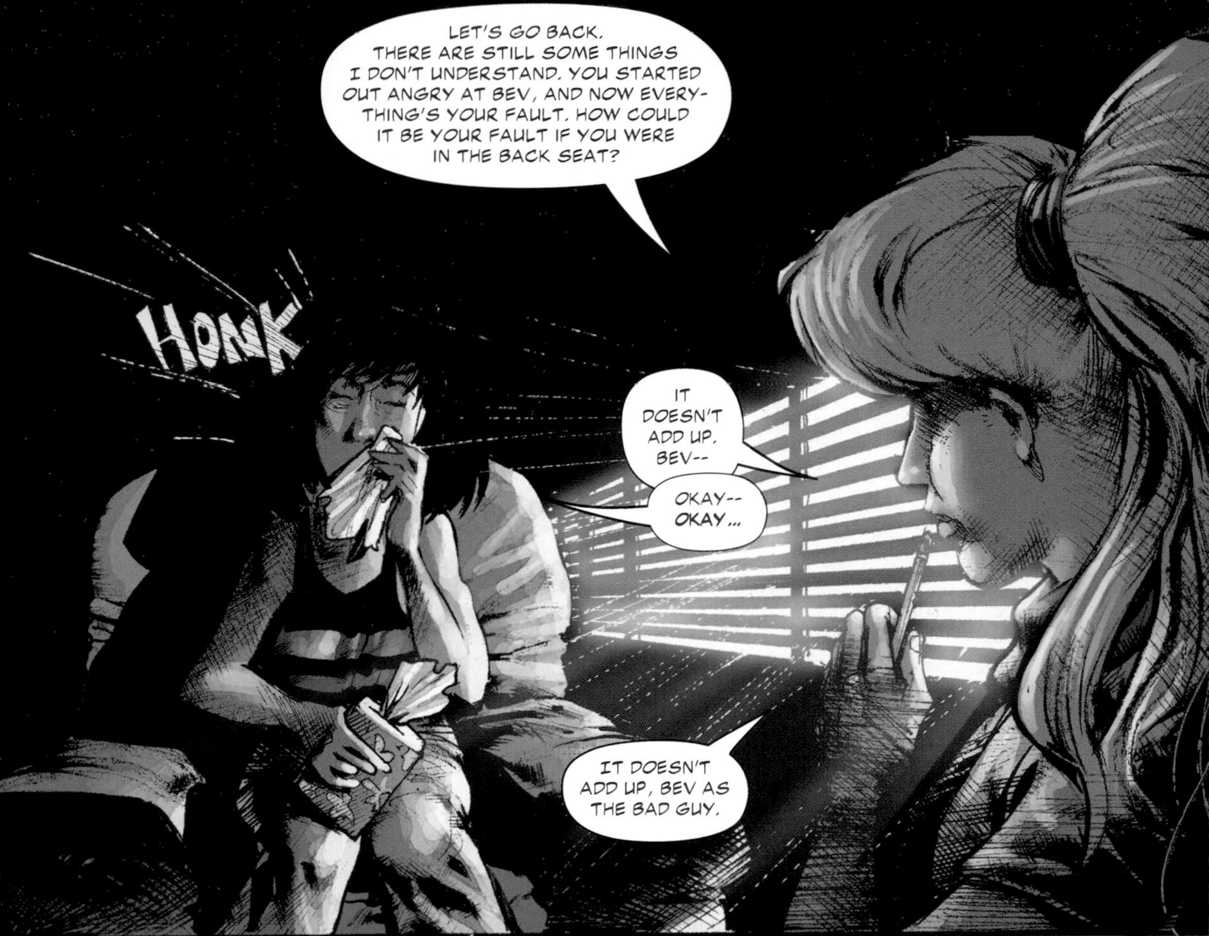
LET'S GO BACK. THERE ARE STILL SOME THINGS I DON'T UNDERSTAND. YOU STARTED OUT ANGRY AT BEV, AND NOW EVERY-THING'S YOUR FAULT. HOW COULD IT BE YOUR FAULT IF YOU WERE IN THE BACK SEAT?
HONK
IT DOESN'T ADD UP, BEV--
OKAY-- OKAY...
IT DOESN'T ADD UP, BEV AS THE BAD GUY.

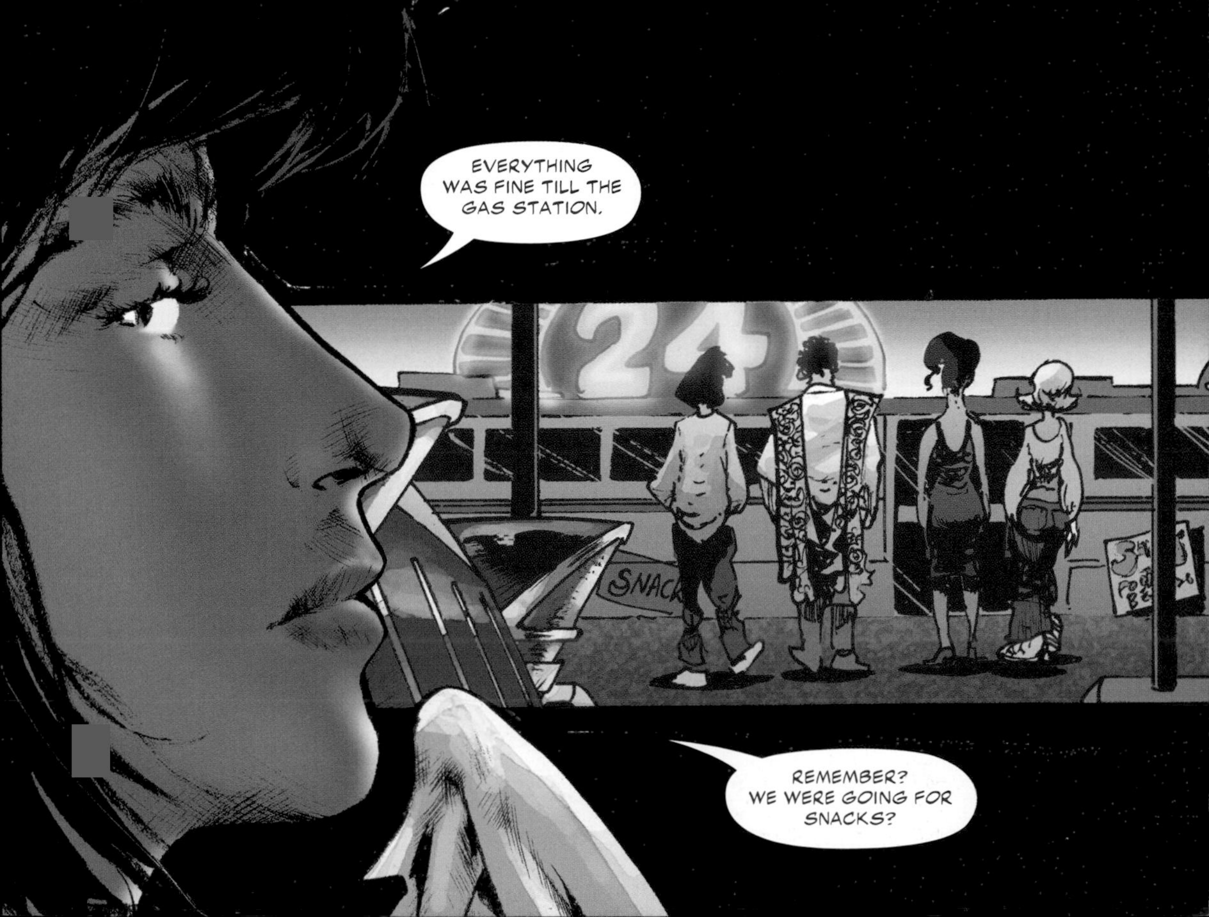
EVERYTHING WAS FINE TILL THE GAS STATION.
24
SNACK
REMEMBER? WE WERE GOING FOR SNACKS?

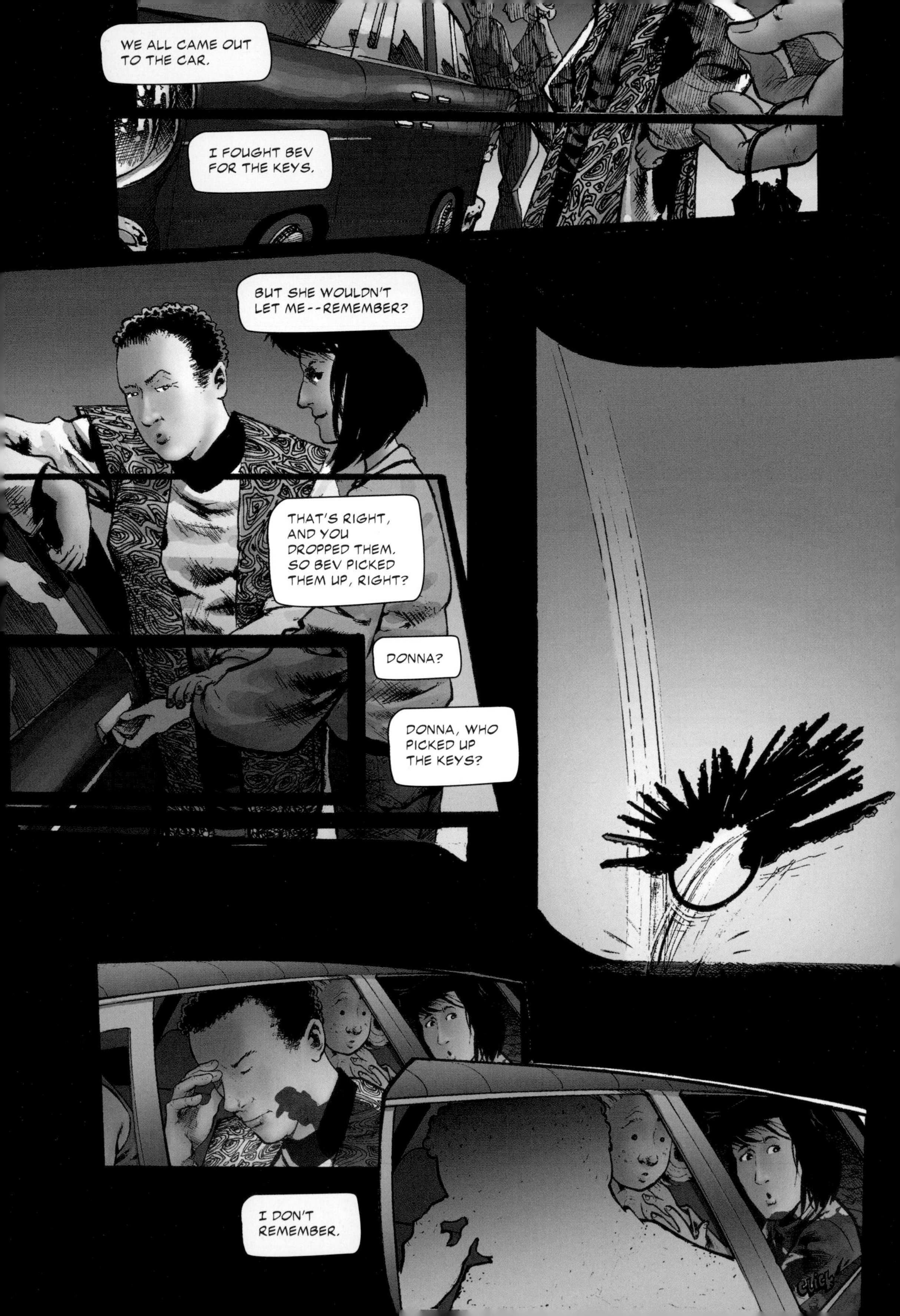
WE ALL CAME OUT TO THE CAR.
I FOUGHT BEV FOR THE KEYS.
BUT SHE WOULDN'T LET ME--REMEMBER?
THAT'S RIGHT, AND YOU DROPPED THEM. SO BEV PICKED THEM UP, RIGHT?
DONNA?
DONNA, WHO PICKED UP THE KEYS?
I DON'T REMEMBER.
CLICK

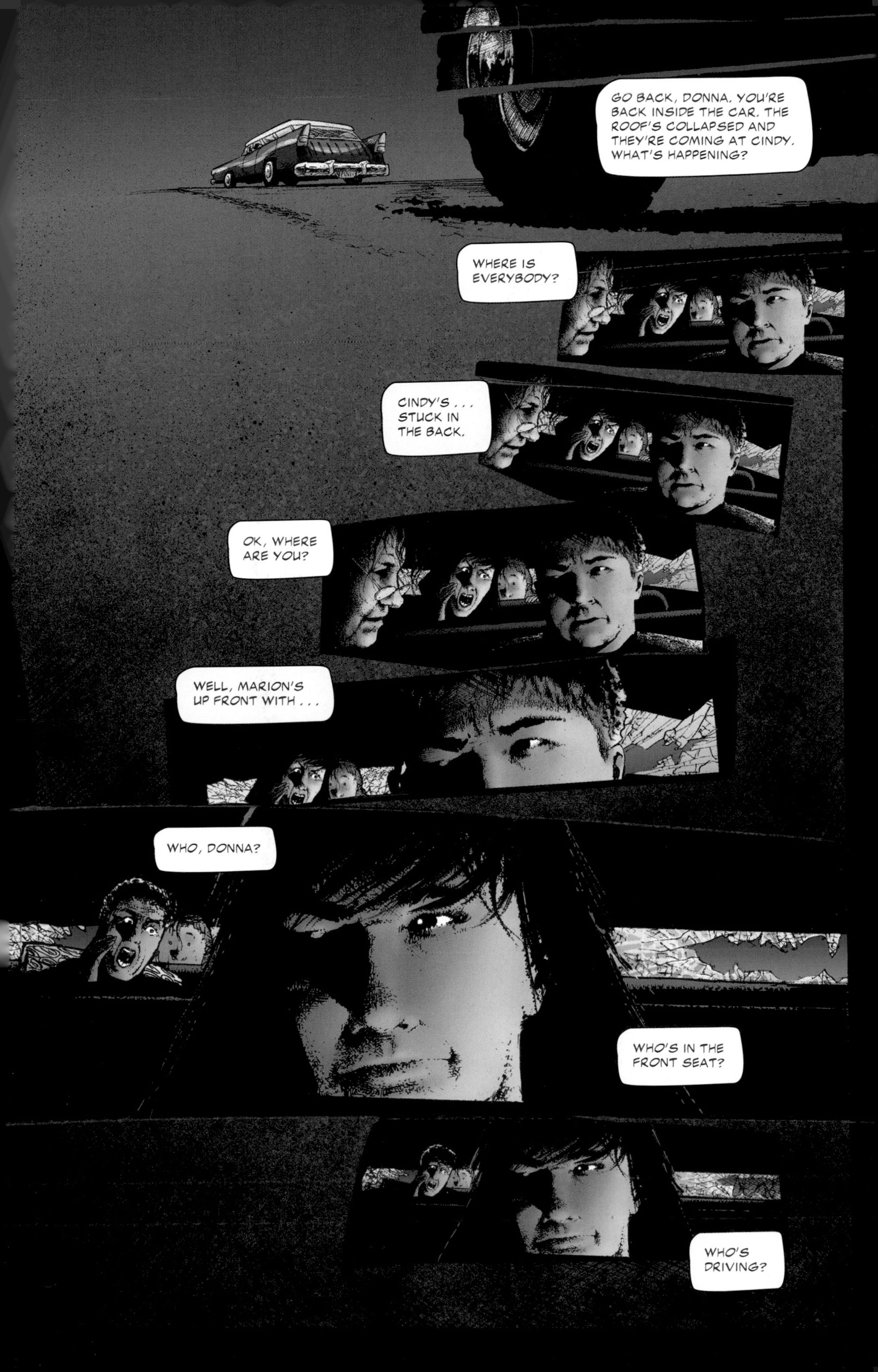
GO BACK, DONNA. YOU'RE BACK INSIDE THE CAR. THE ROOF'S COLLAPSED AND THEY'RE COMING AT CINDY. WHAT'S HAPPENING?
WHERE IS EVERYBODY?
CINDY'S . . . STUCK IN THE BACK.
OK, WHERE ARE YOU?
WELL, MARION'S UP FRONT WITH . . .
WHO, DONNA?
WHO'S IN THE FRONT SEAT?
WHO'S DRIVING?

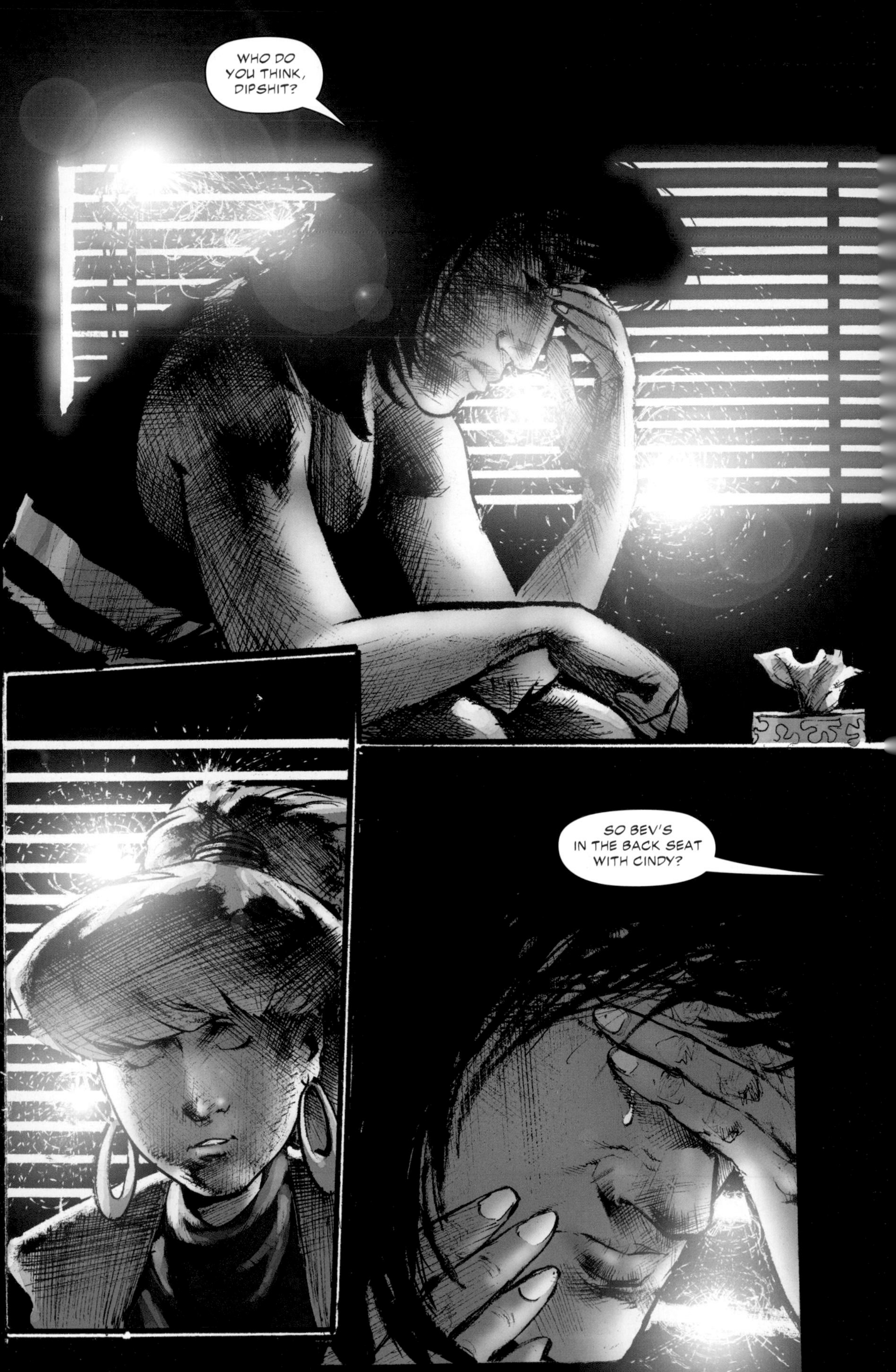
WHO DO YOU THINK, DIPSHIT?
SO BEV'S IN THE BACK SEAT WITH CINDY?

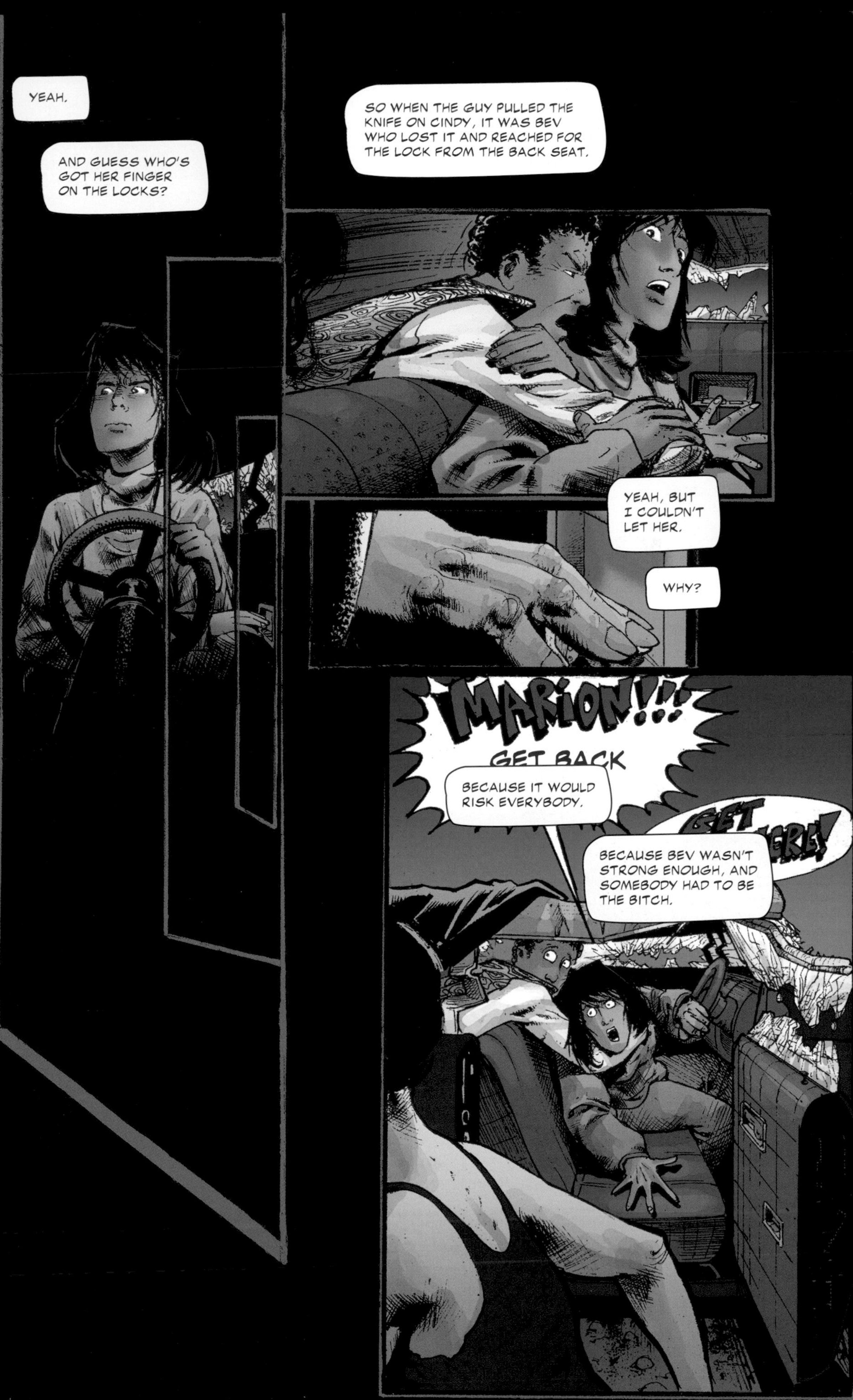
YEAH.
AND GUESS WHO'S GOT HER FINGER ON THE LOCKS?
SO WHEN THE GUY PULLED THE KNIFE ON CINDY, IT WAS BEV WHO LOST IT AND REACHED FOR THE LOCK FROM THE BACK SEAT.
YEAH, BUT I COULDN'T LET HER.
WHY?
MARION!!!
GET BACK
BECAUSE IT WOULD RISK EVERYBODY.
GET
BECAUSE BEV WASN'T STRONG ENOUGH, AND SOMEBODY HAD TO BE THE BITCH.

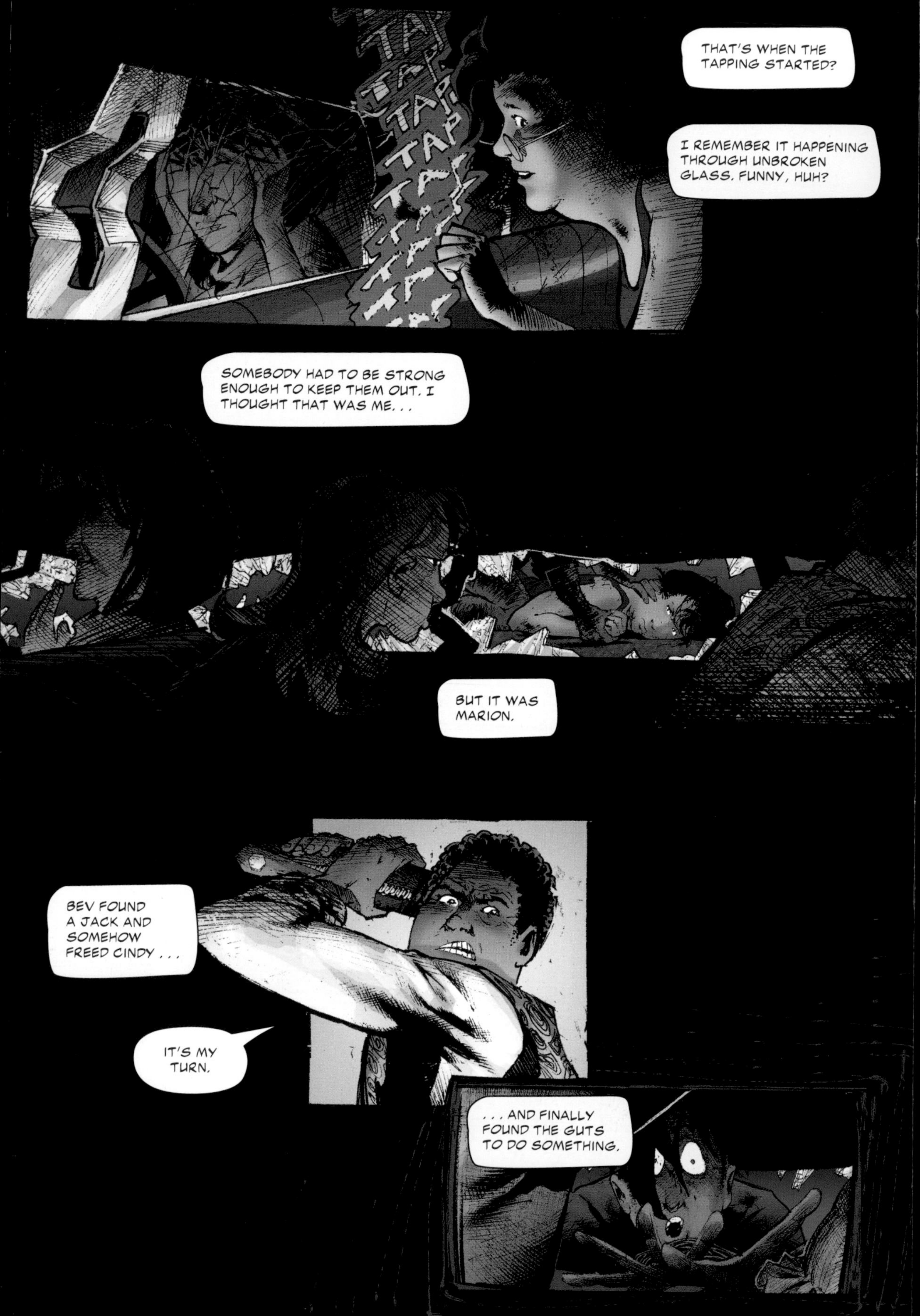
THAT'S WHEN THE TAPPING STARTED?
I REMEMBER IT HAPPENING THROUGH UNBROKEN GLASS. FUNNY, HUH?
TAP TAP TAP TAP TAP
SOMEBODY HAD TO BE STRONG ENOUGH TO KEEP THEM OUT. I THOUGHT THAT WAS ME. . .
BUT IT WAS MARION.
BEV FOUND A JACK AND SOMEHOW FREED CINDY . . .
IT'S MY TURN.
. . . AND FINALLY FOUND THE GUTS TO DO SOMETHING.

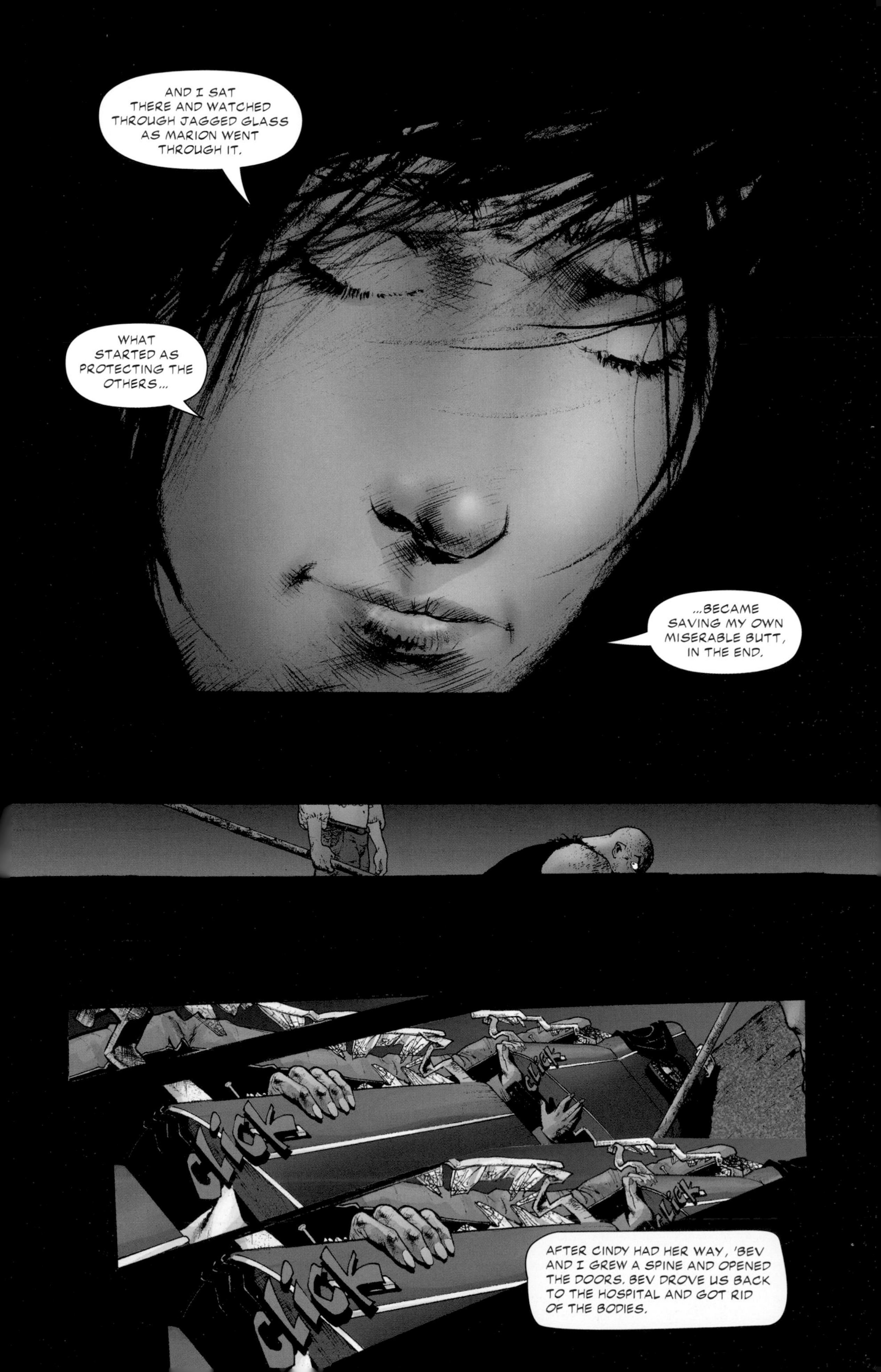
AND I SAT THERE AND WATCHED THROUGH JAGGED GLASS AS MARION WENT THROUGH IT.
WHAT STARTED AS PROTECTING THE OTHERS...
...BECAME SAVING MY OWN MISERABLE BUTT, IN THE END.
CLICK
CLICK
CLICK
CLICK
AFTER CINDY HAD HER WAY, 'BEV AND I GREW A SPINE AND OPENED THE DOORS. BEV DROVE US BACK TO THE HOSPITAL AND GOT RID OF THE BODIES.

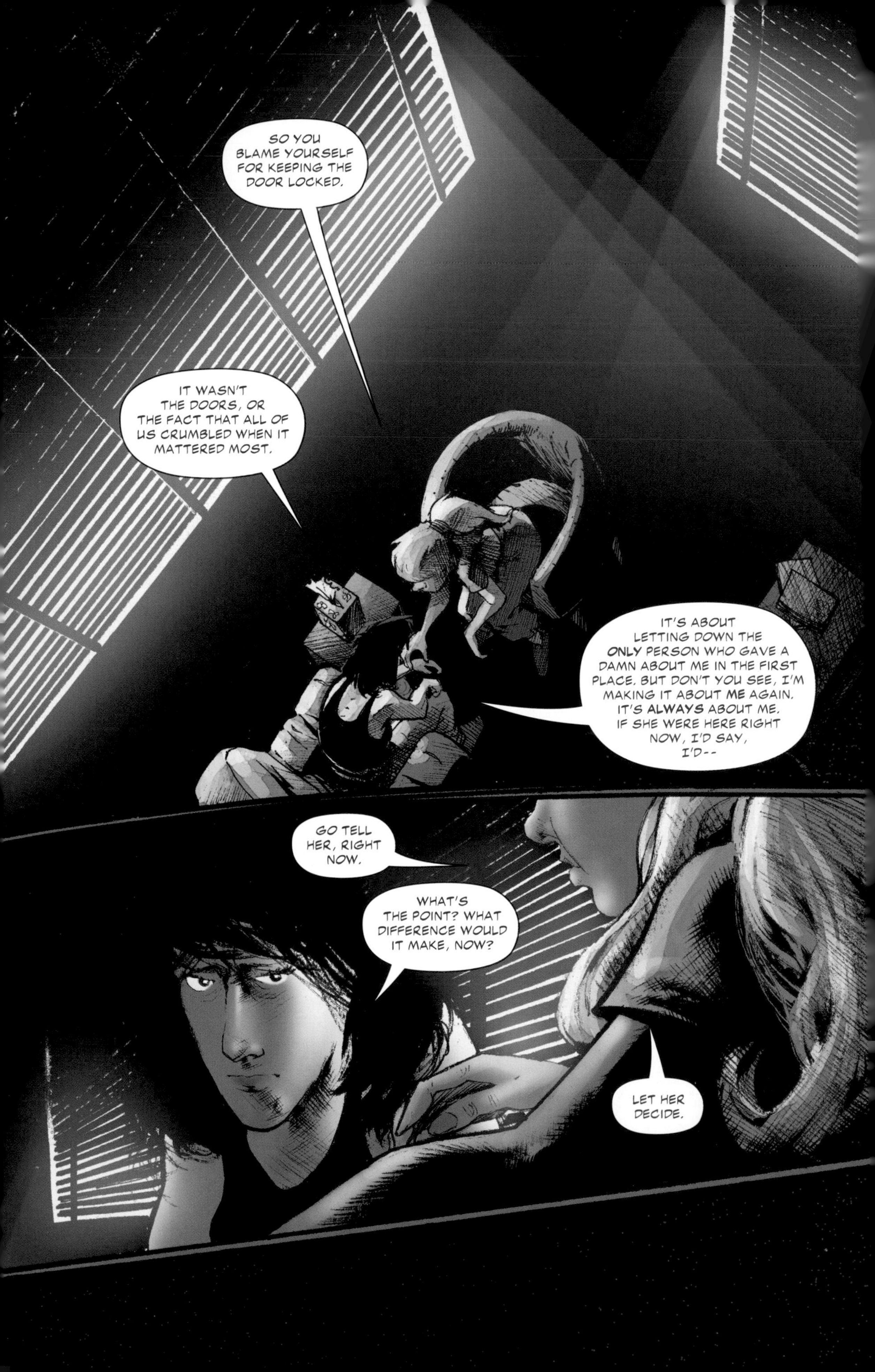
SO YOU BLAME YOURSELF FOR KEEPING THE DOOR LOCKED.
IT WASN'T THE DOORS, OR THE FACT THAT ALL OF US CRUMBLED WHEN IT MATTERED MOST.
IT'S ABOUT LETTING DOWN THE **ONLY** PERSON WHO GAVE A DAMN ABOUT ME IN THE FIRST PLACE. BUT DON'T YOU SEE, I'M MAKING IT ABOUT **ME** AGAIN. IT'S **ALWAYS** ABOUT ME. IF SHE WERE HERE RIGHT NOW, I'D SAY, I'D--
GO TELL HER, RIGHT NOW.
WHAT'S THE POINT? WHAT DIFFERENCE WOULD IT MAKE, NOW?
LET HER DECIDE.

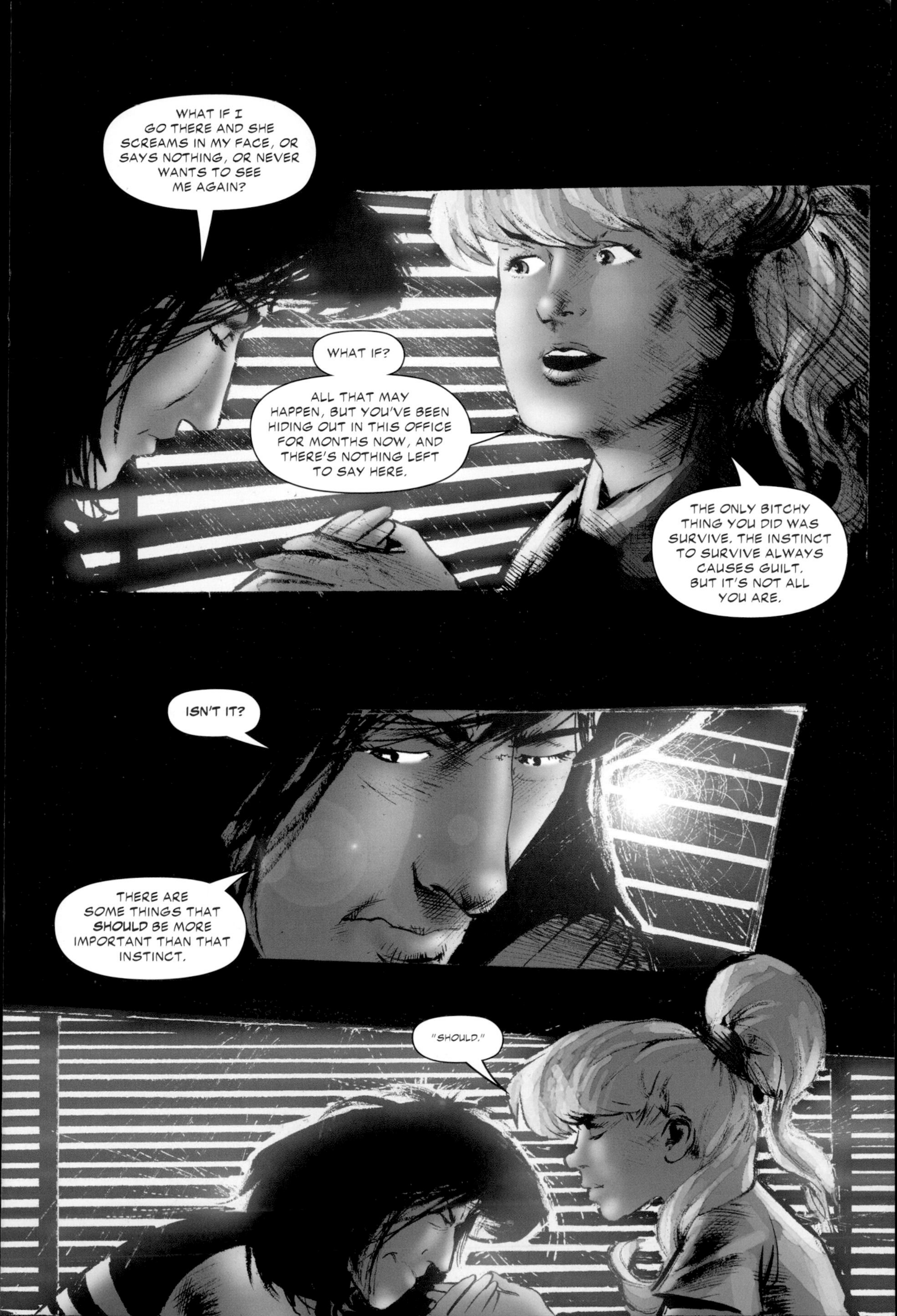
WHAT IF I GO THERE AND SHE SCREAMS IN MY FACE, OR SAYS NOTHING, OR NEVER WANTS TO SEE ME AGAIN?
WHAT IF?
ALL THAT MAY HAPPEN, BUT YOU'VE BEEN HIDING OUT IN THIS OFFICE FOR MONTHS NOW, AND THERE'S NOTHING LEFT TO SAY HERE.
THE ONLY BITCHY THING YOU DID WAS SURVIVE. THE INSTINCT TO SURVIVE ALWAYS CAUSES GUILT. BUT IT'S NOT ALL YOU ARE.
ISN'T IT?
THERE ARE SOME THINGS THAT SHOULD BE MORE IMPORTANT THAN THAT INSTINCT.
"SHOULD."

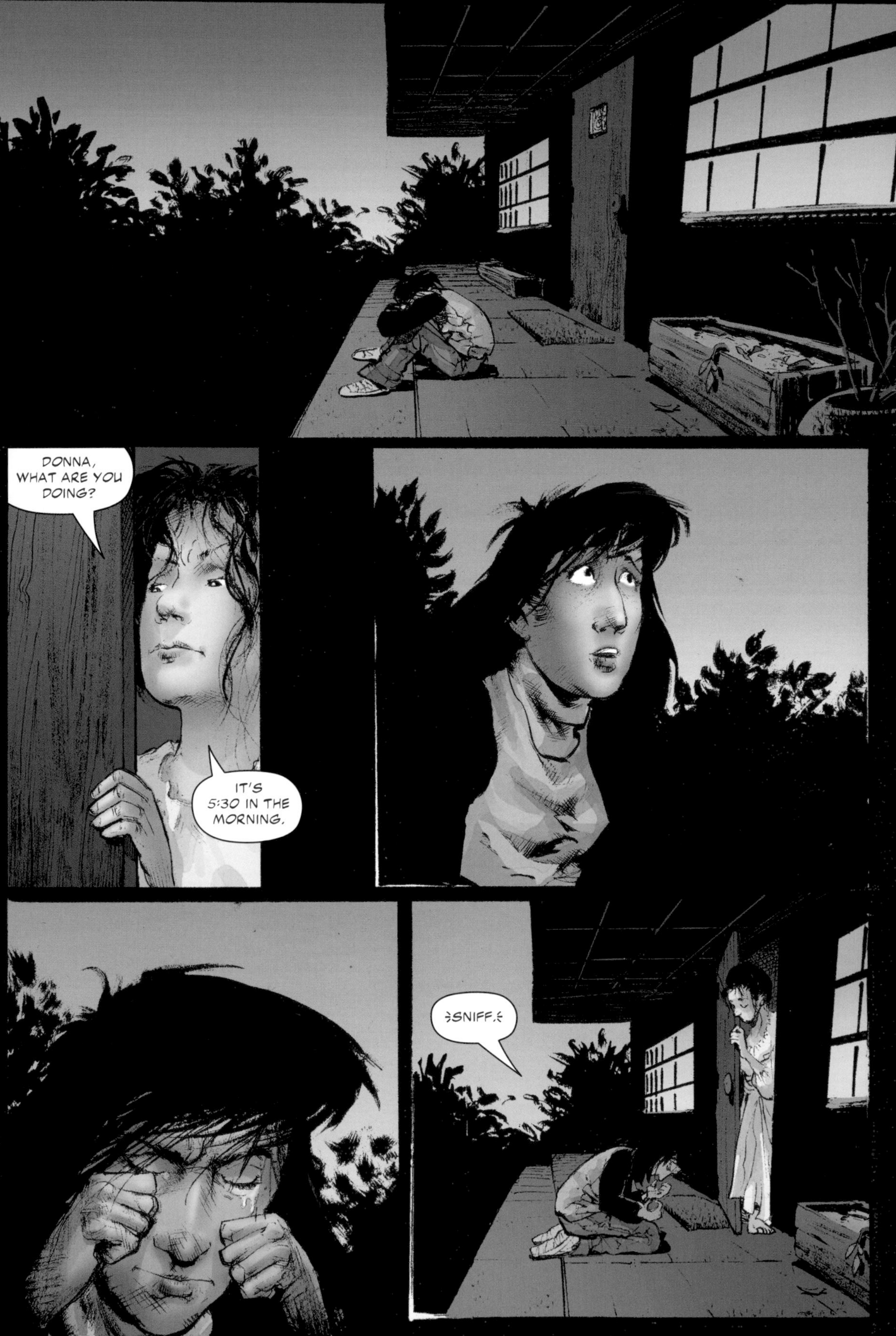
DONNA, WHAT ARE YOU DOING?
IT'S 5:30 IN THE MORNING.
SNIFF.

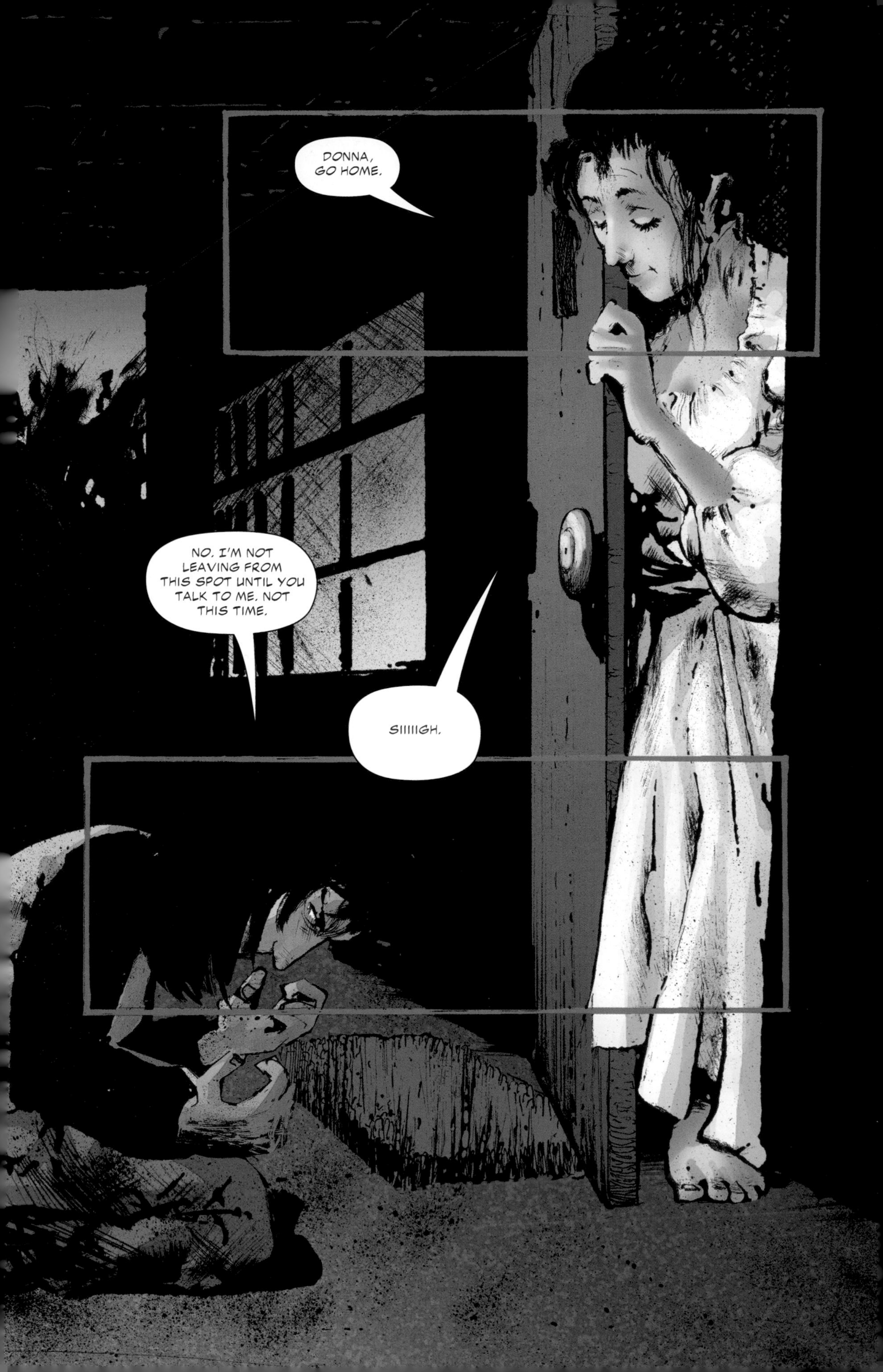
DONNA, GO HOME.
NO. I'M NOT LEAVING FROM THIS SPOT UNTIL YOU TALK TO ME. NOT THIS TIME.
SIIIIGH.

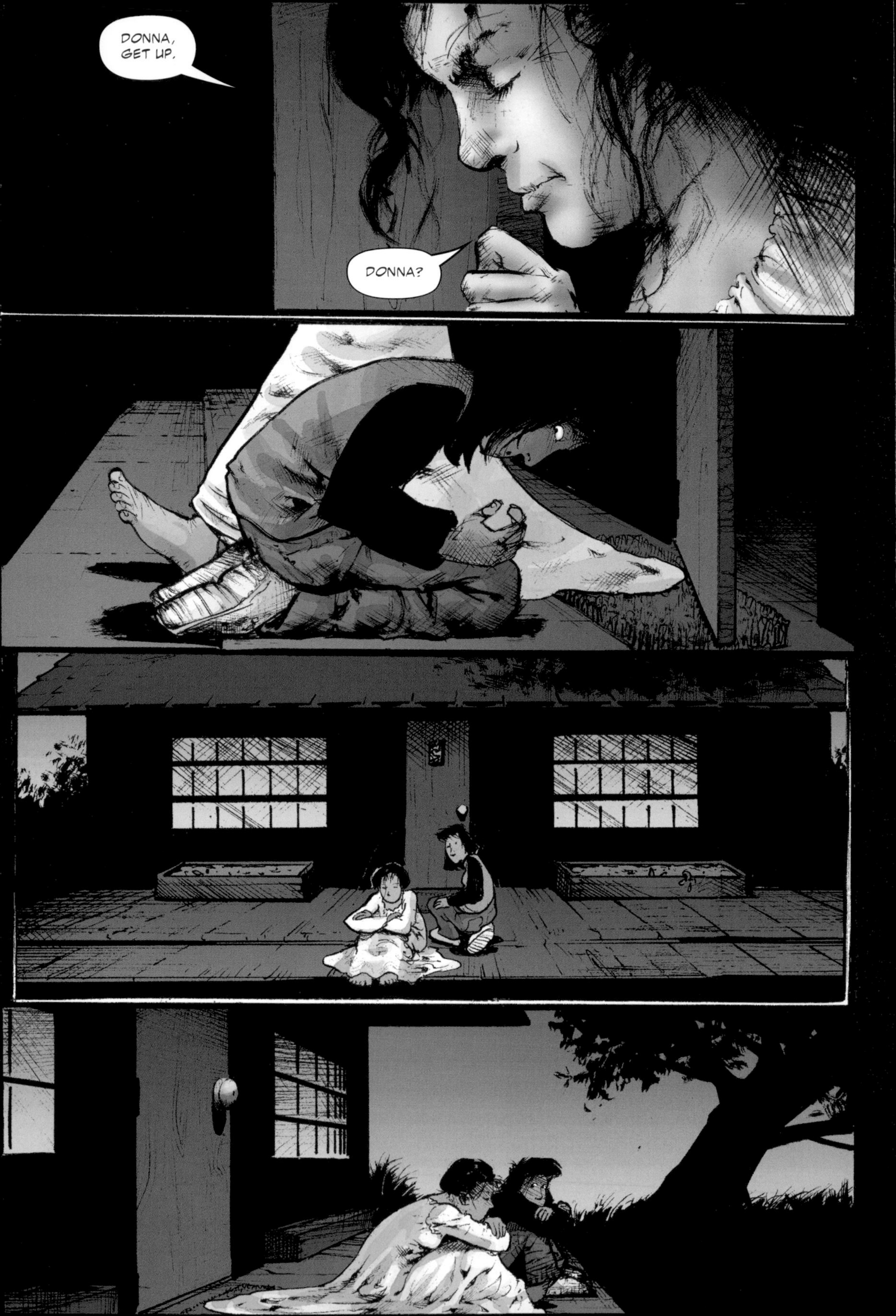
DONNA, GET UP.
DONNA?

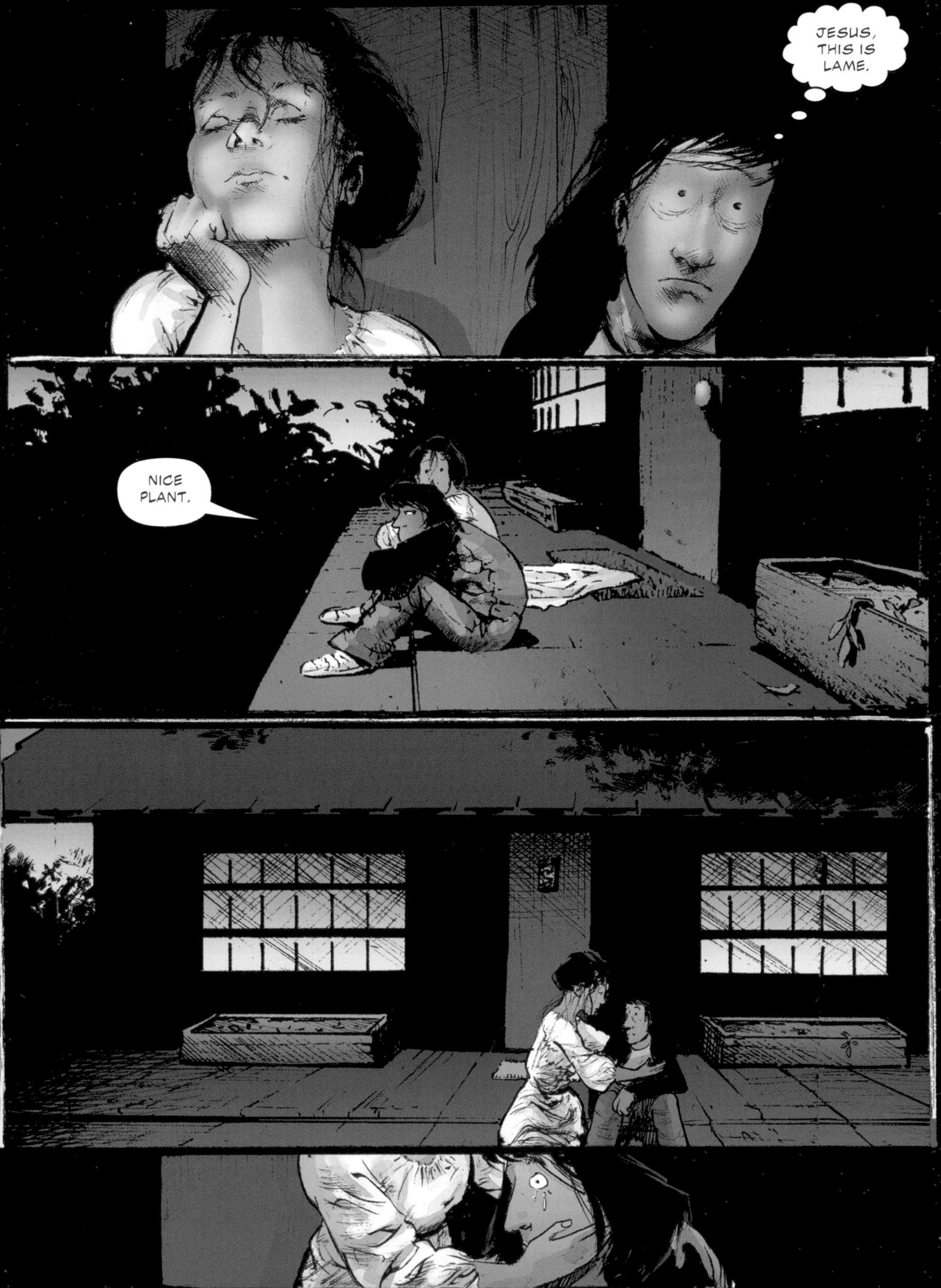
JESUS, THIS IS LAME.
NICE PLANT.

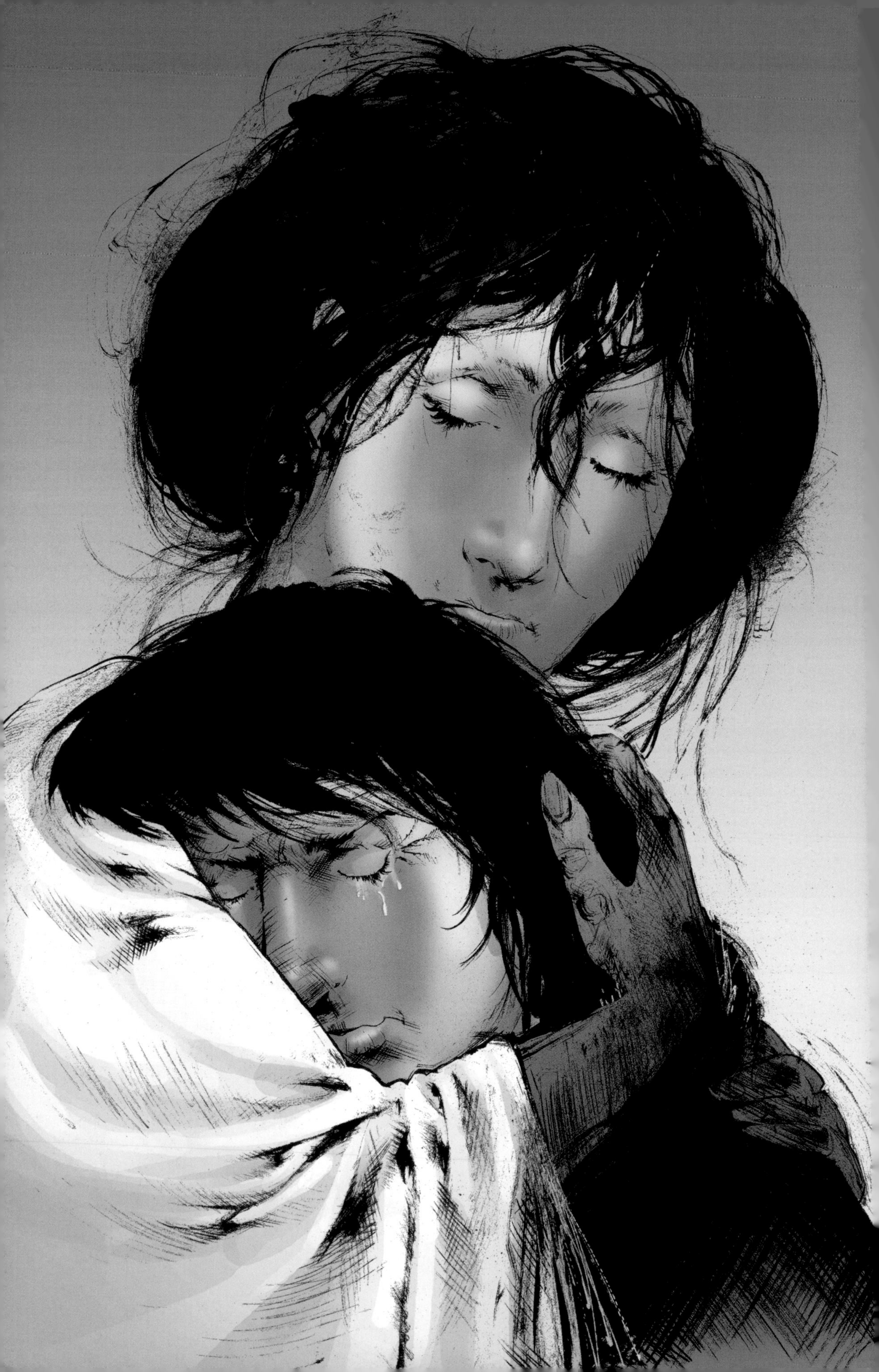

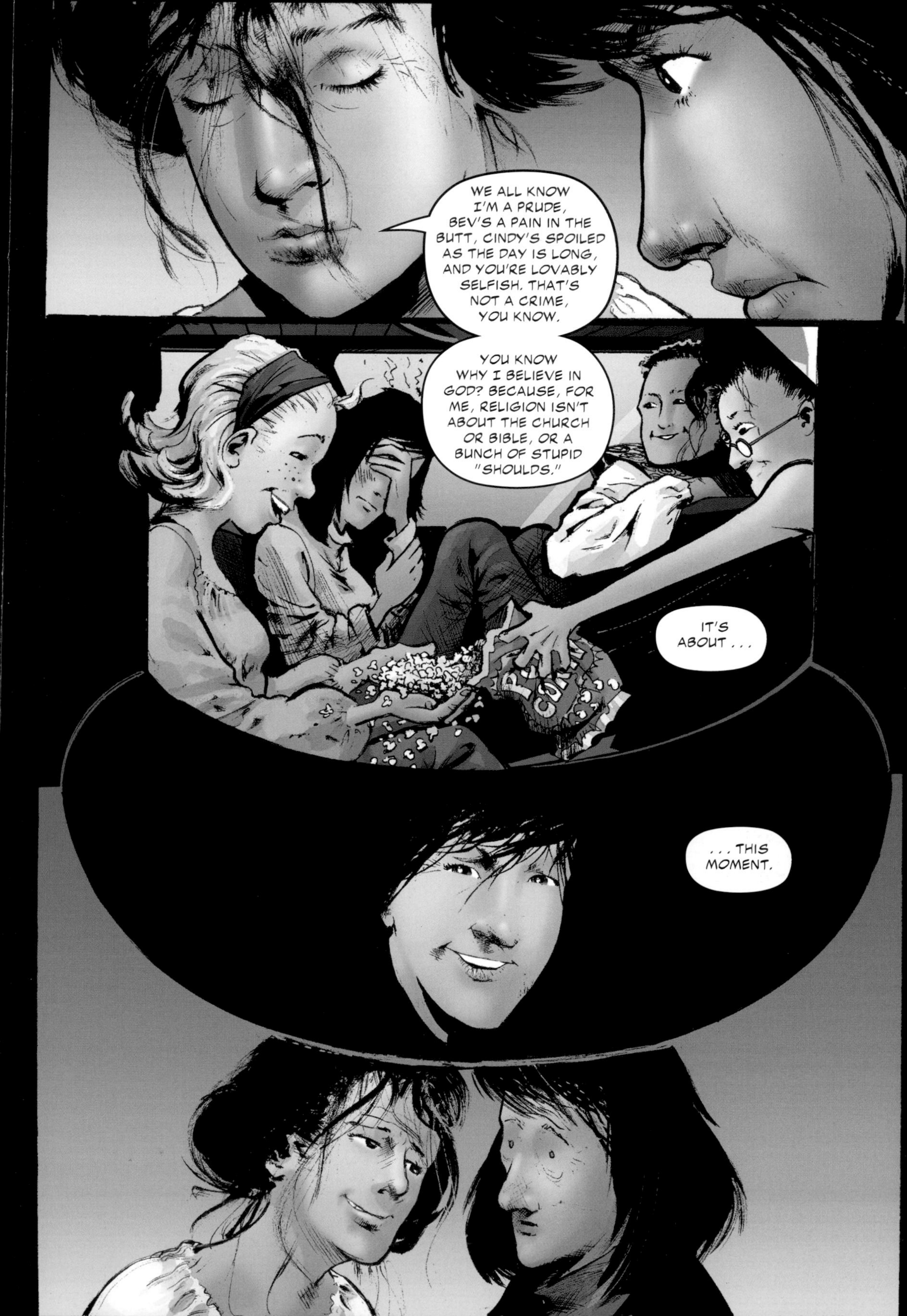
WE ALL KNOW I'M A PRUDE, BEV'S A PAIN IN THE BUTT, CINDY'S SPOILED AS THE DAY IS LONG, AND YOU'RE LOVABLY SELFISH. THAT'S NOT A CRIME, YOU KNOW.
YOU KNOW WHY I BELIEVE IN GOD? BECAUSE, FOR ME, RELIGION ISN'T ABOUT THE CHURCH OR BIBLE, OR A BUNCH OF STUPID "SHOULDS."
IT'S ABOUT . . .
. . . THIS MOMENT.

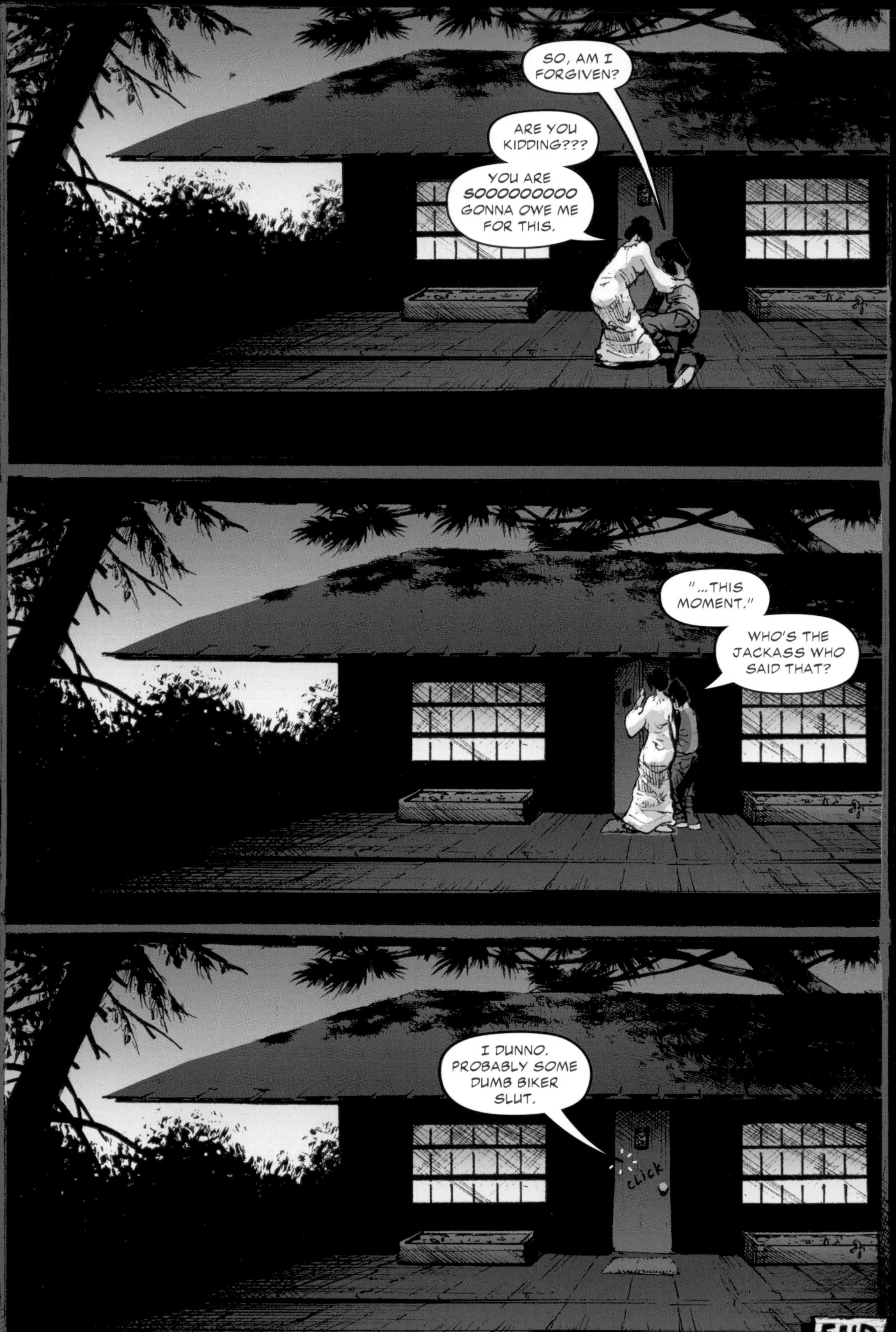
SO, AM I FORGIVEN?
ARE YOU KIDDING???
YOU ARE SOOOOOOOOO GONNA OWE ME FOR THIS.
"...THIS MOMENT."
WHO'S THE JACKASS WHO SAID THAT?
I DUNNO. PROBABLY SOME DUMB BIKER SLUT.
CLICK
END